THEORETICAL MODELS AND EMPIRICAL ANALYSES

Contributions to the Explanation
of Individual Actions and Collective
Phenomena

THEORETICAL MODELS AND EMPIRICAL ANALYSES

Contributions to the Explanation
of Individual Actions and Collective
Phenomena

Edited by

Werner Raub

E.S.-Publications
Utrecht
1982

Explanatory Sociology Publications

For information address:

VOS b.v. booksellers
Rademarkt 10
9711 CV Groningen
The Netherlands

Copyright © 1982 by the contributors

All rights reserved

ISBN 90-70740-01-X

CONTENTS

Preface

Introduction

1. The Structural-Individualistic Approach towards an Explanatory Sociology
   Werner Raub ... 3

Part I
Theoretical Models

2. The Generation of Oligarchic Structures in Constitutionally Democratic Organizations
   Reinhard Wippler ... 43

3. Theories of Revolution and Empirical Evidence
   Siegwart Lindenberg ... 63

4. Rational Actors and Social Institutions: The Case of the Organic Emergence of Norms
   Thomas Voss ... 76

5. From a Classical Attitude-Behavior Hypothesis to a General Model of Behavior, via the Theory of Mental Incongruity
   Frits Tazelaar ... 101

Part II
Empirical Analyses

6. On the Explanation of Contextual Effects on Individual Behavior. The Case of Language Acquisition by Migrant Workers
   Hartmut Esser ... 131

7. Economics, Sociology, and Political Protest
   Karl-Dieter Opp ... 166

8. Explaining Differential Participation in High-Cultural Activities
   - A Confrontation of Information-Processing and Status-Seeking Theories
   Harry Ganzeboom 186

9. Structural Determinants of Objective and Subjective Status
   Ute Kort-Krieger 206

10. Subjective Status Identification, Class Consciousness and Political Attitudes
    Peter Schmidt 227

Notes on Contributors 254
Name Index/Subject Index 259

PREFACE

The papers contained in this volume have been prepared by a group of sociologists from The Netherlands and the Federal Republic of Germany in connection with the Ad Hoc Group 'Explanatory Sociology and the Structural-Individualistic Approach' at the 10th World Congress of Sociology, organized by the International Sociological Association (ISA) and held at Mexico City in August 1982. Preliminary versions of most of the papers were presented by their authors in Mexico City and discussed by the participants of the two sessions of the Ad Hoc Group. Preliminary versions of two contributions (Esser, Opp) were distributed during these sessions, although their authors could not attend the ISA-meeting. One paper (Voss) was completed only after the congress. All of the papers have been revised for this volume as a result of the discussions of the group and some of them have been quite extensively changed and expanded.

The ISA offers a limited number of sessions of their world congresses to Ad Hoc Groups which consist of a substantial number of sociologists from several countries who have already engaged in some collaboration and whose special interest does not properly fit within the province of one of the established Research Committees of the ISA. At the suggestion of some members of the Dutch 'Workgroup Explanatory Sociology', the editor of this volume undertook the organization of an Ad Hoc Group on 'Explanatory Sociology and the Structural-Individualistic Approach'. The application for a place on the program of the 10th World Congress of Sociology was formally approved by the Executive Committee of the ISA.

All the contributions in this volume focus on an explanatory sociology which rests on the assumption that the explanation of social actions of individuals as well as the explanation of collective social phenomena forms a central task of sociology and that such explanations require explicit reference to general principles of individual action as well as to institutional and structural conditions of individual actions and their collective consequences. This assumption, which is elaborated and discussed in the introductory paper, is to be viewed as the common explicit or implicit reference point of the following contributions.

In addition, there is a common view of sociology as theory-guided empirical science underlying all of the pieces appearing in this book. Following this view, the development of sociology can be reconstructed in accordance with Popper's general evolutionary approach as a sequence of problems, tentative solutions of these problems which are tested by various mechanisms and procedures of error-elimination, leading to new problem situations, etc. In the context of an explanatory sociology this sequence may be more precisely characterized as starting with the problem of explaining different explananda, tentative solutions in the form of hypotheses and theories applicable to the explanation, and checks and controls of these solutions, especially in the form of empirical research and empirical tests of hypotheses and theories, producing in turn new problems of explanation. It goes without saying that the substantial themes of the papers in this volume form a rather wide and varied range of explananda, including classical as well as more recent topics of sociology. Naturally, the different contributions also focus on different elements of the sequence of problems, solutions, error-elimination and new problems, putting other elements of this sequence in the background. Hopefully, the variety of explananda treated in this volume will make it clear that an explanatory sociology need not be restricted to a limited field of application. Hopefully, it will also become obvious that a shift from a mere methodological and programmatic discussion of the approach of an explanatory sociology towards substantive theoretical and empirical analyses is not only possible but also fruitful and, in fact, under way.

After the general introduction, the papers are divided into two main groups according to their specific emphasis. The first four papers focus on the construction of theoretical models for the explanation of social phenomena, thus on the first two elements of the above-mentioned Popperian sequence. WIPPLER's paper is the first of those in this volume which take up a classical problem of sociology, namely the occurence of oligarchic tendencies in organizations with a democratic constitution. Wippler gives a new analysis of Michels' problem of the rise of oligarchic structures in terms of a dynamic model, the theoretical core of which is taken from utility theory, paying special attention to structural and institutional conditions such as the size of organizations, their network density and degree of homogeneity, presence/absence of internal opposition and the kind of electoral system. Revolutions are the explanandum of the paper by LINDENBERG, which has a twofold purpose: outlining reasons for the inability of many current theories of revolution to account for available data and sketching an alternative

model by stressing the importance of a combination of an adequate theory of
action with institutional and structural aspects. Next comes the paper of VOSS,
which deals with social norms. In contrast to the majority of sociological
contributions in this field, the focus is not on the explanation of the effects
of social norms on individual behavior, social stability, etc. but on problems
and possibilities of rational-choice explanations of the emergence of norms in
a specific type of situation. The last contribution to the section on theoretical
models is TAZELAAR's paper, which differs from its three predecessors in two ways.
Its explanandum is not a collective phenomenon but individual dispositions and
behavior, especially the relation between an individual's attitudes and behavior.
In contrast to the other theoretical papers as well as to most of the empirical
contributions, it also does not use some version of rational-choice theory (or
utility theory, expectancy-value theory or however it may be called) but develops
instead a formal model of individual dispositions and actions which may be
subsumed under the tradition of the various balance or consistency theories.

Five papers with a strong emphasis on the presentation and analysis of empirical
data and/or empirical tests of general behavioral principles are contained in
the second main part of this volume. The stress of these contributions is thus
on the last two elements of Popper's sequence. The substantial theme of ESSER's
paper is language acquisition by migrant workers. From a theoretical and
methodological point of view, it is of special interest that techniques of
multi-level analysis are used in order to include the influence of contextual
conditions on language acquisition and that the question of a theoretical
explanation of such contextual effects is explicitly dealt with. The next paper
by OPP is on political participation, especially on participation in social
movements and protest behavior. Emphasis is placed on the confrontation of
competing theories applicable to the explanation of protest behavior with
empirical data on this topic. In this way, a utilitarian model is confronted with
competing sociological hypotheses on political participation in order to find out
if there is evidence for a better empirical confirmation of one of these
theoretical alternatives. The following contribution of GANZEBOOM is also
concerned with an empirical test and confrontation of two rival theories of
individual behavior. In this case, participation in different cultural events is
the relevant explanandum, and data from a Dutch survey are used to test the
comparative empirical adequacy of an information-processing and a status-seeking
theory for the explanation of participation in cultural activities. The last two
papers of KORT-KRIEGER and SCHMIDT are closely related. They use data from the

same survey (the ALLBUS survey of the West German voting population from 1980) and the same program for data analysis (LISREL), and have a common substantial interest, namely the determinants as well as the consequences of people's objective social status and their subjective status identification. Whereas Kort-Krieger's contribution centers on the determinants of and the relationship between an individual's objective and subjective status, the paper by Schmidt contains an analysis of the consequences of subjective class identification on class consciousness and political attitudes.

The contributions of three persons, who took a substantial share in the preparation of this volume and in its speedy publication, should not go unnoticed. Thanks are due to Claude Evans (University of Bochum) for his translations and his checking of the translations of most of the papers (those by Lindenberg and Ganzeboom being the only exceptions), to Marjolijn van Osch (University of Utrecht), who prepared the whole manuscript for the reproduction and to Udo Mohn (University of Hagen), who prepared the indices.

Werner Raub

INTRODUCTION

2

Werner Raub

THE STRUCTURAL-INDIVIDUALISTIC APPROACH TOWARDS AN EXPLANATORY SOCIOLOGY

Introduction

The structural-individualistic approach can be roughly characterized such that (a) the explanation of both social behavior and collective effects and processes is viewed as a central task of sociology. In addition, consistent with a naturalistic position it is assumed that (b) such explanations make use of general and lawlike propositions on the one hand and specific assumptions concerning initial and boundary conditions on the other hand. Following the conception of a synthetic theory formation, (c) assumptions concerning individual behavior and its cognitive, motivational etc. foundations function as the general and lawlike propositions of the explanation, and assumptions concerning the social conditions of individual behavior and its consequences are explicitly taken into account as initial and boundary conditions.

In this paper it is not my aim to trace the development of this conception within the framework of a history of sociological theory, nor shall I attempt to give a survey of contemporary research. In these respects I shall restrict myself to a few brief remarks. My main concern here is rather to give a more precise explication of the central characteristics of the structural-individualistic approach. Selected examples should make clear just how the basic assumptions of this approach can be applied within the framework of theoretical sociology. To this end I shall first (Part 1) discuss the idea of the explanation of sociological explananda with the aid of general behavioral assumptions and with reference to social conditions. In the following sections I shall use examples to demonstrate how general behavioral assumptions are used in a structural-individualistic sociology and how social conditions of various kinds can be taken into account. In this context I shall discuss the use of utility theory (Part 2) and the role of interdependencies as social conditions in terms of the example of a competition model (Part 3). Finally, I shall summarize the results and briefly sketch some open problems (Part 4).

1. The explanation of individual and collective effects on the basis of general assumptions and with reference to social conditions

The thesis that the explanation of social phenomena is a central task of sociology is widely accepted. But a more exact specification of precisely what 'explanation' is to mean in this thesis already leads to a delimitation of different lines of thought within theoretical sociology. The structural-individualistic approach follows a naturalistic program in this respect (Albert, 1980), which claims that explanations are to be constructed on the basis of theoretical regularities. In this view, an explanation is a deductive argument which answers the question why the phenomenon to be explained occurs by means of a logical derivation of the description of this phenomenon, the explanandum, from a set of sentences, the explanans, which in addition to initial and boundary conditions essentially contains at least one universal law and which is open to empirical confirmation. Explanations of this kind are generally called deductive-nomological or covering-law explanations [1]. Borrowing a term which is perhaps more current in economics, one could also speak of deductive models of social phenomena.

In sociology we find attempts to give deductive-nomological explanations for a great variety of explananda. Leaving aside the case of the explanation of lawful regularities, which gives rise to special problems (cf. Stegmüller, 1969: 90-96) and restricting our attention to singular explananda, it will be helpful to begin with a few rough distinctions. A first kind of singular explananda encompasses the behavior or the properties of individual actors such as giving advice to or showing respect for colleagues in an office, a worker's joining a union, the degree to which a soldier is satisfied or dissatisfied with the system of promotions in his unit, a person's decision to attend a university, specific characteristics of the conduct of the managers of bureaucratic institutions. With regard to explananda of this kind one can speak of 'individual effects'. In contrast sociologists are also concerned to explain characteristics of collectives of various kinds such as the (informal) status structure in a group of officials, collective actions (such as strikes) or the degree to which a collective good is made available to the members of a group, the total deprivation rate of soldiers in various units, the aggregate demand for long-term and short-term higher education, the productive efficiency of a bureaucracy.

Such explananda will be referred to here as 'collective effects' or as 'collective' processes' (Lindenberg, 1977). In another dimension we can distinguish, again very roughly, between microsociological and macrosociological explananda, whereby the former concern closed networks of small groups (cf. Homans, 1974: 2-4; also Coleman, 1979). Microsociological explananda are, for example, the interactions between colleagues and the resulting status structure, the satisfaction/dissatisfaction of soldiers and the deprivation rates in various units. Phenomena such as the degree to which unions are supported by new members, the availability of collective goods for large groups, the aggregate demand for education or the behavior of bureaucratic managers and its consequences for bureaucratic efficiency would be of macrosociological interest.

Explanations for these various kinds of sociologically interesting explananda, and especially explanations of micro- or macrosociological collective effects, are construed within the structural-individualistic approach such that the given explanans contains general principles concerning the behavior, cognitions and motivations of individuals as lawlike assumptions, thus laws which refer to the characteristics of or relations between individual actors. For the deductive-nomological explanation of singular states of affairs one would, in addition, have to take into account initial and boundary conditions as elements of the explanans. Whereas the general propositions of the explanans refer to individual behavior, in the context of the descriptions of singular initial and boundary conditions the social setting of individual behavior and collective effects is taken into account. The initial and boundary conditions of structural-individualistic explanations will thus contain descriptions of social situations in which individual behavior takes place, and they will describe characteristics of collectives of various kinds [2]. The basic assumptions of the structural-individualistic approach may now be summarized as follows:

> Sociological explananda can be deductive-nomologically explained by making use of general laws of individual behavior and taking explicit account of social conditions [3].

The idea of using general behavioral assumptions in sociological explanations is based on the heuristic assumption of a constancy of human nature (Lindenberg, 1981). It is important to keep in mind the way in which this assumption is to be interpreted. It refers to general theoretical propositions concerning human behavior, thus to general hypotheses which are used in explanations, and it is indeed assumed that they are valid for all actors. But the constancy assumption does not say that all actors are identical with respect to properties of various sorts which are referred to in the general principles of behavior. Thus, it is not assumed that all actors are subject to the same initial and boundary conditions (cf. Homans, 1967: 56). According to this understanding of a uniformity of human nature we should of course expect that different actors in different situations and the same actors in changed situations will exhibit different behavior, since the same regularities of behavior will lead to different modes of behavior in different situations. To put the point in another way: From the same lawlike sentences we can derive different conclusions given different initial and boundary conditions (cf. e.g. Hummell, 1973b: 146).

In addition to this interpretation of the assumption of a constancy of human nature, we must keep in mind that the structural-individualistic characterization of sociological explanations is neutral with respect to the question of the kind of hypotheses concerning individual actors which are to be used as general laws. It thus allows in principle the use of quite different theories of human behavior (Homans, 1964: 967; Schütte, 1976a: 385), and in fact we find quite a variety of different theories being used within the framework of the structural-individualistic approach, such as, for example, utility and decision theories, behavioral theories of learning or various theories of cognitive consistency, so that we must pose the question concerning criteria for the use of these theories in dealing with various problems of explanation.

Evidence for the applicability of specific behavioral assumptions would be provided, for example, by the fact that their use makes it possible to do justice to the other goal as well, namely taking into account social conditions for the occurrence of the given explanandum event. On the one hand, the action-steering function of these conditions must be analyzed, i.e. their influence on individual effects, on the other hand their consequences for the social results of individual actions have to be thematized (cf. Schütte, 1981: 16). For a somewhat more systematic survey it seems appropriate to take interdependencies between individuals as our point of departure, i.e. relations between actors which influence their behavior and/or the results of their behavior, such that the individuals are reciprocally dependent upon one another. Social relations of this kind can rest on interactions between the individuals, as in the case of contact and communicative relations, but they can also occur without interactions between the persons involved and thus be rather indirect (Humell, 1973a: 71, 113-120; Boudon, 1979: 107).

Typical examples for interdependencies which are taken into account in structural-individualistic analyses are complementary control, externalities and co-orientation (cf. Lindenberg, 1977: 60-64). Complementary control is present when each actor has control over certain events and is ready to exchange control over the events in his control for control over the events now controlled by other actors, should he be interested in these events. Individual effects which result from interlockings of complementary controls are, for example, the power of individual actors, whereas phenomena such as markets can be viewed as the collective consequences of specific interlockings of controls (cf. Coleman, 1973). Externalities are present in situations in which the action of an individual has consequences for (at least) one other individual, consequences which this individual evaluates positively or negatively. Such situations can lead to cooperation or conflict between the actors and to collective effects such as collective goods or bads (cf. Olson, 1971). Finally, co-orientations are an example of purely cognitive interdependencies in the sense of reciprocally restricted behavioral expectations. The actors not only have expectations concerning the behavior of the partner, but also concerning the partner's expectations concerning one's own behavior (Scheff, 1967). Co-orientations of this sort are the basis for collective effects such as institutions (cf. Lewis, 1969; Schotter, 1981).

The consequences of interdependencies for individual and collective effects are often dependent on additional social conditions. Thus, group size will have an influence on whether and which behavior-regulating effect externalities have or whether co-orientations can be changed by means of agreements. In addition, with respect to institutions, if they are thematized not with respect to the explanation of their creation and development but rather as initial and boundary conditions for the explanation of other sociologically relevant events, we can pose the question of the manner in which they regulate, for example, interdependencies between individuals, or which interdependencies are created by them. Finally, one must take account of corporate actors (Coleman, 1974, 1975), that is to say, actors of a higher order such as firms, churches, clubs, parties or states, which are characterized by the fact that a number of actors pool their resources and subject the use of these resources as well as the distribution of the results of their use to collective decisions (Vanberg, 1979). Corporate actors of this kind, which in turn are defined as interlockings of individual interdependencies, can, for example, create, control and interpret institutional regulations and in this manner exercise an influence on individual and collective effects.

Structural-individualistic explanations of individual and collective effects have been characterized as deductive-nomological explanations in whose explanans both general behavioral regularities as well as social conditions are taken into account. Thus, it is clear that within the framework of this approach it is quite possible to do justice to the interest of sociologists in finding social causes for social phenomena. If one follows the usual manner of characterizing the initial and boundary conditions of its deductive-nomological explanation as causes of an explanandum event (cf. Hempel, 1965: 347-354), then the social conditions which appear in a structural-individualistic explanation can also be understood as social causes of the individual or collective effects to be explained. The attempt to construct such explanations and the use of general principles of individual behavior which it involves is thus not contrary to the search for social causes. It rather explicitly includes this search in its goals. But the specification of such causes alone cannot be considered to be sufficient for explanatory purposes. An explanation also requires recourse to the laws which, along with the initial and boundary conditions as descriptions of causes, first make the deduction of the explanandum possible (Homans, 1964: 971) and thus, as one might put it, explicate the mechanism by means of which the social causes lead to the social effects (Lindenberg, 1977: 47-49).

If not only individual but also, and especially, collective effects are to be explained, and if in addition to regularities of individual behavior also, and especially, the social conditions of individual and collective actions are to be taken into account, then it becomes clear that the explanans of a structural-individualistic explanation must contain, in addition to the behavioral regularities and the descriptions of the social conditions, sentences which produce a link between the descriptions of the social conditions and the collective effects to be explained on the one hand as well as the general behavioral assumptions on the other [4]. In the first place, we need sentences linking social conditions of individual behavior and the terms of the theories concerning individual actors being used in the given case, i.e. sentences which connect social conditions with the cognitions, motivations, attitudes, utility functions, preferences, stimuli etc., which are dealt with in such theories. Sentences of this kind can be called 'coordination rules'. Along with the behavioral assumptions and assumptions concerning initial and boundary conditions they allow the explanation of individual effects. In a further step a connection must be produced between the general behavioral assumptions and the collective effects which are to be explained. This can be done by connecting the individual effects which were explained in the first step on the basis of general behavioral assumptions, initial and boundary conditions as well as coordination rules, and further social and non-social conditions with the given collective effect. Sentences which yield such a connection can be called 'transformation rules' (Lindenberg, 1977). Deductive-nomological explanations of collective effects are therefore characterized by a double structure (Lindenberg, 1977; Raub and Voss, 1981: Ch. 3, 4). Following the deduction of individual effects in the first step, in a second step collective effects are derived from the transformation rules and a constellation of conditions to which, among other things, the individual effects contained in the first step belong. This amounts to a distinction between the actions of the individuals and the individual and collective consequences of these actions. It goes without saying that the latter need not correspond to the expectations and goals of the individuals, and can, indeed do, often present themselves as unintended consequences (Boudon, 1977; Wippler 1981).

It should be clear by now that from a structural-individualistic point of view not only the empirical test and improvement of general behavioral assumptions but especially the application of these assumptions to various social situations becomes a central task, showing how on the basis of the behavioral assumptions along with a set of further premises among which belong descriptions of social conditions as well as coordination and transformation rules, deductive consequences can be derived, which describe the effects to be explained. Coleman (1964: 34-54, 516-519) and Homans (1967: 105-109) have spoken of a task of synthetic theory formation in this context, distinguishing it from the search for and testing of new lawlike propositions. An adequacy condition for the theories concerning individual actors used in a given case would consist in the fact that it is possible to connect them by means of coordination and transformation rules with the descriptions of social conditions and collective effects and processes which are relevant within the framework of the given explanatory problem. It may turn out that, for example, certain theories such as behavioral theories of learning can be applied more easily in certain contexts, namely in the closed networks of small groups, than is the case with respect to other explanatory problems which refer to more complex social structures and require a macrosociological analysis (cf. Schütte, 1976b).

A consequence of the structural-individualistic approach is the idea of the integration of the social and behavioral sciences. This idea is based on the fact that the same theoretical principles, namely those concerning regularities of individual behavior, are used in the analysis of quite different phenomena which are generally investigated in different social sciences (cf. Homans, 1967: 3; Malewski, 1967; Coleman, 1975). Conceptions closely related to the structural-individualistic approach in sociology can thus be found in a series of other disciplines in the social sciences, such as anthropology (Barth, 1966), political science (Riker and Ordeshook, 1973) and of course economics (Albert, 1977; Becker, 1976). All of the attempts aiming at a unity of the methodological and theoretical foundations of the social sciences carry on in this respect the work of Scottish moral philosophy of the 18th Century represented by Hume, Adam Smith, Ferguson, etc., in which for the first time economic, political and social problems were thematized in a manner consonant with the structural-individualistic approach (cf. the collection edited by Schneider, 1967 and the extensive discussion by Vanberg, 1975).

In recent sociology, the basic ideas of the structural-individualistic approach have been used in the first place in behavioral sociology whose development in the USA was influenced above all by the work of Homans (1974; cf. Burgess and Bushell, eds., 1969) and which was continued in Poland by Malewski (1967) and in West Germany by Opp (1972). In addition, social exchange theory (Thibaut and Kelley, 1959; Blau, 1964), which was partially (cf. Homans, 1974: 56) interpreted as a special application of the hypotheses of behavioral theories of learning to social interactions, orients its attempts at explanation in terms of a structural-individualistic program. In the last few years, the application of behavioral theories of learning for the explanation mainly of microphenomena of elementary social behavior has increasingly taken the back seat to various applications of utility and game theory to macrosociological questions. In this respect, the fundamental works on the 'economic theory of politics' have probably exercised a paradigmatic influence, since the investigations by Arrow (1963) concerning the voting paradox, by Downs (1957) concerning party competition, by Buchanan and Tullock (1962) concerning problems of constitutional choice and by Olson (1971) concerning the way in which groups of different size are provided with collective goods have made clear the manner in which different versions of utility theories or theories of rational action can be applied fruitfully outside of the traditional realm of economics (cf. as a survey Mueller, 1979). New and expanded applications of these theories in the narrower realm of sociology can be found in Coleman's theory of collective decisions and corporate actors, and in Boudon's analyses of the connection between the development of inequality of educational opportunity and social mobility in modern western industrial societies.

The remainder of this paper will pursue the goal of using sketches of a number of case studies to clarify in an exemplary manner the way in which the structural individualistic approach works within the framework of theoretical sociology. The emphasis will lie on the question how not only individual but also collective effects can be explained and how utility theory can be applied to problems of explanation in which interdependencies between individuals play a central role as social conditions.

2. The application of general behavioral assumptions: the case of utility theory

In theoretical sociology as well as in empirical investigations, various theories of individual behavior are often used implicitly. Lindenberg (1981) distinguished two theories thus used, which he terms the 'functionalistic' and the 'empiricist' model of man. According to the former, a process of socialization leads to the internalization of role expectations by the actors. Internal controls by the individual itself and external sanctions by other persons who are also following their role expectations stabilize the social action of the individual which correponds to the role expectations. In contrast, the 'empiricist' model assumes that the individuals are exposed to social influences which have an effect on their attitudes and in this manner affect the social behavior which is guided by their attitudes.

In addition to these roughly characterized models there are various psychological theories which find explicit application in sociology. I have already referred to the use of hypotheses from theories of operant conditioning concerning conditional probabilities of particular behavior patterns in behavioral sociology. The special characteristic of these applications is to be found in the fact that the activities of an individual are discriminative, or reinforcing or aversive stimuli for the reactions of other individuals, whose reactions in turn also function as contingencies, such that the frequencies of behavior patterns are interdependent in this manner (cf. Kunkel, 1975). In addition, various versions of theories of cognitive consistency have been used in sociological explanations, for example Heider's balance theory and the further developments and formalizations of this theory in the theory of social networks which was started by Cartwright and Harary (cf. Davis, 1979) or a theory of mental incongruencies in a series of empirical investigations (cf. Tazelaar and Wippler, 1981). This is not the place to go into these attempts [5]; we shall rather focus our attention on the possibilities of applying utility theory in sociology [6]. Applications of this sort currently constitute the main focus of theoretical analyses within the structural-individualistic approach.

Following a suggestion by Elster (1979: 113), we can in general regard all behavior as a result of two filtering devices. A first filter consists in the set of structural constraints. Here we are dealing with restrictions which lead to a reduction of the set of all abstractly possible behavioral alternatives to the subset of feasible alternatives. A second filter is constituted by a mechanism, for example a decision rule, which determines which element from the opportunity set is chosen. Following this general characterization, the intuitive basic assumptions of utility theory (cf. Meckling, 1976; Lindenberg, 1981) can be explicated in terms of the idea that individuals evaluate the elements of the set of feasible actions and carry out the alternative selected from this set on the basis of a decision rule.

The restrictions which lead to the opportunity set can be of various kinds (cf. Lesourne, 1979: 32-33). They by no means need to comprise only budget restrictions like in traditional neoclassical economics; it can also be a matter of time resources and of restrictions such as legal norms and other normative expectations, for example, role expectations, as well as factually available information and and technical conditions. It is assumed that the actors within these restrictions are capable of broadening their knowledge of opportunities and of conceiving of new courses of action.

As to the alternative courses of action it is assumed that the individual evaluates them positively or negatively with reference to the consequences they involve. These consequences do not necessarily involve (only) the disposition of material goods or economic profit. In principle, any given consequence such as, for example, status, power, the well-being of others, knowledge, the observance of internalized norms, beauty, etc., can fill the role of a utility argument and influence the utility of the opportunities (cf. Furubotn and Pejovich, 1972: 1138). It is assumed that the evaluation of alternative courses of action has the formal properties of reflexivity, connectivity and transitivity, i.e. that the actors have ordered preferences. In addition to the evaluation it is assumed that the individuals have expectations concerning the probability with which the alternatives will lead to the respective consequences. These expectations can be understood as learning effects (cf. Coleman, 1973: 32-37; Blalock and Wilken, 1979: Ch. 3). Expectations and evaluations of the consequences determine together the subjectively expected utility of every alternative course of action, and the central behavioral assumption thus says that an individual carries out an action for which the subjectively expected utility is maximal. The choice of this alternative simultaneously involves the giving up of other alternatives and their consequences, i.e. choice involves opportunity costs. Important in connection with the decision rule of maximizing subjectively expected utility is the fact that an assumption of this kind does not imply consequences for the cognitive processes which take place within the actors. Thus, it is not assumed that the actors consciously weigh their opportunities and their respective advantages and disadvantages, and consciously calculate their utilities. It is merely assumed that the individuals react systematically to the incentives which are involved in the alternatives via their consequences (Frey, 1980).

Finally, if we assume that the maximizing behavior of the actors also relates to actions such as the search for information, thus taking into account information, transaction and decision costs, then Simon's (1957) 'satisficing' can be interpreted as a special case of maximizing behavior, and the idea of a 'limited rationality' of the actors is reflected in the fact that their actions occur on the basis of limited information and in the face of uncertain consequences [7].

If one considers the central behavioral dispositions which the basic assumptions of utility theory refer to, then it is clear that we are dealing with belief and wish dispositions. In the former the expectations, in the latter the evaluations of the persons are reflected. For the purposes of a survey of related theories and suggestions for the further development of utility theory, its ordering in a spectrum of theories concerning belief and wish dispositions proves to be useful (cf. Spohn, 1978: Ch. 1). An initial distinction can be made depending on whether the theories in question deal with qualitative, classificatory, comparative or quantitative belief and/or wish dispositions. In this respect, utility theory is in the first place a theory of quantitative dispositions of the kind in question. In addition, one can differentiate between static theories which investigate the dispositions in question at a fixed point of time, and dynamic theories which deal with the relations between these dispositions at different points of time. In this respect, utility theory is a static theory. Thirdly, we can distinguish between personal and interpersonal theories. The former deal with the belief and wish dispositions of a single actor, the latter with the relations between the dispositions of a set of actors, such that utility theory is in this respect a personal theory. Various variants of utility theories can be distinguished especially with respect to the question whether the actor believes that he is capable of completely predicting the consequences of the action, thus, whether he can make a decision under certainty, whether a decision involves risk such that with respect to his actions he can only assign the consequences a (subjective) probability, or wheter a decision situation involves uncertainty such that he cannot even assign a (subjective) probability.

Savage's (1972) SEU-theory, whose similarity to a whole series of (social) psychological theories of behavior has often been pointed out (cf. already Feather, 1959), can be understood as a fundamental formalization of utility theory for decisions in situations involving risk. It will be sketched here in order to point out the manner in which some of the intuitive ideas on the basis of which utility theory is constructed can be rendered a precise form. We must, thus -following Spohn (1978: 40)- first deal with the question of an appropriate formulation of utility theory on the basis of which we can then deal with the further question of the application of this theory in specific realms.

Consider a situation (cf. Savage, 1972: Ch. 2-5; and the discussion in Spohn, 1978: 42-54) in which an actor in a given situation perceives various alternative courses of action and in which he must decide to carry out one of these alternatives. It is assumed that his decision depends on the consequences of the individual action. The possible consequences are represented by a finite and non-empty set C. The consequences of an action depend on the circumstances of the situation (the 'states of the world'). The central idea in Savage's model

is that the actor does not know with certainty which state is realized in a
given situation and that the occurrence of a state of the world is independent
of the specific act that is implemented. So the actor must depend on subjective
probabilities for the different possible states. On the other hand a given state
univocally determines the consequences of an action in the opinion of the actor.
For the formal representation of states we shall use a non-empty and finite set
W, whose elements constitute an exhaustive and disjunctive partition of the
possible states, such that for the subjective probabilities P we have $\sum_{w \in W} P(w) = 1$.
An action h can then be formally represented as a function which assigns to a
state w a consequence $f(w)$, and the set H of alternative courses of action is
correspondingly a set of functions from W in C. Finally, the subjective evaluations
of the consequences by the actor are modelled by a subjective utility function U,
which, as a function from C in the set R of real numbers assigns a number
$U(f(w))$ to every consequence $f(w)$ as its subjective utility. On this basis, the
subjectively expected utility SEU(h) of an alternative h can be characterized
by a function over the set H of actions, which assigns to every $h \in H$ a real number
such that $SEU(h) = \sum_{w \in W} U(f(w)) \cdot P(w)$. The empirical assertion of utility theory
corresponds to the Bayesian Principle of maximizing subjectively expected utility
and claims that an actor in a situation characterized by W, C, H, P, U and SEU
carries out an action $h \in H$ for which SEU(h) is maximal.

An essential aspect of this theory which has been overlooked and ignored especially
in various attempts to interpret it as a limiting case of a more general psychological theory of action is to be found in the fact that both the quantitative
subjective probabilities as well as the subjective utilities of the consequences
and thus finally also the subjectively expected utilities of the alternative
courses of action can, under certain conditions, be reduced to the preference
relation of the actor concerning the set of possible actions. A strict preference
of the actor for an action h as opposed to h' is present when the actor always
chooses h when forced to choose between the two. If the relations of indifference
and weak preference between actions are introduced in the usual manner, then
with the help of a metrization-theorem it can be shown that in the case of
sufficiently rich sets W, C and H to every complete and consistent (weak)
preference order over H which also satisfies a series of further postulates (such
as continuity assumptions and assumptions of a sure-thing principle), functions
P and U exist such that h is weakly preferred to h' if and only if $SEU(h) \geq SEU(h')$.
In addition, it can be shown that by means of this preference relation the

probability function is uniquely determined and the subjective utility function for consequences is uniquely determined up to positive linear transformations. In connection with the classification of theories concerning belief and wish dispositions, the quantitative utility theory can thus be reduced to a comparative theory of wish dispositions. In this manner it is on the one hand possible to characterize actions in the sense of utility theory as a specific behavior which satisfies (rationality) postulates for preferences and thus to give a precise significance to the claim that actors act as if they maximize the subjectively expected utility of their actions (this point has been emphasized, for example, by Harsanyi, 1977b). On the other hand, on the basis of the metrization-theorem it is also possible to measure the subjective probabilities and utilities of actors on the basis of preferences which manifest themselves in appropriately construed decision situations and thus to study them for example on the basis of the actors' gambling behavior.

Utility theory in the form just sketched refers to actors who do not act circumspectly in the sense (cf. Spohn, 1978: Ch. 4.1) that they do not take account of possible changes in their preferences, subjective probabilities and utilities, and also fail to develop theories concerning other actors who do act circumspectly. For situations in which circumspect action in this sense cannot be left out of account, we must pose the question concerning the possibility of dynamizing utility theory as well as the question of expanding it into an interpersonal theory which takes strategic interdependencies into account. Exemplary attempts at the development of an interpersonal theory can be found in game theory, where we recently find attempts (cf. e.g. Harsanyi, 1977a) which gives solutions not only for the classical case of two-person zero-sum games but also for broader classes of games.
Although we cannot present and discuss the various suggestions here, with respect to the dynamization of utility theory I would like to mention alternatives which consist in either drawing on 'external' theories or in treating the dynamics of utility and probability 'internally', i.e. on the basis of a Bayesian approach. Under the rubric of bringing in external theories I have in mind attempts which amount to using learning theories such as those of classical and operant conditioning to explain the formation, stability and transformation of belief and wish dispositions [9]. In contrast, 'internal' dynamization is at work when, for example, one attempts to deal with the dynamics of subjective probability by assuming that an actor has new experiences between two points in time, i.e. gains information on the basis of which he assumes with certainty or with a

higher or lower subjective probability, that certain events have occurred. The actor's subjective probabilities at the later of the two points in time are then relativized as conditional probabilities in terms of these experiences (cf. as a survey of the dynamization of subjective probabilities by means of such a conditionalization Spohn, 1978: Ch. 4).

A treatment of the dynamics of preferences and subjective utilities, which is in principle similar, is given within the framework of analyses of endogeneous changes in preferences (cf. as a survey Yaari, 1977). Here situations in which preferences change on the basis of past consumption are dealt with (such as e.g. drug consumption). Both with reference to the dynamization of subjective probabilities as well as with respect to preferences one must pose the question how a decision model can be formulated for a finite sequence of points of time (a planning horizon with a finite number of planning periods), a model which specifies a strategy for the actor for every point of time. In the construction of such models one always uses, roughly, a recursive procedure such that initially the last planning period, in which the static version of utility theory can be applied, is considered. The strategy for every earlier planning period can then be determined under the presupposition that a strategy is known for all following periods.

A different possibility for the 'dynamization' of utility theory via immanent means consists in theoretically grounding precisely the stability of preferences and explaining behavioral changes accordingly in terms of changed constraints alone without recourse to changed preferences. Becker has undertaken an attempt of this sort in economics with his household productions function approach (cf. Michael and Becker, 1973). Becker assumes a set of basic objects of choice the preferences for which are more or less the same and stable for all actors. The domain of the utility function of an actor is correspondingly formed out of a set of commodities from which utility is directly obtained. A commodity is produced by the actors, using resources such as market goods and time, and under specific environmental conditions (state of technological development, but of course also political conditions, norms, etc.). This relation is represented by a production function for every commodity. All behavioral changes are explained by means of changes in the (relative) shadow prices of the individual commodities. These depend on the production costs of an additional unit and are correspondingly not determined merely by the prices of the market goods used, but also by the value of the time devoted to their production, by changes in the environmental conditions and by the procuction technique of the actor. In the place of an explanation of behavioral changes with the aid of the assumption of changing wish dispositions we thus have their explanation via application of the assumption of stable tastes in the face of changing productive efficiency with reference to commodities.

After this survey of a possibility of formulating utility theory along with the hints at possible extensions of the theory into a more comprehensive theory of action [10] we can now take up the additional problem of its application in sociology. In this context we must deal with two groups of questions. In the first place, we have to be able to specify for every (group of) actor(s) under consideration an at least approximative characterization both of the decision situation perceived as well as the cognitive and evaluative assessment of this situation. The first task refers to the (approximative) characterization of perceived possible alternative courses of action, circumstances and consequences. The second task concerns the (approximative) specification of preferences or subjective utilities and probabilities. It is clear that in this connection the question concerning which consequences are evaluated by the actors in what way is of special importance. The problem is thus how we can provide a substantive determination of the utility functions by means of appropriate specifications of actors' goals as utility arguments and by determining the relative weights of these goals. If a (simplifying) assumption is not introduced to the effect that a situation of a decision under certainty is present, one furthermore cannot ignore the problem of giving a detailed treatment of the circumstances of the situation perceived by the actors and the subjective probabilities assigned to them.

With reference to this first group of questions, Harsanyi (1977a: 21) speaks of the problem of dominant loyalties. We shall make use of this expression here simply because it is rather comfortable, although it probably emphasizes the necessity of assumptions concerning the wish dispositions of individuals somewhat more than the questions connected with assumptions concerning their belief dispositions. The significance of the problem of dominant loyalties, i.e. the elaboration of substantive assumptions concerning belief and wish dispositions, becomes clear when one recalls that utility theory itself is of course neutral with respect to assumptions of this kind. Thus, empirically significant applications of utility theory in sociology and other disciplines cannot be carried through without such assumptions. On the one hand, we are certainly not interested in retaining at all cost substantive assumptions concerning belief and wish dispositions which, though being empirically significant, are presumably false. Thus, we shall have to search for alternatives to the assumption of profit maximization if it turns out that this assumption, while it is capable of giving empirical content to applications of utility theory, only holds for certain types of firms under specific institutional and organizational conditions (cf. e.g. Albert, 1977: 191-195). On the other hand, it is clear (cf. Tversky, 1975) that we can always introduce ad hoc assumptions concerning (changes of) preferences, subjective probabilities, etc., assumptions which, while they do make arbitrary actions compatible with the abstract assumptions of utility theory, remain methodologically unsatisfying, since they reduce the informative content of the premises of explanatory arguments by postulating for example ever new utility arguments as goals for individuals, which in turn makes the corroboration of assumptions concerning utility arguments more and more difficult (cf. e.g. Lindenberg, 1981). With respect to the problem of dominant loyalties, it becomes clear that the important thing is to introduce and develop substantive assumptions concerning belief and wish dispositions in a systematic and testable manner, and not ad hoc.

The problem of the balance of power (as Harsanyi, 1977a: 21 calls it) poses a second group of questions concerning the application of utility theories in sociology. If on the basis of assumptions concerning the decision situation of the individuals involved and their evaluations of the situation, the calculus of utility theory is used to derive consequences for their action decisions or choices of strategy, we are then faced with the further problem of ascertaining the results of these decisions. Here one must ask which social results ensue from given belief and wish dispositions of the actors involved when further conditions are taken into account, and what influence the actions of the various individuals have on this result. Thus, to mention an example from Schütte (1982), in elections the consequences of the actors' voting behavior with respect to the distribution of seats or the building of the government depend on characteristics of the laws governing the right to vote, the weight given to individual votes, the division of voting districts as well as on the possibilities of coalition formation.

In using utility theory in sociology along the lines suggested by the structural-individualistic approach, it is important that, precisely in the framework of the treatment of the problem of dominant loyalties and the problem of balance of power, the consequences of social conditions for individual behavior and its collective effects be ascertained. In connection with the problem of dominant loyalties it is thus important that we discover just how interdependencies, institutional regulations, size, etc., influence the decision situation of the actors, i.e. specify as restrictions the kind and number of feasible actions, or determine possible circumstances and consequences. Furthermore, the implications of these conditions for the evaluations of the situation by the actors have to be pointed out (cf. Lindenberg, 1981). An example of coordination rules of the relevant kind which can be found in the economic theory of politics is provided by Olson's theory (1971), in which the size of a group is connected with the subjective probability of successful influence by means of participation. A series of additional relevant examples of suggestions for solutions to the problem of the coordination of social conditions with individual dispositions can be found in various attempts to simply ignore the task of giving a more exact formulation of all motives or goals of individuals, choosing instead to deal with the question of which means specific groups of actors must make use of under certain institutional conditions if they are to realize their personal goals, regardless of what these goals might be. The economic theory of democracy has also gone this direction (cf. Schumpeter, 1942: Ch. 22; Downs, 1957). The coordination rules formulated here make use of the fact that for politicians taking control of the government is independently of their private goals at least an instrumental goal. Within the institutional framework of a representative democracy and under suitable assumptions concerning the internal structure of political parties and properties of the electorate, this implies the further instrumental goal of maximizing the number of votes one receives in an election. Thus, the objective function of the politician is specified by means of a single utility argument and the presence of such an objective function is connected with specific institutional conditions. Finally, as a sociological example we can mention Boudon's (1974: Ch. 2) utility-theoretical explanation of the (dynamics of) the inequality of educational opportunities in an ideal-typical western industrial society. Here we are confronted with a situation in which students or their families must decide about the continuation or ending of the student's educational career, and the theory attempts to use a set of assumptions to establish relations between the relevant utility and probability evaluations of the actors and the social status of the family as a social condition.

A structural-individualistic sociology must solve the problem of dominant loyalties by linking social conditions with the decision situations of actors and their dispositions by means of coordination rules, in order to derive consequences concerning decisions and actions of individuals. In the context of the problem of the balance of power we are confronted with the question as to the results of these decisions and actions. Here we must make use of transformation rules which determine how collective effects result from individual effects and additional conditions. Here too one must attempt to take into account the social context of the individual effects. Thus, Boudon's theory of the inequality of educational opportunities deals with the collective effects of the development of school attendance rates of groups of students with different social background with reference to a sequence of student cohorts and with the development of inequality between the groups with respect to these school attendance rates. Individual effects in Boudon's model are the probabilities with which the students will remain in the school system when they or their families at so-called branching points (e.g. the end of a school year) must make decisions concerning staying in or leaving school. Relevant institutional conditions, which along with the individual effects yield the collective effects which are to be explained, are, above all, regulations concerning the kind and number of branching points the student is confronted with during his career, thus, for example, regulations concerning the number of years a student must attend school or the number of school years which are a prerequisite for attending a college or university. Transformation rules specify the connection between these institutional conditions and the individual effects on the one hand with the collective effects concerning the development of the (inequality of) school attendance rates on the other hand. In conjunction with assumptions concerning the presence of these regulations we can then produce explanations of the collective effects.

These few examples should have made it clear that utility-theoretical explanations of a structural-individualistic kind cannot avoid simplifying and idealizing assumptions (cf. e.g. Boudon, 1977: Ch. 7). These concern both utility theory itself and its postulates concerning formal properties of preference relations and subjective probability and utility functions as well as the additional substantial assumptions which must be made when they are used to analyse individual and collective effects. Simplifications and idealizations will often be unavoidable when it is a matter not of giving detailed descriptions of sociologically relevant effects and processes, but rather of giving deductive arguments which provide at least 'potential explanations' (Hempel, 1965: 338) for such explananda.

3. Interdependencies as social conditions: the case of a competition model for the explanation of relative deprivation and inefficient allocation of resources

The general characterization of the structural-individualistic approach and the discussion of the application of utility theory within this approach have already provided us with opportunities of referring to a number of attempts at giving explanations of sociologically relevant individual and collective effects. The somewhat more detailed discussion of one such attempt will serve the purpose of opening up the possibility not only of presenting the application of general utility-theoretical behavioral assumptions in terms of a further example, but more especially of studying the manner in which a special type of social conditions, namely interdependencies, can be taken into account. In addition, the example is so chosen that the explanation of certain collective effects constitutes the central problem. We shall focus on Boudon's (1977: Ch. 4, 5) theoretical model for the explanation of relative deprivation and sub-optimal allocation of resources, in which both kinds of explanandum events are explained in terms of the presence of specific competitive structures. These competitive structures produce interdependencies between the individuals, interdependencies which steer both their strategy decisions and the social results which ensue from these decisions. The discussion will first sketch the background ideas for the construction of the model and specify its explananda more precisely. On this basis the assumptions which are found in Boudon's explanans are then reconstructed.

Phenomena of the kind for which Stouffer et al. introduced the term 'relative deprivation' in their well-known study The American Soldier, have often been dealt with in sociological investigations as well as by the predecessors of modern sociology. Following Boudon (1977: Ch. 5), we can refer to Tocqueville, who in the fourth chapter of the third book on L'ancien régime et la révolution describes the increasing public prosperity in France prior to the revolution and the increasing general public dissatisfaction which arose on this basis. Durkheim's interest focused on a similar theme in his investigation of anomic suicide in Le Suicide. Suicide rates rise not only during periods of economic and financial crisis, but also and especially in periods of economic boom. The reason for this is, according to Durkheim, that in such situations there is no social control of individual demands and expectations. Finally, we can mention the investigations by Stouffer et al., which established a higher degree of satisfaction with the system of promotions among members of the military police than among members of the air corps, although the objective chances of being promoted are greater in the case of air corps men.

In addition to effects of this sort, Boudon's model can also be drawn on in the case of a further problem. The situations assumed, which lead to relative deprivation, are namely situations in which we find simultaneously an inefficient allocation of resources. The decisions of the actors lead to social results, which are pareto-inferior, i.e. there are other possible results which are not less preferred by all actors while they are strictly preferred by at least one actor. An example for such a situation can be found in Boudon's (1977: Ch. 4) analysis of the failure of the introduction of short-term higher education in France in the 1960s and 70s, which were chosen by much fewer students than the original plan had assumed. The application of his model in terms of the relevant constellation of conditions leads to the results that the educational investments of the students in a traditional long-term curriculum prevent an outcome in terms of the distribution of the students in professional positions, average income, etc. which is pareto-optimal with regard to the utility of the educational investments.

The basic idea of Boudon's analysis consists in attributing relative frustration and inefficient allocation of resources to special competitive situations. These are roughly characterized by the fact that the individuals either, by making an investment (e.g. enrolling in a traditional long-term institution of higher education) and accepting the corresponding costs (e.g. tuition, loss of income, temporary social marginality), can enjoy a specific profit (e.g. the social status proper to a certain occupational position or life-time earnings) with a higher or lower probability or, on the other hand, can dispense with both the investment and the possible profit. The decisive thing is that the probability of realizing the profit by means of the investment decreases the more actors decide for the investment. The competition for scarce goods which arises on this basis is then analysed with game-theoretical tools. In this analysis it is assumed that the assumptions of the game-theoretical analysis, while they may not necessarily represent adequately the behavior of each individual actor, are capable of giving an approximately correct characterization of the behavior of the individuals on the average. The assumptions thus amount to simplifications which are acceptable given the explanatory goals Boudon sets and which are now to be discussed.

Boudon's explananda consist of collective effects in connection with relative deprivation and inefficient allocation of resources. Relative deprivation is present when individuals perceive inequalities which they themselves evaluate negatively when they compare their own situation with that of other individuals, which constitute their 'reference group' (cf. Runciman, 1966: Ch. 1). In the above-mentioned competitive situations it is assumed that the actors feel themselves deprived if they do not realize the possible profit. Within this group of deprived actors, however, there is an additional distinction between those who have made the investment in question and those who have not made it. In the latter case one speaks of 'resignative' in the former of 'discordant deprivation'. The discordantly deprived like the winners and unlike those who are resignatively deprived have made the investment, but like the resignatively deprived and unlike the winners cannot enjoy the projected advantages of their investment and can thus be expected to consider their situation to be unjust. Thus, a first collective effect requiring explanation is the total deprivation rate of a population, defined as the proportion of discordantly deprived persons within the population as a whole. With respect to the total deprivation rate and in the light of the examples from Tocqueville, Durkheim and Stouffer, there is a special interest in those cases in which an improvement in the social conditions in the sense of an increase in the possible profit or in the number of actors who can realize a profit is combined with an increase in the total deprivation rate [11]. With reference to inefficient allocation of resources one must correspondingly investigate whether and to what degree the investment decisions of individuals lead to pareto-suboptimal results with reference to the (expected) utility of the actors. Again, of special interest are cases which are characterized by an improvement in the social framework combined with pareto-deterioration of the results.

The assumptions appearing in the explanans assume in the first place (a) a homogeneous population of individuals. The persons thus perceive their situation in the same manner and are characterizable by the same belief and wish dispositions. Concerning the alternative courses of action it is assumed (b) that the actors have to choose between an investment involving a cost C_1 and an investment involving a cost C_2. The set of possible consequences consists (c) of three elements, namely the investment of C_1 and receipt of a profit B_1, the investment of C_1 and the receipt of a profit B_2, as well as the investment of C_2 and the receipt of B_2. The relevant parameters of the model are (d) the number N of actors, the number n_1 of winners of C_1 and the relations between the costs and the profits. Here we have the following relations: $B_1 > B_2$, $C_1 > C_2$, $B_1 > C_1$, $B_2 \geq C_2$, $B_1 - C_1 > B_2 - C_2$ [12]. The subjective utility of the possible consequences results from subtracting costs from profit, such that we have the following relations concerning net profit: $B_1 - C_1 > B_2 - C_2 > B_2 - C_1$. An additional assumption (e) says that we are dealing with the situation of a non-cooperative N-person game. Thus, the actors cannot enter into negotiations and, most importantly, cannot enter binding agreements.

According to an assumption (f) concerning the distribution rule for the profit, every actor who has risked the higher investment C_1 receives the higher profit B_1 if for the number x_1 of individuals who risk C_1 it holds $x_1 \leq n_1$. If, on the other hand, $x_1 > n_1$, then an actor who has risked C_1 receives B_1 with probability $\frac{n_1}{x_1}$ and B_2 with probability $(1 - \frac{n_1}{x_1})$. Individuals who risk C_2 receive B_2 in any case. By means of a distribution rule of this kind and the non-cooperative nature of the game, an indirect interdependence between the actors is established: the decisions of each individual are (as it turns out: for specific values of the model parameters) dependent on his assumptions concerning the strategy choices of other actors, and these strategy choices influence the consequences of the investment decisions.

If, in addition, (g) veridical perceptions of the situation are imputed to the actors, then their subjectively expected utility for the two feasible actions can be specified. The expected value in the case of risking C_1 depends on the total number of individuals who risk C_1. For the expected value $E_1(x_1)$ of the alternative of risking C_1, in case x_1 actors risk C_1, we have

$$(1) \quad E_1(x_1) = \begin{cases} B_1 - C_1, & \text{if } x_1 \leq n_1 \\ (B_1 - C_1)\frac{n_1}{x_1} + (B_2 - C_1)(1 - \frac{n_1}{x_1}), & \text{if } x_1 > n_1 \end{cases}$$

For the expected value E_2 of risking C_2 on the other hand:

$$(2) \quad E_2 = B_2 - C_2$$

For the further analysis the decisive question is whether the risk of C_1 is a dominant strategy for the actors in contrast to the risk of C_2, thus, independent of the decisions of the other actors has at least as high an expected value as the risk of C_2. This is the case when

$$(3) \quad E_1(N) \geq E_2$$

that is, when

$$(4) \quad \frac{B_1 - B_2}{C_1 - C_2} \geq \frac{N}{n_1}$$

Whereas we have thus far only considered the pure strategies of the actors, in the absence of a dominant pure strategy it is helpful to take mixed strategies into consideration, in this case strategies of risking C_1 with a probability p and C_2 with (1-p). Here we have to investigate N-tuples of strategies $S_1, \ldots S_N$ of individuals $1, \ldots, N$, which constitute an equilibrium, i.e. are such that no actor has an advantage from the choice of another strategy as long as the other actors do not change their strategy choices. It can be shown (cf. Raub, 1982) that in the absence of dominant pure strategies the strategies $S_1 = \ldots = S_N = S$ constitute an equilibrium and in fact the only equilibrium if S is the mixed strategy of risking C_1 with probability p^+ and C_2 with $(1-p^+)$, whereby

$$(5) \quad p^+ = \frac{n_1(B_1 - B_2)}{N(C_1 - C_2)}$$

On this basis we can specify the behavioral assumption (h) which appears in Boudon's model. In the formulation we shall make use of the distinction between the cases in which dominant strategies exist or do not exist. In the former case, while for every actor his payoff may depend on the decision of others, strategy choices can be made independently from assumptions concerning the decision of others. In situations where no dominant strategies exist assumptions concerning other actors are relevant for each individual's decision. In cases of the first kind, Elster (1976) speaks of games in the 'weak', in the second case of games in the 'strong' sense. With regard to the situation discussed here we can assume that in the case of a game in the weak sense the actors choose the dominant pure strategy [13]. For the consequences of Boudon's competition model with respect to the (development of) total deprivation rates and the efficiency of resource allocation under various social conditions it is decisive in the case of games in the strong sense that the behavioral assumption implies that there is a decrease in the number of actors who risk the higher investment C_1. Thus, for example, the maximin strategy of risking C_2 with probability 1 would have such an effect. A less drastic decrease in the number of actors who risk C_1 is yielded by the assumption that in the absence of a pure dominant strategy and in the case of games in the strong sense there is a transition to mixed strategies of the kind S which determine the only equilibrium. It is precisely this sort of assumption which Boudon makes in his model. As a coordination rule which connects the assumptions (a) to (g) concerning individual and social inital and boundary conditions with the general behavioral assumption (h) there is no difficulty in introducing the assumption (i) that under the conditions (a) to (g) and in the presence of (3) a game in the weak sense, in the absence of (3) however, a game in the strong sense is being played.

The strategy choices of the players follow from the assumptions (a) to (i) as individual effects. The proportion A of individuals who risk the higher investment C_1 is equal to 1 in the case of a game in the weak sense, whereas in the case of a game in the strong sense an expected value for A of $\frac{n_1(B_1 - B_2)}{N(C_1 - C_2)}$ results [14]. In the first instance the total deprivation rate is a collective effect which calls for explanation. The transformation rule which connects the individual effects and additional conditions with the collective explanandum can be formulated as assumption (k): If in correspondence with (g) we have a case of veridical situational perception and if there is a distribution rule in correspondence with assumption (f) and if the strategy choices of the individuals have been made, then for the expected value G of the total deprivation rate we have:

$$
(6) \quad G = A - \frac{n_1}{N} = \begin{cases} 1 - \frac{n_1}{N}, & \text{if } \frac{B_1 - B_2}{C_1 - C_2} \geq \frac{N}{n_1} \\ \\ \frac{n_1(B_1 - B_2)}{N(C_1 - C_2)} - \frac{n_1}{N}, & \text{if } \frac{B_1 - B_2}{C_1 - C_2} < \frac{N}{n_1} \end{cases}
$$

From the assumptions (a) to (k) we can now derive the expected value for the total deprivation rate.

An improvement of the chances of the actors can be modelled by an increase of n_1, i.e. of the number of winners of B_1, or by an increase of the quotient $Q = \frac{B_1 - B_2}{C_1 - C_2}$, i.e. by means of appropriate changes of the costs and profits. Via partial differentiation with respect to n_1 or Q we can then derive consequences for the changes in the expected total deprivation rate in the face of changing chances of the individuals. It turns out that with an increasing number of winners of the higher profit the expected value of the total deprivation rate grows, reaching its maximum when, as a result of the increase of n_1, the risk of C_1 for every actor becomes the dominant pure strategy, only to fall once more as n_1 continues to grow. In the case of a rising Q, the expected value of the total deprivation rates rises likewise up to the point that the pure strategy of risking the higher investment becomes dominant and then remains constant. Thus, the assumptions built into the model do in fact yield the result that under specifiable presuppositions an improvement in the social conditions leads to an increase in the total deprivation rate, since this improvement can have the effect that the number of actors who risk the higher investment grows more rapidly than the number of those who can receive the higher profit. The assumptions also specify the intervals within which the model parameters must fall if such effects are to appear.

The question concerning the efficiency of resource allocation under various conditions can now be easily answered in the same spirit. A pareto-optimal situation is present when n_1 actors risk C_1, since this yields a utility of $B_1 - C_1$ for these actors, for $N - n_1$ actors a utility of $B_2 - C_2 < B_1 - C_1$, and for no actor a utility of $B_2 - C_1 < B_2 - C_2$. A situation T_2 with improved chances of the individuals in contrast to a situation T_1 is thus pareto-inferior with respect to T_1 if and only if the expected value of the total deprivation rate in T_2 is larger than in T_1.

Finally, what are some possibilities for a further development of the competition model which we have outlined here? It is, of course, possible to increase its technical complexity by introducing a larger number of different investment possibilities or profits, thus of action alternatives or consequences. By the same token, it would be possible to introduce additional assumptions which would allow the treatment of additional kinds of explananda. For example, one might try to determine the consequences of higher total deprivation rates or of distribution rules which the actors hold to be illegitimate. Another question would be the one concerning conditions which aid and which hinder the development of coordination mechanisms which secure a more efficient allocation of resources.

In addition to the more obvious questions of this sort, however, we might mention two additional lines of research which Boudon (1977: 150-155) has suggested. On the one hand we may try to relax the assumption of a homogeneous population of actors. In its place we might assume a stratified population whose members control resources of greater or lesser quantities. Once we have made this move, the most obvious additional assumption would be that individuals with fewer resources are inclined to avoid the risk of losses which is bound up with larger investments. The consequences would be on the one hand a decrease of the total deprivation rate under specific constellations of model parameters, on the other hand, however, also a reproduction of inequality. A second presumably fruitful line of investigation for this model might be seen in the possibility of taking positional goods into account (Hirsch, 1977). In this case possible profits must be understood as goods the utility of which is a decreasing function of the number of persons who likewise possess them.

4. Closing remarks and some open problems

A summary of the basic elements and exemplary applications of the structural-individualistic approach provides an appropriate opportunity to cast some light on the cogency of some opinions concerning this approach which are apparently widespread among sociologists. Orienting itself in terms of the goal of the explanation of sociological explananda with the aid of general propositions concerning individual behavior derived from, in our examples, utility theory, and taking account of social conditions, our discussions began with an interpretation of the fundamental constancy assumption such that, whereas constancy is assumed to apply to the universal and lawlike premises of explanatory arguments, identical initial and boundary conditions on the part of the actors involved are not assumed. Thus, the structural-individualistic approach does not lead to the assumption that different individuals or groups of individuals exhibit the same behavior. The explicit recourse to the social conditions of individual behavior and its collective consequences makes it clear that this approach is not an attempt to base the singular premises of the explanans merely on endogeneous variables of the personality system such as instincts and innate behavioral tendencies, motives, needs and intentions as 'independent variables'. A 'psychologism' is avoided in that the theoretical problem of analyzing the consequences of interdependencies, group size, institutional regulations, corporate actors, etc. for individual actions and their social consequences is explicitly posed. In the framework of the general discussion of the application of utility theory it became clear how it is in principle possible to take into account such conditions in dealing with the problem of dominant loyalties and the balance of power, and Boudon's competition model demonstrated in somewhat more detail how specific interdependencies have consequences for individual preferences and decisions and also for their social results.

Whereas these remarks concern the general structure of the explanans of structural-individualistic explanations, it was emphasized that the explananda by no means encompass merely individual behavior but precisely also collective effects and processes. Thus, in the competition model the analysis of individual strategy choices was only an intermediate step in the derivation of the consequences for the total deprivation rate in a collective or for the optimality of the social results of individual strategy choices. By the same token, those collective effects which are regarded as being in need of explanation and in principle open to explanation are not only microsociological explananda such as status and power structures in the closed networks of informal small groups. Above and beyond explananda of this kind we find especially attempts at the explanation of effects and processes of macrosociological interest. The in recent years dominant applications of utility theory and the comparatively diminishing interest in behavioral theories of learning can be considered to be an evidence for a problem shift. In the 'classical' contributions to the economic theory of politics, in Coleman's theory of corporate actors and collective decisions as well as in Boudon's studies of inequality of educational and social opportunity, such attempts at explaining macrophenomena using utility theory have had their effect. For the competition model, too, it is characteristic that it not only makes possible a potential explanation of microsociological phenomena, such as those presented by Stouffer et al., but precisely also makes it possible to deal with macrosociological questions such as those which were posed by Tocqueville and Durkheim in an exemplary manner.

I should like to close this attempt to clarify the methodological and theoretical foundations of the structural-individualistic approach by asking some questions concerning open problems and desiderata for the further development of this line of investigation. It goes without saying that it would be desirable to go beyond the programmatic explication of the approach and its exemplary application in starkly simplified models of potential explanation, and to place a greater emphasis on the elaboration of explanations in which one can also assume an empirical confirmation of the universal and singular assumptions of the explanans, thus approaching the goal of effective explanations of social effects and processes. If one holds the approximation of such goals to be desirable, then one must correspondingly lay greater value on the empirical test of the assumptions used in a given explanation. Is it possible to predict some specific difficulties which will arise in the course of such attempts?

A first problem might concern the general behavioral assumptions used in a given explanation. It has often been pointed out that, for example, the assumptions of utility theory have an idealizing character and in the final analysis cannot be considered to be nomological principles of individual action. Thus, the sketch of Savage's SEU-theory should have made clear the very strong presuppositions concerning individual behavior and the dispositions which underlie it. It is questionable whether in this context the simple statement that the application of presuppositions and assumptions of this sort has the desired effect of simplifying the argumentation and enabling the construction of deductive models at all can be considered to be sufficiently satisfying. It would be necessary to investigate whether it is not possible to specify conditions in the presence of which utility theory might be granted an at least approximative validity as a theory of individual action, or whether at least for specific types of situations it is not possible to elaborate behavioral assumptions which exhibit a sufficient deductive content while also being open to adequate empirical confirmation, such as Lindenberg's (1980) model of repetitive choice. One might see an alternative third possibility in justifying the use of idealizing assumption of utility theory in a more rigorous sense such that it would be systematically demonstrated how the given explananda might be won even if one assumes other behavioral tendencies than the maximizing of subjectively expected utility. Becker (1976: Ch. 8) has gone just in this direction in his demonstration that specific microeconomic theorems, for example, concerning negatively inclined demand curves, also result even on the assumption of 'irrational' behavior (impulsiveness, inertia), if the consequences of changes in prices for the opportunities of actors are taken into account.

The structural-individualistic approach is also likely to have consequences - as yet largely ignored - for the realm of data collection and data analysis. It has long since been pointed out (cf. Coleman, 1958/59) that the interest in taking account of the social context, for example in the form of relations and interdependencies between individuals, has implications for research designs and sampling procedures. It appears that a systematic discussion of these questions explicitly in the light of the structural-individualistic approach has been more or less neglected up to now. In addition, against the background of the goal of on the one hand explaining individual effects and on the other hand making all premises in explanations explicit in order to produce deductive arguments, there is the obvious problem that the empirical foundations of data which must be drawn on in explanations are actions of individuals in research contacts or results of individual actions. Thus, we are faced with the task of developing adequate theories of individual behavior in research contacts and with the question of developing models of data analysis which are capable of taking into account assumptions concerning systematic measurement errors which are deducible from an appropriate theory of reactions in research situations (cf. Esser, 1980).

In connection with the discussion of the logical foundations of structural-individualistic explanations we have pointed out the necessity of developing transformation and coordination rules which establish a connection between social conditions and individual dispositions as well as between individual and collective effects. In concluding these fragmentary remarks concerning possible lines of research in the further development of the structural-individualistic approach, I would like to pose the question as to which methods and techniques are needed for the formulation and, to the extent that they are empirical propositions, verification of these rules and whether these methods and techniques are already available. Here one would have to examine the contribution which, for example, multi-level analysis might make to the solution of the coordination problem or which the theory of consistent aggregation (Hannan, 1971) might make to the elaboration of transformation rules.

Notes

(1) Concerning the deductive-nomological concept of explanation cf. Hempel (1965). Homans (1967, 1974: 8-11) sees the elaboration of explanations in the deductive-nomological sense as the most important task of sociology. It can be shown (de Vos, 1981) that programmatic statements by classical sociologists such as Durkheim, Marx and Weber can also be interpreted as pleas for deductive-nomological explanations. For brief references to other ways of using the concept of explanation in sociology, cf. Wippler (1978: 139). Distinctions between deductive-nomological and inductive-statistical explanations will not be taken into account in this paper.

(2) For the distinction which is normally made by both proponents and critics of the structural-individualistic approach between assertions about individuals and assertions about collectives, a distinction which is made on the basis of the terms used in such assertions, cf. for example the discussion between Homans (1970) and Blau (1970). Additional elaborations can be found, for example, in Malewski (1967: 14-16) and Opp (1979). In contrast to Homans, I shall not speak of psychological propositions in connection with general assumptions concerning individuals, since the behavioral assumptions which will be discussed here are, in contrast to Homans' preference for hypotheses from behavioral theories of learning, by no means a specific product of psychology. References to problematic limiting cases in the differentiation

between assertions concerning individuals and collectives can be found, for example, in the discussion in Keuth (1973).

(3) As a representative of such theses we can, of course, name above all Homans (e.g. 1967, 1974). In addition to a series of other authors we could also name Coleman (e.g. 1979), Boudon (e.g. 1979) and Opp (e.g. 1979). The expression 'structural-individualistic approach', which goes back to Opp (1978) and Wippler (1978) emphasizes both the aspect of the use of general behavioral assumptions as well as taking into account social conditions. For expressions used by other authors see Wippler (1978: 143).

(4) Logical problems of the structural-individualistic explanations which are relevant in this context are discussed in Raub (1982).

(5) For brief references to the possibilities as well as the problems of the theories listed in their use in explanations in sociology cf. e.g. Schütte (1976b) and Lindenberg (1981).

(6) Some authors, such as Harsanyi (1977a) and Coleman (1973, 1975) prefer to speak of a 'theory of rational action' rather than 'utility theory'. Opp (1978: 55-56) has pointed out misunderstandings which the former expression can lead to especially in sociology. We shall therefore follow his suggestion and avoid this expression. One also often finds the expression 'decision theory'.

(7) For an extended discussion not only of the problem of 'satisficing' but also of further foundational problems in connection with the central assumptions of utility theory, cf. Elster (1979).

(8) For surveys of this 'indirect' way of measurement and for other procedures of measuring utilities, probabilities and preferences cf. e.g. Lee (1971), Blalock and Wilken (1979: Ch. 2, 3).

(9) Homans (1974: 43-47) has argued for a procedure of this kind. Similar attempts are elaborated in detail by Blalock and Wilken (1979: Part 1).

(10) For remarks concerning some connections between these attempts at dynamizing

utility theory and themes from general sociological theory, cf. Raub and Voss (1981: 38-58).

(11) Thus, Boudon's model deals with neither the determinants of the selection of reference groups nor with the individual or collective consequences of (discordant) deprivation and (high) total deprivation rates. A series of questions in the literature concerning relative deprivation and reference groups as well as concerning dissonance and equity theory are left open at that point. The point here merely concerns the consequences of central characteristics of a specific class of competitive situations for the total deprivation rate under the presupposition that specific individuals orient themselves in terms of a specific reference group and feel themselves relatively deprived in a certain respect.

(12) In Boudon the assumption $B_1 - C_1 > B_2 - C_2$ is lacking. A presupposition of this kind turns out to be unavoidable.

(13) At this point the relevance of the assumption $B_1 - C_1 > B_2 - C_2$ becomes clear. Namely, if it is not fulfilled, the risk of C_2 becomes the dominant alternative. This trivial case is, however, of no interest in the framework of the social situations which are dealt with by means of Boudon's model.

(14) For the deduction of the collective effects which are in need of explanation it is decisive that we can derive on the basis of the general behavioral assumption along with the additional assumptions of the model such expected values for the number of individuals who risk the higher investment. I.e. it is decisive that in games in the strong sense this value is smaller than 1.

References

ALBERT, H., (1977) 'Individuelles Handeln und soziale Steuerung', pp. 177-225 in H. Lenk (ed.), Handlungstheorien - interdisziplinär, Vol. 4. München: Fink.

ALBERT, H., (1980) 'Die Einheit der Sozialwissenschaften', pp. 53-70 in E. Topitsch (ed.), Logik der Sozialwissenschaften. Königstein/Ts.: Hain.

ARROW, K.J., (1963) Social Choice and Individual Values. New Haven: Yale University Press.

BARTH, F., (1966) Models of Social Organization. Glasgow: Royal Anthropological Institute.

BECKER, G.S. (1976) The Economic Approach to Human Behavior. Chicago: University Press.

BLALOCK, M. and P.H. WILKEN (1979) Intergroup Processes. New York: Free Press.

BLAU, P.M., (1964) Exchange and Power in Social Life. New York: Wiley.

BLAU, P.M., (1970) 'Comment (on Homans)', pp. 329-339 in R. Borger and F. Cioffi (eds.), Explanation in the Behavioural Sciences. London: Cambridge University Press.

BOUDON, R., (1974), Education, Opportunity, and Social Inequality. New York: Wiley.

BOUDON, R., (1977), Effets pervers et ordre social. Paris: PUF.

BOUDON, R., (1979), La logique du social. Paris: Hachette.

BUCHANAN, J.M. and G. TULLOCK, (1962), The Calculus of Consent. Ann Arbor, Mich.: University of Michigan Press.

BURGESS, R.L. and D. BUSHELL (eds.)(1969), Behavioral Sociology. New York: Columbia University Press.

COLEMAN, J.S. (1958/59) 'Relational Analysis', Human Organization 17: 28-36.

COLEMAN, J.S. (1964), Introduction to Mathematical Sociology. New York: Free Press.

COLEMAN, J.S., (1973), The Mathematics of Collective Action. London: Heinemann.

COLEMAN, J.S., (1974), Power and the Structure of Society. New York: Norton.

COLEMAN, J.S., (1975), 'Social Structure and a Theory of Action', pp. 76-93 in R. Harrison (ed.), Rational Action. Cambridge: University Press.

COLEMAN, J.S., (1979), 'Rational Actors in Macrosociological Analysis', pp. 75-91 in R. Harrison (ed.), Rational Action. Cambridge: University Press.

DAVIS, J.A., (1979), 'The Davis/Holland/Leinhardt Studies: An Overview', pp. 51-62 in P.W. Holland and S. Leinhardt (eds.), Perspectives on Social Network Research. New York: Academic Press.

DE VOS, H., (1981), *Verklaring en interpretatie in de sociologie*. Utrecht: Van Loghum Slaterus.

DOWNS, A., (1957) *An Economic Theory of Democracy*. New York: Harper and Row.

ELSTER, J., (1976), 'Boudon, Education and the Theory of Games', *Social Science Information* 15: 733-740.

ELSTER, J., (1979), 'Problematic Rationality: Some Unresolved Problems in the Theory of Rational Behaviour', pp. 112-156 in *Ulysses and the Sirens. Studies in Rationality and Irrationality*. Cambridge: University Press.

ESSER, H., (1980) 'Research Reaction as Social Action and the Problem of Systematic Measurement Error', in M. Brenner (ed.), *Social Method and Social Life*. London.

FEATHER, N.T., (1959) 'Subjective Probability and Decision under Uncertainty', *Psychological Review* 66: 150-164.

FREY, B.S., (1980), 'Ökonomie als Verhaltenswissenschaft', *Jahrbuch für Sozialwissenschaft* 31: 21-35.

FUROBOTN, E. and S. PEJOVICH, (1972), 'Property Rights and Economic Theory: A Survey of Recent Literature', *Journal of Economic Literature* 10: 1137-1162.

HANNAN, M.T., (1971), *Aggregation and Disaggregation in Sociology*. Lexington, Mass.: Lexington Books.

HARSANYI, J.C., (1977a), *Rational Behavior and Bargaining Equilibrium in Games and Social Situations*. Cambridge: University Press.

HARSANYI, J.C., (1977b), 'On the Rationale of the Bayesian Approach', pp. 381-392 in R.E. Butts and J. Hintikka (eds.), *Foundational Problems in the Special Sciences*. Dordrecht: Reidel.

HEMPEL, C.G., (1965), 'Aspects of Scientific Explanation', pp. 331-496 in *Aspects of Scientific Explanation and other Essays in the Philosophy of Science*. New York: Free Press.

HIRSCH, F., (1977), *Social Limits to Growth*. London: Routledge.

HOMANS, G.C. (1964), 'Contemporary Theory in Sociology', pp. 951-977 in R.E.L. Faris (ed.), *Handbook of Modern Sociology*. Chicago: Rand McNally.

HOMANS, G.C. (1967), *The Nature of Social Science*. New York: Harcourt, Brace & World.

HOMANS, G.C. (1970), 'The Relevance of Psychology to the Explanation of Social Phenomena', pp. 313-328 in R. Borger and F. Cioffi (eds.), *Explanations in the Behavioural Sciences*. London: Cambridge University Press.

HOMANS, G.C. (1974), *Social Behavior: Its Elementary Forms*. New York: Harcourt, Brace, Jovanovich.

HUMMELL, H.J., (1973a), 'Methodologischer Individualismus, Struktureffekte und Systemkonsequenzen', pp. 61-134 in K.-D. Opp and H.J. Hummell, Soziales Verhalten und soziale Systeme, Probleme der Erklärung sozialer Prozesse, Vol. 2. Frankfurt a.M.: Athenäum.

HUMMELL, H.J., (1973b), 'Für eine Struktursoziologie auf individualistischer Grundlage', pp. 135-177 in K.-D. Opp and H.J. Hummell, Soziales Verhalten und soziale Systeme, Probleme der Erklärung sozialer Prozesse, Vol. 2. Frankfurt a.M.: Athenäum.

KEUTH, H., (1973), 'Zwischen Sein und Schein, oder die 'Mehrebenenanalyse' (Review of Hummell, Probleme der Mehrebenenanalyse)', Zeitschrift für Sozialpsychologie 4: 378-380.

KUNKEL, J.H., (1975), Behavior, Social Problems, and Change. Englewood Cliffs, N.J.: Prentice-Hall.

LEE, W., (1971), Decision Theory and Human Behavior. New York: Wiley.

LESOURNE, J., (1979), 'Economic Dynamics and Individual Behaviour', pp. 29-47 in L. Lévy-Garboua (ed.), Sociological Economics. London: Sage.

LEWIS, D., (1969), Convention: A Philosophical Study. Cambridge, Mass.: Harvard University Press.

LINDENBERG, S., (1977), 'Individuelle Effekte, kollektive Phänomene und das Problem der Transformation', pp. 46-84 in K. Eichner and W. Habermehl (eds.), Probleme der Erklärung sozialen Verhaltens. Meisenheim: Hain.

LINDENBERG, S., (1980), 'Marginal Utility and Restraints on Gain Maximization: The Discrimination Model of Rational, Repetitive Choice', Journal of Mathematical Sociology 7: 289-316.

LINDENBERG, S., (1981), 'Erklärung als Modellbau: Zur soziologische Nutzung von Nutzentheorien', pp. 20-35 in W. Schulte (ed.), Soziologie in der Gesellschaft. Bremen: Zentraldruckerei der Universität.

MALEWSKI, A., (1967), Verhalten und Interaktion. Tübingen: Mohr.

MECKLING, W.H., (1976), 'Values and the Choice of the Model of the Individual in the Social Sciences', Schweizerische Zeitschrift für Volkswirtschaft und Statistik 112: 545-559.

MICHAEL, R.T. and G.S. BECKER, (1973), 'On the New Theory of Consumer Behavior', Swedish Journal of Economics 75: 378-395.

MUELLER, D.C., (1979), Public Choice. Cambridge: University Press.

OLSON, M., (1971), The Logic of Collective Action. 2nd ed., Cambridge, Mass.: Harvard University Press.

OPP, K.-D. (1972), Verhaltenstheoretische Soziologie. Reinbek: Rowohlt.

OPP, K.-D. (1978), Theorie sozialer Krisen. Hamburg: Hoffman und Campe.

OPP, K.-D. (1979), Individualistische Sozialwissenschaft. Stuttgart: Enke.

RAUB, W., (1982), 'Erklärende Sozialwissenschaft auf strukturell-individualistischer Grundlage', Mimeo.

RAUB, W. and T. VOSS, (1981), Individuelles Handeln und gesellschaftliche Folgen. Darmstadt: Luchterhand.

RIKER, W.H. and P.C. ORDESHOOK, (1973), An Introduction to Positive Political Theory. Englewood Cliffs, N.J.: Prentice Hall.

RUNCIMAN, W.G., (1966), Relative Deprivation and Social Justice. London: Routledge.

SAVAGE, L.J., (1972), The Foundation of Statistics. New York: Dover.

SCHEFF, T.J., (1967), 'Toward a Sociological Model of Consensus', American Sociological Review 32: 32-46.

SCHNEIDER, L. (ed.), (1967), The Scottish Moralists on Human Nature and Society. Chicago: Phoenix.

SCHOTTER, A., (1981), The Economic Theory of Social Institutions. Cambridge: University Press.

SCHUMPETER, J.A., (1942), Capitalism, Socialism and Democracy. New York: Harper.

SCHÜTTE, H.G., (1976a), 'Durkheim vs. Bentham. Anmerkungen zu zwei soziologischen Forschungsprogrammen', Mens en Maatschappij 51: 382-397.

SCHÜTTE, H.G., (1976b), 'Het dilemma van de macrosociologie', pp. 51-74 in W. Arts, S. Lindenberg and R. Wippler (eds.), Gedrag en Struktuur. Rotterdam: Universitaire Pers.

SCHÜTTE, H.G., (1981), 'Plädoyer für eine Soziologie der praktischen Vernunft', Mimeo.

SCHÜTTE, H.G., (1982), 'Zur Renaissance des utilitaristischen Denkens in der Soziologie', Mimeo.

SIMON, H.A., (1957), 'A Behavioral Model of Rational Choice', pp. 241-260 in Models for Man. New York: Wiley.

SPOHN, W., (1978), Grundlagen der Entscheidungstheorie. Kronberg: Scriptor.

STEGMÜLLER, W., (1969), Probleme und Resultate der Wissenschaftstheorie und Analytischen Philosophie, Band I, Wissenschaftliche Erklärung und Begründung. Berlin: Springer.

TAZELAAR, F. and R. WIPPLER, (1981), 'Die Theorie mentaler Inkongruenzen und ihre Anwendung in der empirischen Sozialforschung', Mimeo.

THIBAUT, J.W. and H.H. KELLEY, (1959), The Social Psychology of Groups. New York: Wiley.

TVERSKY, A., (1975), 'Critique of Expected Utility Theory: Descriptive and Normative Considerations', Erkenntnis 9: 163-173.

VANBERG, V., (1975), Die zwei Soziologien. Tübingen: Mohr.

VANBERG, V., (1979), 'Colemans Konzeption des korporativen Akteurs - Grundlegung einer Theorie sozialer Verbände', pp. 93-123 in J.S. Coleman, Macht und Gesellschaftsstruktur. Tübingen: Mohr.

WIPPLER, R., (1978), 'The Structural-Individualistic Approach in Dutch Sociology', Netherlands Journal of Sociology 14: 135-155.

WIPPLER, R., (1981), 'Erklärungen unbeabsichtigter Handlungsfolgen: Ziel oder Meilenstein soziologischer Theoriebildung?', pp. 246-261 in J. Matthes (ed.), Lebenswelt und soziale Probleme. Frankfurt a.M.: Campus.

YAARI, M.E., (1977), 'Endogeneous Changes in Tastes: A Philosophical Discussion', Erkenntnis 11: 157-196.

Part I

THEORETICAL MODELS

Reinhard Wippler

THE GENERATION OF OLIGARCHIC STRUCTURES IN CONSTITUTIONALLY DEMOCRATIC ORGANIZATIONS

Introduction

One of the classical problems of sociology is the following question, raised by Michels early in this century: 'But if the main theoretical concern of the social revolutionary and democratic parties consists of opposing oligarchy in all its forms, how can it be explained that they internally give rise to the same tendencies they oppose?' (Michels, 1909: 231). Michels spent many years of his life in search of an answer to this question, but in spite of this the problem has not lost much of its challenge.

In Michels' view, the occurrence of oligarchic tendencies in formally democratic organizations required an explanation because he apparently rejected the common sense theory according to which group members always act in accordance to their common ideology. The complementary common sense theory - blaiming malevolent leaders for their failure to observe democratic principles - seemed to him equally unacceptable given his high esteem for many of the leading social democrats of his time.

For explanations of oligarchic tendencies, Michels did not look so much in the direction of individual shortcomings as in the direction of structural conditions within organizations. The result of his studies was summarized in what became known as the 'iron law of oligarchy': 'It is organization which gives birth to the dominion of the elected over the electors, of the mandatories over the mandators, of the delegates over the delegators .... . The formation of oligarchies within the various forms of democracy is the outcome of organic necessity, and consequently affects every organization, be it socialist or even anarchist' (Michels, 1962: 365-366).

Michels' lively and colorfully presented argument requires a systematic reconstruction (Casinelli, 1953; May, 1965; Hands, 1971; Wippler, 1979; Grunwald, 1980). The core of his theory of oligarchy consists of hypotheses postulating

structural effects, that is effects of the structural characteristics of an
organization on the degree to which its functioning is effectively controlled by
its members. Psychological factors are considered to be of secondary importance [1]
in the sense of merely strengthening or weakening the structural effects. This
focus on structural effects is characteristic of most sociological studies on
organizational democracy - among which Union Democracy is to be considered as the
most prominent one (Lipset et al., 1956).
The postulation of structural effects does not specify the means by which
structural conditions affect the functioning of organizations. Specifying
structural conditions under which formally democratic organizations develop
oligarchic tendencies does not yet explain these tendencies as long as reference
to a mechanism generating these tendencies is missing.

This paper aims to specify the mechanisms generating the oligarchic phenomena
which have been described by Michels and other sociologists. The strategy I am
using - the strategy of generating models - is borrowed from Boudon (1979). The
model to be presented will give a strongly simplified representation of real
social processes. It will contain explicit behavioral assumptions as well as
assumptions concerning structural conditions restricting individual choices.

Within a structural individualistic framework [2], organizational processes are
considered to be the - often unintended - result of individual actions and their
interdependencies, whereby individual actions are considered to be channeled by
the structural characteristics of the organization in question. Therefore, two
questions have to be taken into account for the modelling of the rise of oligarchic
structures in democratic organizations. Firstly, in what way does the structure
and the context of an organization affect the behavior of its members, and
secondly, in what way does the behavior and interaction of different categories
of organization members result in a specific organizational functioning?

Utility theory represents the behavioral part of the model. This theory postulates
that from the behavioral alternatives given in a specific situation, the
alternative with the highest expected utility is chosen. The expected utility of
an action is a function of the utilities and disutilities of its consequences
for the actor and of the actor's subjective probability with which he expects
these consequences to occur.

For the model to be presented, Boudon's general heuristic scheme developed for
the analysis of social change (1979: 148, 153) is used. Its three components are

a system of interaction, the environment of this system of interaction, and the outcome generated by this system of interaction. The three components are causally linked, sometimes - depending on the type of change process - with the inclusion of feedback relations.

I shall introduce the model in several steps, starting with the modelling of some of the structural conditions, which form the center of Michels' theory of oligarchy. Then those dynamic consequences of these conditions which form the core of the iron law of oligarchy, are derived. Secondly, some structural conditions conducive to outcomes counteracting oligarchic tendencies are introduced. Finally, the conditions enhancing and inhibiting oligarchic tendencies are combined in order to explore the margin for organizational democracy.

My analysis of oligarchic tendencies focusses on those types of organizations which take a central place in the classical studies of this fields: political parties and labor unions. One of their common characteristics is a voluntary membership. This has at least two theoretically relevant implications. Firstly, members face a choice problem; they have to weigh the costs of membership (i.e. money, time, the risk involved in transferring control over resources to a corporate actor) against the expected benefits of membership (i.e. the pooling of resources yields higher gains than the separate use of these resources). Secondly, members have two ways of expressing their satisfaction or dissatisfaction with organizational performance; they can either articulate their opinion or leave the organization (Hirschman, 1970). A further common characteristic of the organizations to which the analysis is restricted consists of their democratic constitution. This implies (a) the right to decide on organizational issues is delegated to organization leaders and (b) these leaders are selected by internal elections.

1. Conditions enhancing oligarchic tendencies

For our purpose, we will restrict ourselves to two categories of actors: organization members and organization leaders. To the actors of each category, two behavioral alternatives are open. Members may keep track of the organizational performance and express their opinions; that is to say, they protest in case of bad performance, and give support in the opposite case. Following Hirschman (1970), this behavioral alternative is called 'voice' (V). 'Voice' can take different forms, varying in efficacy and cost. The weakest and cheapest form is participation in internal elections, followed by oral or written criticism or support, while organizing an opposition or adherence group may be considered to be the strongest form of voice. The second behavioral alternative, open to members, is inactivity (IN); that is to say, the actor remains a member of the organization, while abstaining from voice.

The first behavioral alternative of organization leaders corresponds with the common sense notion of democratic leadership: in decisions of organizational issues, the highes priority is given to the promotion of members' interest. Serving the interest of members (MI) is the main characteristic of leadership behavior in the classical theory of democracy, but recent economic theories have drawn attention to leadership behavior serving the private goals of organizational decision makers (Herder-Dorneich, 1973: 15-16). Therefore, if the highest priority in deciding organizational issues is given to the promotion of private goals, the second behavioral alternative of organizational leaders is enacted; I shall call this alternative promoting private goals (PG)

The determination of the subjectively expected utility of the four behavioral alternatives described above requires specification of relevant costs and benefits (i.e. utilities and disutilities U) and of subjective probabilities P. The core model of member behavior in voluntary and formally democratic organizations is summarized in the following equations.

(1) $SEU_V = U_{cg}(P_{wc} + P_c) + U_i - U_m - U_v$

(2) $SEU_{IN} = U_{cg}P_{wc} - U_i - U_m$

where:

SEU_V : expected utility of behavioral alternative 'voice'

SEU_{IN}: expected utility of behavioral alternative 'inactivity'

U_{cg} : utility of a situation where the interest of the members is realized (a collective good)

U_i : utility of ideological gratification received by acting in accordance with democratic principles or disutility of violating these principles

$-U_m$: disutility (costs) of membership (dues etc.)

$-U_v$: disutility (costs) of voice (gathering information on organizational performance; investing time in elections, meetings, or consultations)

P_{wc} : probability that the interest of members will be realized without own distribution

P_c : change in probability P_{wc} expected from own contribution

Simplifying assumptions contained in the core model of member behavior are: ideological gratification, membership costs and costs associated with voice are expected with certainty.

The core model of leader behavior is also summarized in two equations:

(3) $SEU_{MI} = U_{gv} P_{cv} + U_i - U_{mc} - U_{pp}$

(4) $SEU_{PG} = U_{pp} - U_{lv} P_{cv} - U_i$

where:

SEU_{MI} : expected utility of behavioral alternative 'serving the interest of the members', when deciding on organizational issues

SEU_{PG} : expected utility of behavioral alternative 'promoting private goals' when deciding on organizational issues

U_{gv} : utility of gaining votes in internal elections

U_{pp} : utility of actual or future personal privileges due to leader position (financial benefits, career perspective, etc.)

$-U_{lv}$: disutility (costs) of losing votes

$-U_{mc}$: disutility (costs) of intensive contact with members (gathering information about changes in member interest, explaining strategic moves to members etc.)

P_{cv} : probability that organizational decisions will lead to a change (gain or loss) of votes received in internal elections

Like before, the symplifying assumption is introduced, stating that some consequences are expected with certainty to follow from the alternative chosen, namely ideological gratification as well as gain or loss of personal privileges, and the costs of intensive member contact (transaction costs). Another simplifying assumption which will be dropped later is that serving the interest of the members requires leaders to sacrifice personal privileges.

Stated in terms of behavioral alternatives, oligarchy in democratic organizations corresponds with a situation where members choose inactivity and leaders choose the promotion of private goals. Since the iron law of oligarchy predicts that any formally democratic organization will develop oligarchic tendencies in course of time, it can be derived from Michels' theory that finally a state will be reached where $SEU_{IN} > SEU_V$ and $SEU_{PG} > SEU_{MI}$.

In Michels' theory, the development of oligarchic structures is assumed to follow inevitably from a specific constellation of structural conditions (Michels, 1962). In order to model this process we need assumptions that link the terms of the equations of the behavioral model with structural characteristics of organizations (Lindenberg, 1981a). To begin with, only three of these characteristics are introduced. 'Size' refers to the number of members of an organization, 'network density' indicates how many informal relations relative to size exist between members, and 'homogeneity' alludes to the diversity of ability and aptitude (energy, cognitive and social skills etc.) among actors within an organization. In which way do these three structural variables affect organizational functioning? The organizations Michels was concerned with were typical mass organizations, that is to say they were characterized by large size and small network density. Furthermore, Michels assumed a great diversity in natural endowment within organizations (i.e. little homogeneity).

A combination of large size and small network density is characteristic of those groups that have been named 'latent groups' by Olson (1965). In latent groups, rational actors will not participate in efforts aiming at the realization of a common interest (i.e. the production of a collective good) because eventually they can benefit from the efforts of other group members (the 'free rider' phenomenon); furthermore, the probability of exerting a decisive influence is extremely low when a large number of group members is involved. Applying Olson's theory to our behavioral model and structural conditions means that in large organizations with little informal relations the change in probability of a realization of members' interest as expected from one's own effort (P_c) approaches zero. Consequently, members expect equal chances of the realization of their interest, whether they choose voice or inactivity. Voice will only be chosen in case of strong ideological commitment. More precisely, it will be chosen if the costs of neglecting ideological commitment are higher than half of the costs associated with the enactment of voice. As the average costs of voice are rather high, such a cost ratio will probably be rare. Furthermore, the weakness of ideological motivation even in social democratic parties was the very condition leading Michels to his search for structural conditions as causes for oligarchy [3].

Organization size and network density have still another influence on the expected utility of the behavioral alternatives of members and leaders. The larger the organization and the smaller its network density, the higher the costs of voice ($-U_v$): with increasing size and few informal relations it becomes more difficult for members to gather information about organizational performance (information costs) and to consult other members or coordinate activities (transaction costs). As to the behavioral alternatives of leaders, the smaller the network density is, the smaller the likelihood that organizational decisions will result in gains or losses of votes in internal elections (P_{cv}). In organizations with little informal relations, members cannot get a clear picture of the decisions taken because communications between members and leaders cannot be transferred through personal channels of communication and will therefore be rather ineffective. As organizational decisions are quite unlikely to change the votes received in internal elections, the attractiveness of the democratic behavioral alternative will weaken as more weight will be given to the costs associated with this alternative ($-U_{mc}$).

Little homogeneity of the actors within an organization is related to both of the democratic behavioral alternatives of the model. 'Voice' as well as 'serving the interest of the members' require for their enactment some cognitive and social skills. Lack of homogeneity means that these skills are unevenly distributed among the actors. Since the costs of voice ($-U_v$) and the costs of intensive leader contact with members ($-U_{mc}$) count less for skilled members and leaders than for actors with little cognitive and social skills, the relative attractiveness of the democratic alternatives differs among persons. If Michels' assumption that in the average organization leaders have more cognitive and social skills than organization members [4] is correct, then the lesser the homogeneity of an organization, the heavier the costs of choosing the democratic alternative will count, in a disproportional way for members than for leaders.

To summarize: the effects of the three structural variables on the behavioral alternatives of members and leaders all point in the same direction. Under the conditions described by Michels, the expected utility of the 'democratic' alternatives is lower than the expected utility of the 'oligarchic' alternatives: $SEU_V < SEU_{IN}$ and $SEU_{MI} < SEU_{PG}$.

2. Changes in time

Up to now, only two components of Boudon's heuristic scheme for the analysis of social change have been taken into account. The core models of member and leader behavior, the structural variables, and the assumptions linking behavioral models and structural conditions describe the system of interaction, while the resulting behavioral choices represent the outcome generated by this system. However, some conditions in the environment of the system of interaction have been implicitly taken for granted. I will briefly mention two of these boundary conditions.

Firstly, by introducing only two behavioral alternatives for members and by neglecting differences in the environment of organizations, one might get the impression that members are forced to keep their organization membership even when the organizational performance is purely detrimental to them. Such a situation would run counter to the principle of voluntary membership. In the model thus far presented, I have tacitly assumed (a) that the environment does not offer an alternative arrangement for the realization of members' interest, and (b) that membership benefits never are lower than membership costs. Later I will drop these assumptions.

Secondly, the environmental conditions determining the margin within which the realization of members' interest is feasible, also have not been taken into account. Obviously, it matters for the actors whether an organization is operating under adverse or propitious circumstances. Thus far, I have tacitly assumed a middle level of environmental restriction. This assumption too, will later be dropped.

The question which behavioral choices will be made under given structural and environmental conditions requires a static mode of analysis. However, in Michels' theory of oligarchy the variable 'time' plays an important role. Oligarchic tendencies are assumed to be generated from an initially 'democratic' situation by way of an irreversible cumulative process. Modelling this process requires that the consequences of the outcomes at t_1 for the system of interaction at t_2 are specified (i.e. a dynamic mode of analysis). The general heuristic scheme for the analysis of cumulative processes comprises one feedback relation from outcome to system of interaction (Boudon, 1979: 153).

FIGURE-1:   Scheme of a cumulative process

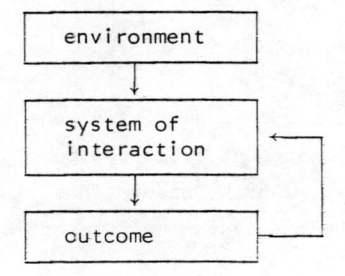

```
┌─────────────────┐
│   environment   │
└────────┬────────┘
         │
         ▼
┌─────────────────┐
│    system of    │◄──┐
│   interaction   │   │
└────────┬────────┘   │
         │            │
         ▼            │
┌─────────────────┐   │
│     outcome     │───┘
└─────────────────┘
```

I shall now describe such a cumulative process for several consecutive time periods. At t_1 the organization is characterized by a modest number of members, a middle level of network density and a modest amount of homogeneity. Furthermore, it is assumed that for the members $SEU_V > SEU_{IN}$ and for leaders $SEU_{MI} > SEU_{PG}$. That is to say, in the situation to start with the organization is functioning democratically.

If it is assumed that new members will be attracted to the organization when the interest of the members is served, the outcome of the system of interaction at t_1 (i.e. the choice of the democratic behavioral alternatives having a high probability) leads to a change of organization members. This increase in organization size will, firstly, reduce network density, and secondly, will change the cost benefit relations of the behavioral alternatives. Because of larger size and smaller network density, the probability of voice being effective (P_c) decreases while the costs of voice ($-U_v$) increases. As a consequence, the relative attractiveness of the behavioral alternatives of the members is reversed, so that the probability of choosing inactivity slightly exceeds the probability of voice ($SEU_{IN} > SEU_V$). With regard to the behavioral alternatives of the leaders, the larger size and smaller network density of the organization at t_2 reduce the likelihood that organizational decisions will result in gains or losses of votes (P_{cv}). As a consequence, the difference in relative attractiveness of the behavioral alternatives gets smaller; that is to say, the probability that the democratic behavior will be chosen exceeds the probability of the other choice at t_2 less than at t_1. The other variables of the model do not change between t_1 and t_2.

The outcome of the alteration in the system of interaction at t_2 is a situation in which organization members are slightly inclined to choose inactivity while organization leaders are still - but not very convincingly - serving the members' interest.

If it is assumed that organization members acquire organizational skills by carrying into effect voice (because voice requires the gathering and processing of information about organizational policies, opportunities etc.), then the outcome of the system of interaction at t_2 leads to new alterations in this system at t_3, namely an increase of the difference between the average cognitive and social skills of members and the same average of leaders [5]. Consequently, the cost benefit relations of the behavioral alternatives are changing. For those who fall behind with regard to cognitive and social skills because of their inactivity, the costs for carrying out voice ($-U_v$) increase relatively to the situation at t_1. As a consequence, the relative attractiveness of voice is further weakened. Additionally, during the period between t_2 and t_3, the number of organization members is increasing further because the probability that organizational decisions are serving the interest of the members is still higher than the probability that these decisions promote private goals of the leaders. This strengthens the earlier mentioned effects of increasing size and decreasing network density on the cost benefit relations of the behavioral alternatives. As a consequence, the probability of members choosing inactivity instead of voice increases. Because the inactivity of members at t_2 leads at t_3 to a lower subjective probability of leaders to expect the result of internal elections (P_{cv}) to be affected by their decisions, the relative attractiveness of the behavioral alternatives of leaders is reversed so that the probability of choosing a promotion of private goals is slightly higher than the probability of serving members' interest ($SEU_{PG} > SEU_{MI}$). Other variables of the model do not change between t_2 and t_3.

The outcome of the alteration in the system of interaction at t_3 consists of a state of the organization in which organization members are strongly inclined to choose inactivity while organization leaders are slightly inclined to give priority to private goals instead of members' interests when deciding on organizational issues.

This outcome, again, leads to changes in the system of interaction at t_4. Because of the organizational performance which serves members' interest less than it serves personal goals of leaders, the benefits associated with organization membership (the collective good aspects of membership U_{cg}) are reduced. This strengthens the significance of ideological motives (U_i) for choosing voice. Because of the more widespread inactivity among members, more and more members fall behind with regard to cognitive and social skills. This makes voice more costly ($-U_v$) for an increasing number of people. Consequently, the probability of members choosing voice is again lowered further. With regard to the organization leaders, the outcome of the system of interaction at t_3 does not change the relative attractiveness of their behavioral alternatives at t_4.

In terms of the behavioral choices of the actors, the outcome of the system of interaction at t_4 is an oligarchic situation. That is to say, the organization members remain inactive while the organization leaders are giving priority to personal goals instead of members' interest. Assuming that for members the cumulative process of falling behind with regard to cognitive and social skills is periodically compensated by the fact that experienced and skilled leaders are replaced by young and less skilled people, the functioning of the organization at t_4 can be described as a stable state of oligarchy. This is exactly what Michels had in mind when developing his theory of oligarchy.

The cumulative feedback effects and their outcome, transforming an initial situation of internal democracy in course of time into a stable state of oligarchy, are schematically summarized in figure 2.

FIGURE-2: Outline of cumulative feedback effects

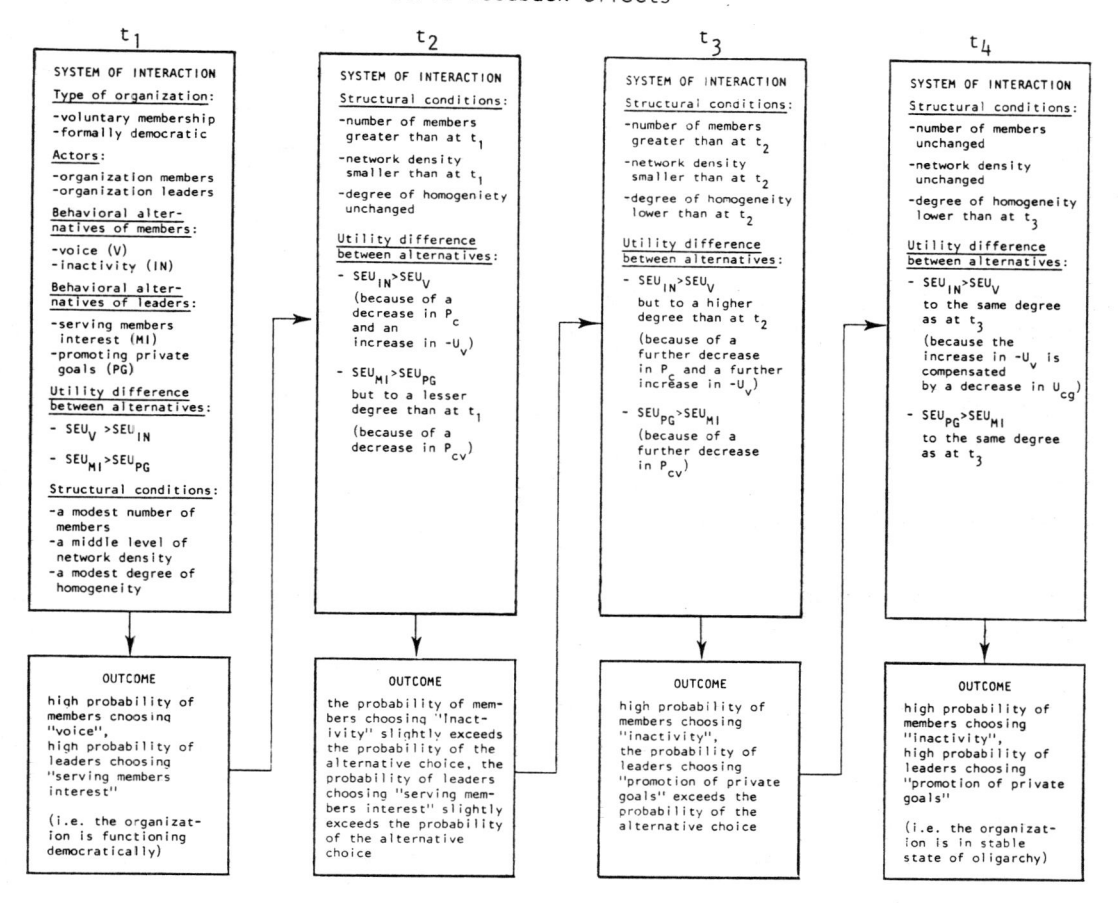

t_1	t_2	t_3	t_4
SYSTEM OF INTERACTION Type of organization: -voluntary membership -formally democratic Actors: -organization members -organization leaders Behavioral alternatives of members: -voice (V) -inactivity (IN) Behavioral alternatives of leaders: -serving members interest (MI) -promoting private goals (PG) Utility difference between alternatives: - $SEU_V > SEU_{IN}$ - $SEU_{MI} > SEU_{PG}$ Structural conditions: -a modest number of members -a middle level of network density -a modest degree of homogeneity	SYSTEM OF INTERACTION Structural conditions: -number of members greater than at t_1 -network density smaller than at t_1 -degree of homogeneity unchanged Utility difference between alternatives: - $SEU_{IN} > SEU_V$ (because of a decrease in P_c and an increase in $-U_v$) - $SEU_{MI} > SEU_{PG}$ but to a lesser degree than at t_1 (because of a decrease in P_{cv})	SYSTEM OF INTERACTION Structural conditions: -number of members greater than at t_2 -network density smaller than at t_2 -degree of homogeneity lower than at t_2 Utility difference between alternatives: - $SEU_{IN} > SEU_V$ but to a higher degree than at t_2 (because of a further decrease in P_c and a further increase in $-U_v$) - $SEU_{PG} > SEU_{MI}$ (because of a further decrease in P_{cv})	SYSTEM OF INTERACTION Structural conditions: -number of members unchanged -network density unchanged -degree of homogeneity lower than at t_3 Utility difference between alternatives: - $SEU_{IN} > SEU_V$ to the same degree as at t_3 (because the increase in $-U_v$ is compensated by a decrease in U_{cg}) - $SEU_{PG} > SEU_{MI}$ to the same degree as at t_3
OUTCOME high probability of members choosing "voice", high probability of leaders choosing "serving members interest" (i.e. the organization is functioning democratically)	OUTCOME the probability of members choosing "Inactivity" slightly exceeds the probability of the alternative choice, the probability of leaders choosing "serving members interest" slightly exceeds the probability of the alternative choice	OUTCOME high probability of members choosing "inactivity", the probability of leaders choosing "promotion of private goals" exceeds the probability of the alternative choice	OUTCOME high probability of members choosing "inactivity", high probability of leaders choosing "promotion of private goals" (i.e. the organization is in stable state of oligarchy)

For a better understanding of the model representing this cumulative process, I would like to clarify two points. Firstly, the model merely demonstrates how an initially democratic situation, given certain structural conditions, may generate a state of oligarchy. However, oligarchy could also be the result of another constellation of conditions. Secondly, the cumulative process described is neither unavoidable nor irreversible as Michels tried to make us believe, since several conditions inhibiting oligarchic tendencies can be specified. I will now describe those conditions

3. Conditions inhibiting oligarchic tendencies

Until now it has been assumed that organization members have to choose either 'voice' or 'inactivity'. However, voluntary membership does not merely refer to the possibility of entering an organization, but also implies that members can choose to leave [6]. Following Hirschman (1970), this third behavioral alternative for members is called 'exit'. The core model of member behavior can be extended by addition of this alternative. I shall confine myself to a mere sketch of the consequences of this extension.

Generally, the costs of voice are greater than those of exit. Voice requires investment of time and energy in order to keep informed about organizational performance and to participate in meetings and internal elections, while cancelling organization membership in most cases does not involve any costs. It is only in organizations of a specific type - in case of ideological commitment or strong loyalties towards other members - that exit costs may be considerable; in political parties with a strong ideological bent, for instance, 'renegades' do have to face severe negative sanctions.

Given the low average cost of exit, the relative attractiveness of this alternative depends, firstly, on the utility of the collective good to be provided by the organization (i.e. the higher the utility, the less attractive the exit opinion is) and secondly, on the availability of alternatives in the environment of the organization by which these goods could equally be provided (i.e. the less there are competing organizations for the provision of a certain collective good, the less attractive is the exit alternative) [7]. However, if the good to be provided by the organization is highly valued and no alternative organizations are available, then the probability of voice increases. Lack of external alternatives advances internal democracy.

When exit is taken into account, the behavioral alternatives of leaders are also affected. Assuming that a large scale exit is perceived by leaders as a threat to the persistence of the organization and a weakening of their own position, a new utility argument can be added to the core model of leader behavior, namely expected loss of members as costs when 'promotion of private goals' is chosen and expected gain of members as benefits when 'serving members' interests' is chosen. The anticipation of sensible member exit as a consequence of the organizational decisions taken increases for leaders the relative attractiveness of the 'democratic' alternative [8].

In Michels' theory of oligarchy, a modest degree of homogeneity was assumed to exist in the initially democratic situation. Dropping this assumption, one could ask what the consequences of little homogeneity on one side, and a high degree of homogeneity on the other are. According to the theory of power distance reduction (Mulder, 1977; Grunwald, 1980: 278-285) the effects of a great difference between the average cognitive and social skills of members and the same average of leaders should even be worse than Michels had predicted. Under these circumstances, member participation even leads to an increase of power distance between members and leaders. On the other hand, in almost homogeneous organizations (e.g. professional associations) the cumulative process resulting in oligarchy is drastically slowed down [9].

Other conditions inhibiting oligarchic tendencies have been analyzed in Union Democracy (Lipset et al., 1956). Two of them will be mentioned here [10]. Previously it was argued that the probability of 'voice' is extremely low when large organizational size is combined with small network density (analogous to the 'free rider' problem in latent groups). The International Typographical Union, however, was an organization in which large size and high network density were combined. The network density in the ITU (i.e. the existence of an 'occupational community') follows from the specific work organization and task structure in the printing industry. Network density increases the likelihood of organizational democracy. Firstly by facing members with the risk of negative sanctions in case of abstention from voice, and secondly by facilitating contacts of leaders with members and thus lowering the costs associated with the choice of the 'democratic' alternative.

The other condition counteracting oligarchic tendencies refers to the existence of a two party system in the International Typographical Union. Whether such an organized internal opposition will arise and persist, depends on environmental factors. In the case of the ITU this means firstly that the union came into existence through the federation of existing independent locals instead of having been organized 'from the top down', and secondly, that internal cleavages were a result of differences in ideology rather than differences in interest (cf. Wippler 1979: 23). The existence of an organized internal opposition changes the relative attractiveness of the behavioral choices in favour of the 'democratic' alternatives. For members, the information costs required to carry out voice are reduced, because the leaders no longer monopolize the channels of communication in the organization. For leaders, the probability increases that their decisions on organizational issues will have consequences for the result of internal elections. This change in probability is likely to occur because organization leaders have to compete for votes with opposition leaders, i.e. their potential successors. Thus, the existence of an organized opposition works as a counter force to oligarchic tendencies in democratic organizations [11].

4. Behavioral choices and organizational functioning

The analysis presented thus far focussed on the question how differences in organizational structure and environment affect behavioral choices. This may give rise to the impression that the way an organization functions is exclusively determined by the behavioral choices of its members and leaders. This impression is wrong because there are several boundary conditions under which either democratic behavioral choices produce an unintended outcome, experienced by the actors as a state of oligarchy, or oligarchic choices that are not experienced to contradict a state of internal democracy. I will sketch just two of these conditions.

So far I have assumed that organizations operate in an environment restricting the realization of members' interest only moderately. When this assumption is dropped, the question rises how adverse or propitious external circumstances with regard to the realization of members' interest affect internal democracy. Under favorable external circumstances (e.g. for labor unions a period of economic growth or for political parties a period of strong voters' support), members' interest can be served even when members are inactive and leaders pursue private goals. In such situations, leaders have a large enough margin to serve members' interest without being obliged to sacrifice many personal privileges. In terms of the third behavioral equation, this means that the sign of the utility argument U_{pp} may even become positive. That is to say, under favorable external circumstances, the members may not experience the outcome of oligarchic choices as a violation of democratic principles. On the other hand, when external circumstances prevent the realization of members' interest, massive voice will be ineffective, even if leaders act in the interest of the members. In such a situation, the organization is experienced to function in an oligarchic way because of the ineffectiveness of democratic behavior.

By introducing gain and loss of votes in internal elections as a utility argument in the behavioral equation of leaders, I did not mention differences in the electoral system. However, the effects of election outcomes on the degree of internal democracy can vary considerably, depending on the number of election steps existing between ordinary members and the organization top (Herder-Dorneich, 1973: 168-177). In a multistep electoral system, those elected in the first step form the electoral college in the second step, and so on; the top is then elected by those elected in the last step. Such electoral chains offer the opportunity of coalition formation at each step. When electoral chains are long and opportunities for coalition forming numerous, the electoral outcome of the last step may be totally different from the outcome of the first step. If this is the case, the decisions taken by the top leaders of an organization will be contrary to the interest of the majority of ordinary members, even if these decisions are taken with the aim of serving the interest of their electors (cf. Wippler, 1981a). Multi-step electoral systems may thus unintentionally transform democratic behavioral choices into an organizational functioning which is experienced as oligarchic by the majority of the organization members [12].

5. Conclusion

In this paper, I have described a model version of Michels' theory of oligarchy and, next, added to this model behavioral, structural and environmental assumptions. My argument is summarized in figure 3, using Boudon's general heuristic scheme for the analysis of social change. Compared to figure 1, two feedback relations have been added, one from the system of interaction to the environment and one from the outcome to the environment (cf. figure 3). Because of these new relations, the scheme refers to what is called 'transformation processes' (Boudon, 1979: 188-196). How are these feedback relations to be interpreted?

Both relations indicate that characteristics of the organizational environment (the boundary conditions 1 and 5 in figure 3) can be altered through initiatives of actors from the system of interaction. With regard to alternatives in the environment of an organization which could equally serve the interest of its

FIGURE-3: Outline of the variables in the model

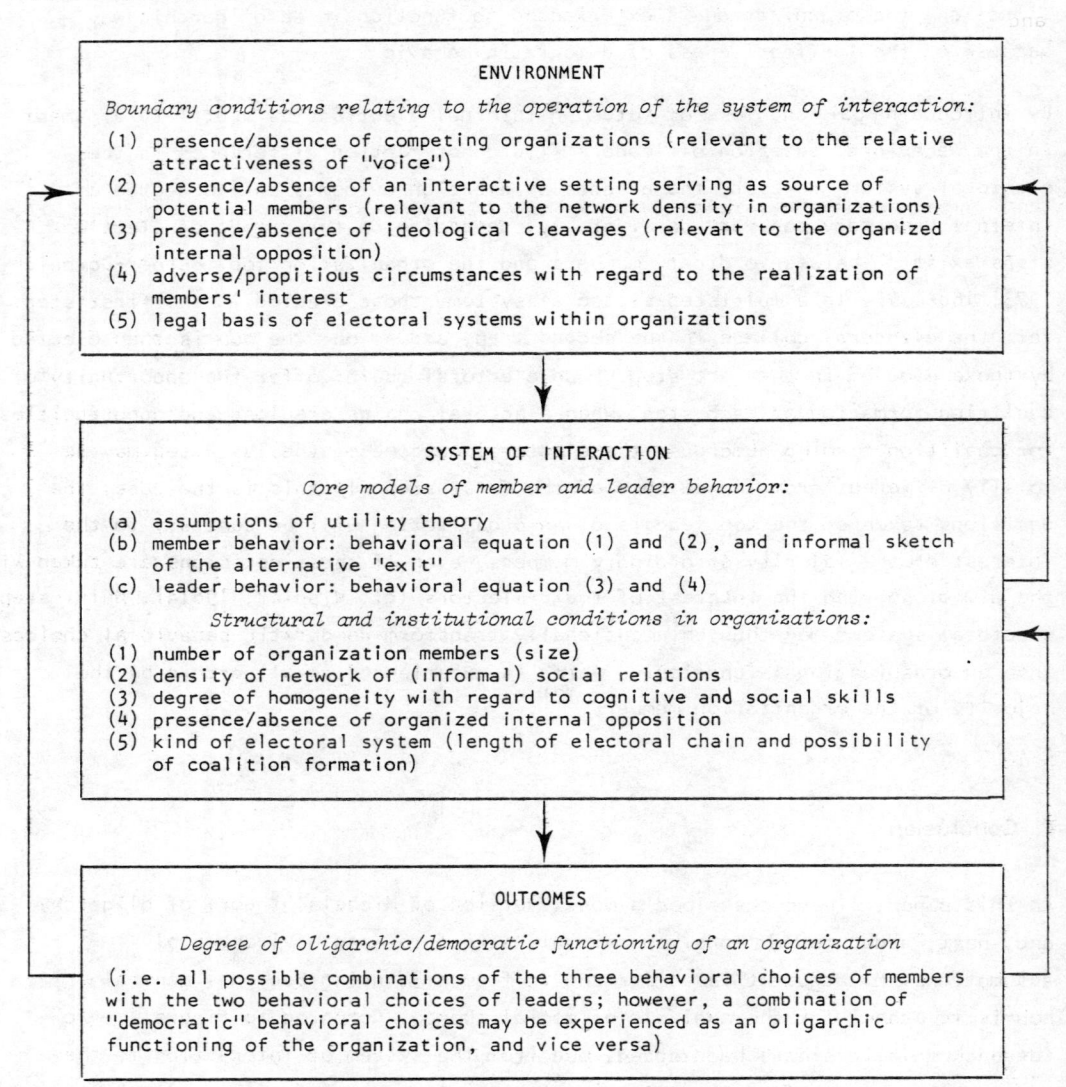

ENVIRONMENT

Boundary conditions relating to the operation of the system of interaction:

(1) presence/absence of competing organizations (relevant to the relative attractiveness of "voice")
(2) presence/absence of an interactive setting serving as source of potential members (relevant to the network density in organizations)
(3) presence/absence of ideological cleavages (relevant to the organized internal opposition)
(4) adverse/propitious circumstances with regard to the realization of members' interest
(5) legal basis of electoral systems within organizations

SYSTEM OF INTERACTION

Core models of member and leader behavior:

(a) assumptions of utility theory
(b) member behavior: behavioral equation (1) and (2), and informal sketch of the alternative "exit"
(c) leader behavior: behavioral equation (3) and (4)

Structural and institutional conditions in organizations:

(1) number of organization members (size)
(2) density of network of (informal) social relations
(3) degree of homogeneity with regard to cognitive and social skills
(4) presence/absence of organized internal opposition
(5) kind of electoral system (length of electoral chain and possibility of coalition formation)

OUTCOMES

Degree of oligarchic/democratic functioning of an organization

(i.e. all possible combinations of the three behavioral choices of members with the two behavioral choices of leaders; however, a combination of "democratic" behavioral choices may be experienced as an oligarchic functioning of the organization, and vice versa)

members, members may leave their organization and set up a new competing one. Members will take this role of a 'political entrepreneur' only as far as the expected benefits from a future leadership position exeed the actual costs of setting up an organization. If such initiatives succeed, the environment of the original organization is altered, in such a way that the likelihood of democratic member behavior decreases and the likelihood of democratic leader behavior increases.

With regard to the legal basis of electoral systems within organizations, members and/or leaders may try to bring about legislative changes in order to reduce the likelihood of election outcomes that are merely the product of a multi-step electoral system instead of a reflection of the preferences of members. Such legislative changes would have to aim at a restriction of possible coalitions as well as at a shortening of electoral chains. If these changes in the organizational environment are realized by actions of organization members or leaders, then the likelihood of unintended oligarchic tendencies is reduced.

One may ask what has been gained by modelling some classical sociological ideas about oligarchy in democratic organizations. I believe at least two things have been gained.

Firstly, explicitly linking structural and institutional conditions with behavioral assumptions sheds some light on the mechanisms by which the influence of social circumstances on organizational performance is mediated. This facilitates the tracing of 'disturbing factors' which have to be taken into account when empirical generalizations on an aggregate level are tested and the test results are interpreted (cf. Lindenberg, 1981b).

Secondly, modelling oligarchic tendencies facilitates the determination of the limits as well as the possibilities of policies aiming at an advancement of internal democracy. With the help of our model, those structural and institutional conditions which inhibit oligarchic tendencies can easily be identified. Relevant conditions are, on the one hand, circumstances which activate members for efforts to further their common interest (.i.e. circumstances which reduce the attractiveness of free rider behavior), and on the other hand circumstances which strengthen the effectiveness of vote and membership fluctuations as a means of steering leader behavior (i.e. circumstances which reduce the attractiveness of neglecting members' interest).

However, knowing the conditions under which oligarchic tendencies are weakened does not yet mean that these conditions can easily be brought about. Even with this knowledge, the prospects of internal democracy are bad, since only a few of the relevant conditions, internal and external to organizations, are accessible to policy measures.

Notes

(1) This general idea is summarized in the statement 'What was initiated by the need for organization, administration and strategy, is completed by psychological determinism' (Michels, 1962: 205).
(2) The structural-individualistic approach in sociology is described for instance in Arts et al. (1976), Wippler (1979), Boudon (1979) and Raub and Voss (1981).
(3) None the less, Michels seems to admit that oligarchic tendencies may in exceptional cases be counteracted by actors who are strongly motivated by ideology, especially when 'the incurable idealism of youth' or 'fanatic political dogmatism' (1908: 114) are involved.
(4) Michels discusses these differences under the headline 'Accessory qualities requisite to leadership' (1962: 98-104).
(5) Groser (1979: 106) calls this a 'Selbstverstärkung des Informationsgefälles. Sind die Entscheidungskompetenzen erst ungleich verteilt, so reduziert sich der Nutzen, den das einfache Mitglied aus der Aufnahme von Informationen zieht, noch weiter. Selbst ein gut informiertes Mitglied wird es unter Umständen schwer haben, seine Meinung zum Tragen zu bringen'. The labels Michels uses for this phenomenon are 'psychologische Metamorphose' and 'psychische Transmutation' (1911: 200, 204; cf. Wippler, 1979: 10-13).
(6) A more detailed and comparative analysis of the two options 'exit' and 'voice' is given by Hirschmann (1970).
(7) Hirschmann (1970: 84) introduces the hypothesis that the relevance of Michels' theory of oligarchy is restricted to multi-party systems, such as those which were characteristic for continental Europe early in this century. However, this may not hold for those multi-party systems which are characterized by what the Dutch call 'verzuiling' (cf. Wippler, 1979: 57).
(8) Herder-Dorneich (1973: 13-25) presents an analysis of the homo organisatoricus whose behavior is aimed at maximizing financial means, members, and votes in internal elections.
(9) A similar hypothesis about the consequences of homogeneity for internal democracy has been suggested by Lipset et al. in Union Democracy (1956: 465).
(10) A more detailed reconstruction of the hypotheses from Union Democracy is given in Wippler (1979: 17-28).
(11) Coleman (1981: 13-17) discusses these two conditions inhibiting oligarchy in the context of his 'theory of social action'. The central defect of any

conjoint structure is the free rider problem, and the network density in the ITU operates as a counterforce to the attractiveness of free rider behavior. The fundamental defect of any disjoint structure is that the superordinate pursues his own interests at the expense of the subordinate, and the existence of an internal opposition may counteract this tendency.

(12) The problem of unintended consequences of purposive actions and the analysis of composition effects are discussed in Wippler (1981a) and in the studies quoted there.

References

ARTS, W., S. LINDENBERG and R. WIPPLER (eds.), (1976), Gedrag en Structuur. Rotterdam: Universitaire Pers.

BARRY, B., (1974), 'Review Article: Exit, Voice and Loyalty', British Journal of Political Science 4: 79-107.

BOUDON, R., (1979), 'Generating Models as a Research Strategy', pp. 51-64 in R.K. Merton, J.S. Coleman and P.H. Rossi (eds.), Qualitative and Quantitative Social Research. New York: Free Press.

BOUDON, R., (1979), La Logique du Social. Paris: Hachette.

CASINELLI, C.W., (1973), 'The Law of Oligarchy', American Political Science Review 77: 773-784.

COLEMAN, J.S., (1981), 'A Theoretical Framework for Social Indicators for Organizational Change', Washington D.C.: Social Science Research Council, Paper prepared for Conference on Indicators of Organizational Change.

GROSER, M., (1979), Grundlagen der Tauschtheorie des Verbandes. Berlin: Duncker & Humblot.

GRUNWALD, W., (1981), 'Das "eherne Gesetz der Oligarchie": Ein Grundproblem demokratischer Führung in Organisationen', pp. 245-285 in W. Grunwald and H.G. Lilge (eds.), Partizipative Führung. Bern: Paul Haupt.

HANDS, G., (1978), 'Roberto Michels and the Study of Political Parties', British Journal of Political Science 1: 155-172.

HERDER-DORNEICH, Ph., (1973), Zur Verbandsökonomie. Berlin: Duncker & Humblot.

HIRSCHMAN, A.O., (1970), Exit, Voice and Loyalty. Cambridge, Mass.: Harvard University Press.

LINDENBERG, S., (1981a), 'Erklärung als Modellbau: Zur soziologischen Nutzung der Nutzentheorie', pp. 20-35 in W. Schulte (ed.), Soziologie in der Gesellschaft. Bremen: Zentraldruckerei der Universität.

LINDENBERG, S., (1981b), Van Hypothese naar model: een voorbeeld. Groningen: Sociologisch Instituut.

LIPSET, S.M., M. TROW and J.S. COLEMAN, (1956), Union Democracy. Garden City, N.Y.: Doubleday.

MAY, J.D., (1965), 'Democracy, Organization, Michels', American Political Science Review 59: 417-429.

MICHELS, R., (1908), 'Die oligarchischen Tendenzen der Gesellschaft. Ein Beitrag zum Problem der Demokratie', Archiv für Sozialwissenschaft und Sozialpolitik 27: 73-135.

MICHELS, R., (1909), 'Der konservative Grundzug der Partei-Organisation', Monatsschrift für Soziologie 1: 228-236.

MICHELS, R., (1962), Political Parties. New York: Collier.

MULDER, M., (1977), The Daily Power Game. Leiden: Stenfert Kroese.

OLSON, M., (1965), The Logic of Collective Action. New York: Schocken.

RAUB, W. and T. VOSS, (1981), Individuelles Handeln und gesellschaftliche Folgen. Darmstadt: Luchterhand.

WIPPLER, R., (1978), 'The Structural-Individualistic Approach in Dutch Sociology. Toward an Explanatory Social Science', Netherlands Journal of Sociology 14: 135-155.

WIPPLER, R., (1979), 'Zum Problem verbandsinterner Demokratie: Rekonstruktion und Vergleich verschiedener Lösungsvorschlage', Bad Homburg: Deutsche Gesellschaft für Soziologie, Beitrag Arbeitstagung "Theorienvergleich in den Sozialwissenschaften".

WIPPLER, R., (1981a), 'Erklärung unbeabsichtigter Handlungsfolgen: Ziel oder Meilenstein soziologischer Theorienbildung?', pp. 246-261 in J. Matthes (ed.), Lebenswelt und soziale Probleme. Frankfurt a.M.: Campus.

WIPPLER, R., (1981b), 'Zur Theorie der Oligarchie in Organisationen und Verbänden', Hagen: Fernuniversität, Beitrag Symposium 'Soziale Bedingungen und soziale Konsequenzen individuellen Handelns'.

Siegwart Lindenberg

THEORIES OF REVOLUTION AND EMPIRICAL EVIDENCE

Introduction

There are many and varied theories of revolution and there is much evidence compiled. Yet, on this topic of revolutions there seem to be endemic problems with regard to the match between theories and data. Exceptions are legion, conclusions are dubious, and ad hoc adjustments are frequent [1]. Of course there are many extenuating circumstances for such a state of affairs. Historical records are often very incomplete; the phenomenon 'revolution' itself is elusive; post-hoc interpretations by post-revolutionary governments and historians create a thick veil of tailor-made historical 'insight' surrounding the events leading up to the revolution. None the less, the poor state of the arts cannot be blamed on these circumstances alone. What else is wrong with the theories and/or the empirical evidence and what can be done about it? The purpose of this paper is to make a contribution towards answering these two questions. It is decidedly not the purpose of this paper to present an overview with regard to either theories of revolution or empirical evidence. There is no dearth of these overviews in the literature [2].

1. Major flaws

1.1. The 'major-group-hypothesis'

Many theories of revolution proceed explicitly or implicitly from the assumption that there is one major group in a society that engages in a revolution: the bourgeois, the proletariat, the underprivileged, the oppressed, the peasants, the military, the aristocracy, the clergy, the privileged, etc. What is wrong with this hypothesis?

Of course, it would be sufficient to find out whether it stands up to test by confronting it with empirical evidence, would it not? Attempts to do so are not completely lacking in the sense that there is controversy over the identification of the 'major' group. Was the Russian Revolution a proletarian or a peasant revolution? Was the French Revolution a bourgeois or a peasant revolution? What was the 'major' group in the Chinese Revolution? As 'major' groups are selected on the basis of theoretical notions the empirical evidence will not tell us whether the general hypothesis ('always a major group') or any of its specifications ('this one is the major group') 'stand up to test'. Quite to the contrary, the relationship between theory and data, so characteristically troublesome when revolutions are concerned, is troubled only more deeply.

While more historically oriented analyses are hampered by the 'major-group-hypothesis', they at least have no trouble dealing with all sorts of groups, even if they are characterized as 'minor' or 'catalyzing' or 'supportive'. The real harm is done in more theoretically oriented analyses. Here we find no mitigating influence by historical material. The translation of the major-group-hypothesis into a theoretical framework is, then, the following: revolutions are revolts by larger groups, so that the difference between revolts and revolutions is only a matter of scale. What needs explaining, therefore, is revolts [3].

The question here is not whether these theories indeed explain revolts. The point is that a theory based on the premise that a revolution is a large-scale revolt is bound to influence the representation of the empirical evidence. The analyst has to concentrate on growth of a group (say, 'the frustrated') without receiving any help from his theory in connecting the conditions that make that group grow. Disjointed pieces of historical evidence must therefore be glued together by common sense or ad hoc assumptions. For example, in his account of the Russian Revolution, Davies (1962) attempts to show how a large revolting group was slowly built up. Peasants had always been discontent, but after the emancipation of serfs in 1861 rural violence increased because 'virtual personal slavery was exchanged for financial servitude'. Yet, since rapid economic growth afforded the chance of economic betterment in the towns and cities, many peasants went to the towns and cities, swelling the ranks of industrial workers; these, in turn, enganged in strikes. Judicial reforms after the emancipation of serfs brought the intelligentsia into the act: 'Public joy at these reforms was widespread. For the intelligentsia, there was increased opportunity to think and write and to criticize established institutions, even sacrosanct absolutism itself'. Alexander III suppressed criticism but 'when it became apparent that Nicholas II shared his father's ideas but not his forcefulness, opposition of the intelligentia to absolutism joined with the demands of peasants and workers ...'. The middle class joined this group of the frustrated too when 'peaceful proletarian petitioners marched on the St. Petersburg palace and were killed by the hundreds. The myth that the Tsar was the gracious protector of his subjects, however surrounded he might be by malicious advisers, was quite shattered. The reaction was immediate, bitter, and prolonged and was not at all confined to the working class. Employers, merchants, and white-collar officials joined in the burgeoning of strikes which brought the economy to a virtual standstill in October'. What happened to the peasants in this scenario? Were they a separate group after all? No, for 'after the October strike, the peasants ominously sided with the workers and engaged in riots and assaults on landowners'.

This summary of Davies' account of the growth of the frustrated is not an unfair portrayal of Davies' line of argument. A few remarks are in order. Observe that the emancipation of serfs, the judicial reforms, the economic growth and the waves of repression are all unrelated events. They simply happen and each is said to have an effect on the growth of the group of frustrated people. Furthermore, the way Davies explains the burgeoning of this group is completely ad hoc. First the peasants became even more violent because virtual personal slavery was exchanged for financial servitude. Why would renting or buying land increase violence? Why did the industrial workers strike? The intelligentia began to become critical when they were allowed to write. Why? And they supposedly joined the workers and peasants when they found out that Nicholas II did 'not have the forcefulness of his father', Alexander III. What did they have to do with the peasants and workers? The middle class, finally, joined the group when hundreds of peaceful proletarian demonstraters were shot down. Supposedly, this brutality just went one step too far for the otherwise quiet merchants, employers and white-collar workers. The peasants seem to have had a similar reaction to this brutality because they 'ominously sided with the workers' after this strike.

The way empirical evidence is presented by Davies actually hides more than it reveals. Seemingly, we do not have to learn anything about the institutions, nor do we need to know anything about the interest of the people involved. All that matters is that events can be found in the historical records that can be

interpreted as frustrating, i.e. as thwarting expected want-satisfaction.
One may object, that I have chosen a particularly weak strawman in order to knock him down. There is no reason to assume that the premise 'revolution is a large-scale revolt' would necessarily result in such a bad handling of empirical evidence. This is quite true but I do think that the extreme case of Davies' analysis shows the weakness more clearly than more sophisticated studies in which this premise is used. Such sophisticated studies do not even attempt to connect the historical events, they move right away to factor models in which various factors present in a society are modeled as causing a revolutionary potential (or a potential for severe internal war). The underlying premise is still the same: revolution is a large-scale revolt. For example, Gurr (1968 and 1970) built very sophisticated models in order to explain the likelihood of internal war (revolution). One links frustration ('deprivation') to the magnitude of internal war via intervening factors such as 'legitimacy', 'institutionalization', 'coercive potential', 'facilitation'. Another model explains the likelihood of internal war by such factors as 'equality of dissident and regime institutional control', 'equality of dissident and regime coercive control' provided there is widespread discontent among both elite and masses. The society is divided into regime and 'dissidents' (the frustrated or the deprived or the discontented) who are more likely to revolt if they consider the regime illegitimate, if there are not many binding rules (low institutionalization), if the regime has few or disloyal military and internal security forces and if dissidents receive arms and training ('facilitation') from other nations.

The point here is not that these models are trivial but that the empirical evidence gathered to test the models is necessarily disjointed and therefore hides more than it reveals, just as in Davies' account. Everybody who has some ax to grind whith the regime is thrown into one group and all 'factors' are seperate even if it is stated that they all reinforce or block each other. Why would such a constellation of factors ever be present?[4]. Since the theory offers almost no guide to the analyst to connect historical events, the way to improve the theory is to cast around for better predictor variables and these are inevitably the variables that jointly describe a highly unstable situation (such as 'equality of dissident and regime institutional control' and 'equality of dissident and regime coercive control'). Thereby, even more historical events are shut out from the analysis. This is good for the explained variance, but not good for explanation.

1.2. The lack of an adequate theory of action

It is not surprising that theorists who subscribe to the major-group-hypothesis and to its specification (revolution is a large-scale revolt) also tend towards the frustration-aggression hypothesis. Revolting is an aggressive act and nobody revolts unless he or she is frustrated by the way things are. Frustration is mostly taken to mean a discrepancy between expectations and need satisfaction or aspirations and achievement. Davies (1971) explicitly includes four selections on the frustration-aggression hypothesis in his reader; Gurr (1970) also makes this hypothesis the central theoretical focus of his book, to mention only the two authors discussed above. There has been much criticism of this hypothesis and some very useful suggestions for improving it for the purpose of explaining political violence [5]. But even the best version of this hypothesis, if there is one, makes a poor theory of action except in highly infrequent incidences when the desire to harm an object or person controls behavior. Again, the image of a revolution being a large-scale revolt may also have induced the image of people armed with ax, pichfork and scythe attacking the tax collector and his small guard. But by and large revolutions don't happen that way [6].

Without an adequate theory of action, action is either explained ad hoc or removed from the analysis. For example, Davies (1962: 12) has to explain why the peasants turned quiet after supposedly siding with the workers 'ominously'. His explanation is: a bad harvest and the Stolypin agrarian reform: 'Between these acts of God and government, peasants were so preoccupied with hunger or self-aggrandizement as to be dulled in their sensitivity to the revolutionary appeals of radical organizers'. Earlier, Davies let the peasants be more violent on account of poor food supply, now they are 'dulled by hunger', the intelligentia became more radical, by new opportunities (to write) while the peasants who got new opportunities through the Stolypin reform became absorbed into self-aggrandizement and dulled in their sensitivity to radical appeals. Anything goes with such a theory of action and empirical evidence is neither organized nor restrained.

Gurr (1970) has again taken the more sophisticated step: he completely dropped concern with action from his theoretical endeavor. For readers who have missed this point, Gurr and Duvall (1976) set the record straight: 'All that we claim in this regard is that manifest conflict is apt to be of greater magnitude to the extent that individuals in the social system are deeply and extensively dissatisfied. What the theory does deal with are conflict processes at the macro- or system level'. (p. 148)

Whether action is explained ad hoc or removed from the analysis, in both cases crucial theoretical questions and empirical evidence cannot be handled. To begin with, institutions are ways to organize behavior. If the effect of certain institutions is to frustrate the larger part of the population, why not change them, why a revolution? Why would the government not want to oblige the larger part of the population? Where does resistance come from? Could it also be that although there is a large group of frustrated people there is not one set of institutional arrangements that would satisfy them all? How could we find out? Without an adequate theory of action, conflict itself is an emergent property of social systems not to be explained but to be taken for granted.

These questions are so basic that they are almost ludicrous and yet even a rudimentary attempt to answer them would force us to introduce various interests and various groups, leaving the major-group hypothesis and its specification behind. Why would some groups form coalitions with some other groups and not with just any group? Why would coalitions change? How is it possible for some groups to mobilize many people and others only few? How can concerted action ever get under way? How can we deal with 'non-action' as when the police refuses to intervene but does not join either? How can we explain the effect of institutional changes for a particular group? Without an adequate theory of action empirical evidence pertaining to these questions will find no place in the analysis.

2. An adequate theory of action

What then is an adequate theory of action? In sociology and other social sciences we are interested in the more or less idealized behavior of kinds of people rather than in the clinical analysis of one person. The theory of action should be adequate to this purpose. We are equally interested in relating the behavior of kinds of people to various social phenomena and we are interested in being able to adjust the action theory to our state of knowledge: we must be able to replace simplifying assumptions by more realistic ones as our knowledge grows. As I have argued in some more detail elsewhere (Lindenberg, 1981), the only theory (at present) that seems adequate to these three purposes is the theory of rational action in its most general form [7]. But I also argued that by itself, i.e. without 'bridge-assumptions' about alternatives, subjective probabilities and utility arguments, this theory will explain nothing.

Introducing the theory of rational action means essentially the following: human beings are said to be resourceful and able to learn from their mistakes; they are restricted in what they can do and not do (i.e. they have to choose among alternatives); they are able to evaluate events past, present and future for themselves; they are able to have expectations regarding the occurrence of these events; and they choose the alternative that maximizes the expected utility (i.e. the alternative for which the sum of the products of evaluation and expectation is highest). Aside from some technicalities, this theory is quite common sensical in the sense that people also use it extensively without being social scientists. If one bridge-assumption is added, namely that people are generally capable only of limited generosity, this otherwise empty theory turns into a powerful tool. The assumption of limited generosity is as old as the hills and as well corroborated as it is old, but as such it has been introduced into social sciences by Adam Smith. It means that other people's joy and sorrow have generally only a limited capacity to make us joyous or sad.

Armed with this theory, Olson (1965) has drawn our attention to a basic problem regarding collective action in general and revolutions in particular. If there is a good which does not only benefit me but also others, then the larger the group of people who benefit from this good, the less likely will I sacrifice for obtaining it. The reason is that my own sacrifice becomes less and less significant as the group grows larger and so I expect my contribution to have less and less effect on the occurrence of this good, thereby tilting the balance in favor of using my means for something else where they do make a difference. For example, a union may be empowered to negotiate wages for members and non-members alike. My few dollars for union dues do not make much difference whether the union is able to negotiate a considerable wage increase or just a small one. So why should I pay my dues? If a high wage increase is negotiated, I benefit from it anyway, if it is not negotiated, nothing is lost. In Olson's terms, I am likely to become a 'free rider'.

Revolutions consist of such public good episodes: protests, negotiations, fights, etc. for the purpose of achieving something that will also benefit others. The larger the group of people who benefit, the more free riders and therefore the smaller the percentage of people who will participate unless there are also private goods (such as individual salvation, individual loot etc.) involved which people only get if they participate. Tullock (1974) has written extensively on this subject and his conclusion is that 'true revolutions (uprisings from outside the government apparatus) are extremely rare and perhaps non-existent' (p. 47). While this statement is exaggerated or at least ambiguous, it does draw attention to the unlikelihood that people would participate in revolutionary episodes at considerable risk and costs to themselves if the group is very large and if the proposed aim of the episode is supposedly benefitting everyone in the group. So-called 'revolutionary masses' are very differentiated in their composition and their interests, as Rudé (1959, 1964) has shown.

However, if one smaller group rebels, even a military weak government is able to repress it. For any revolution to occur there must be many groups engaging in some revolutionary episode, within a rather short span of time. For this reason alone, the premise that a revolution is a large-scale rebellion must be mistaken; and for this reason alone this premise excludes a fundamental theoretical question: how do many different groups get drawn into revolutionary episodes within a rather short period of time? [8]

3. Sketch of an alternative

It is essential that the two major flaws of many theories of revolution be avoided. But that does not mean that if one does so, the alternative is in sight. Only the obstacles for looking for an alternative are removed. Drawing on the work of Moore and Tilly, Skocpol (1979) has provided a pioneering lead. Avoiding even the vestiges of the two flaws in the work by Tilly and by Moore, she set out to focus on the state and its international position. She also considered revolution a basically unintended outcome of various protests, rebellions and other events.

Briefly summarized, her line of argument is as follows: In France, Russia and China the prerevolutionary state was able to protect its hegemony and its dominant classes against revolts from below. In order for these revolts to have any chance

for success, the administrative and military power of these imperial states had
to break down first. This power broke down because these states got drawn into
military competition or intrusions from abroad while their agrarian class
structures and political institutions, facilitating wide-spread peasant revolts,
prevented them from reacting adequatly to these challenges from abroad. Thus it
was the cross-pressure of external and internal threats that made these
revolutions possible.

It is not the place to present Skocpol's work in any detail. She clearly attempts
to move away from the historical description towards the formulation of hypotheses
without falling into the pitfalls of many more formal theories. Yet, she has not
attempted (yet) to drive the analysis a step further by building a model that
would allow her to deal with revolutions in general. What would the outline of
such a model be?

3.1. Negative transfers and destabilization

The power of any state government comes from the resources it can wield. Where
do these resources come from? Only in the earliest beginnings of states properly
so called did the ruler derive its resources from his own patrimonial estates.
And even then did he have to draw resources from his subjects (be it manpower,
produce or money) in case of war against an outside power. Slowly, these
extraordinary ways of drawing resources from his subjects became regular in some
way, with extraordinary levies on top of these. In order to draw resources from
his subjects, the ruler has to overcome recalcitrance because people do not like
to give things away. Compromises had to be agreed upon to various degrees with
the more powerful sections of the population. There developed a 'negative transfer'
system in which burdens (manpower demands, fees, crop demands, money demands etc.)
would be transferred down from the government. Some groups would have managed to
be exempted, others to be able to shift the burden to yet other groups; and some
groups had no choice but to accept the burdens that were handed down. In modern
equivalents one can say that the tax system evolved to be regressive to various
degrees in different states, depending on the circumstances of its development.

Take a very regressive negative transfer system and assume that the state needs
a considerable increase in resources to finance a war, or to modernize the army

due to international competition and military invention abroad. Anticipating
revenues or borrowing on future revenues, the state will go ahead and wage war
or modernize the army, creating a factual problem of resources for running
expenses. The negative transfers have to be increased meeting with recalcitrance.
New compromises have to be made with more powerful groups and some more repression
has to be used to break resistance of less powerful groups to accept the increased
burdens that are transferred down. Let this happen a number of times. Then the
negative transfer system will block. Breaking resistance of less powerful groups
(who establish a tradition in 'tax revolts' and become more skillful at it) will
not be worth the military effort because returns are smaller and smaller;
privileges to the more powerful groups will not bring more because the less
powerful groups cannot even be milked with their assistance. At this point
something curious will happen: the government will initiate reforms to either tap
the wealth of the privileged and/or to improve the economy through industrialization
Either way, the government will destabilize the old order by changing the negative
transfer system: degrading formerly privileged groups, upgrading economically
promising groups, changing the traditional (if hated) way for the least powerful
groups and possibly creating new groups that have no standing in the old order.
Because the government has a severe lack of current resources, its repressive
abilities are also reduced at the same time that it destabilizes the old order.
This constitutes a potential revolutionary situation.

The crucial question is this: how regressive is the negative transfer system?
The more regressive it is, the more radical the government reforms must be in
order to raise more revenue. The more radical the reforms, the less likely that
the needed revenue is forthcoming. And the less likely that the government can
raise the revenue the more likely that resistance to the reforms and/or the
consequences of the reforms lead to a revolution.

Many observations about revolutionary situations can be found in this sketch of
a framework: Tocqueville's observation that the government being overthrown is
normally better than the government preceding it and that the most dangerous
moment for a bad government is when it starts to reform itself. Brinton also
observed that reforms are an essential part of the conditions that issued
revolutions. Davies idea of rising expectations may be connected to reforms but
only for some groups (for others, they are a concrete threat). States with
strongly regressive negative transfer systems are also very repressive and show

great social injustices (Moore, 1978). But none of these elements taken
seperately or taken together make for a revolutionary situation. The government
must also be weak.

The framework sketched above is able to combine the weakness of the government
and the need for drastic reforms. In its elaboration it can consider mobilization,
coalitionforming, political conflict, changes in property rights, conditions for
collective action etc. The negative transfer system is itself a system of
property rights and around this system traditions of collective action have
evolved long before the revolution either to gain privileges or to avert further
burdens. A more formal elaboration would begin by formalizing the model with
strongly simplifying assumptions and then bit by bit replace these assumptions
by more realistic ones. Thanks to the use of the theory of rational action, this
is possible in principle and hopefully we [9] will be able to present it in the
not so distant future.

Notes

(1) See Zimmermann (1981) for a recent survey.
(2) See for example Aya (1979), Salert (1976), Tilly (1975), Skocpol (1976 and 1979a), Zimmermann (1981).
(3) Geschwender (1968: 128) claims explicitly: 'conditions which produce a revolution are no different in principle from those which produce a smaller or even an unsuccessful protest movement. The major difference between the two would be in the number of individuals aroused to revolutionary activity'. Many other theories of revolution follow the same logic even if their authors are not quite as explicit about it as Geschwender (for example Davies (1962 and 1969), Tanter and Midlarsky (1976), Schwarz (1970), Gurr (1968 and, less so, 1970)). It is interesting to note that even Barrington Moore moved in this direction as can be seen from a comparison of Moore (1966) and Moore (1978).
(4) This question is not equal to shifting the phenomena to be explained; it is asking for a different explanation of the same phenomena. Creating a 'process' model for such a static model alone does not meet the objections, as can be seen from Gurr (1970: 349).
(5) Portes' (1971) contribution is particularly interesting in this regard;

adding 'structural blame' as a necessary condition.
(6) See also Tilly et al. (1975: 282). Gurr (1970: 259) warns us that retaliation may become the overriding motive, but he does not thereby discredit the theory of rational action, nor does he intend to do so. But he draws no clear conclusion from his remarks regarding the theory of rational action or any other theory of action.
(7) In Lindenberg (1980), it is shown that Marx' theory of revolution runs into difficulty because Marx took rational action theoretically as a historical phenomenon while in practice he assumed it for all historical periods.
(8) 'Short' is here taken to be relative to the government's ability to deploy military and internal security forces at different places.
(9) Thanks to a generous grant from the Dutch Foundation for Pure Scientific Research, Marjolein 't Hart and I are working on a project that aims at both formalizing the model and collecting the empirical evidence for the French, Russian and Chinese revolutions.

References

AYA, R., (1979), 'Theories of Revolution Reconsidered: Contrasting Models of Collective Violence', Theory and Society 8: 39-99.

DAVIES, J.C., (1962), 'Toward a Theory of Revolution', American Sociological Review 6: 5-19.

DAVIES, J.C., (1969), 'The J-Curve of Rising and Declining Satisfaction as a Cause of Some Great Revolutions and a Contained Rebellion', pp. 690-730 in H. Graham and T. Gurr (eds.), Violence in America. New York: Praeger.

GESCHWENDER, J.A., (1968), 'Explorations in the Theory of Social Movements and Revolutions', Social Forces 47: 127-135.

GURR, T.R., (1968), 'A Causal Model of Civil Strife: A Comparative Analysis Using New Indices', American Political Science Review 62: 1104-1124.

GURR, T.R., (1970), Why Men Rebel. Princeton, N.J.: University Press.

GURR, T.R. and R. DUVALL, (1976), 'Introduction to a Formal Theory of Political Conflict', pp. 139-154 in L.A. Coser and O.N. Larsen (eds.), The Uses of Controversy in Sociology. New York: Free Press.

LINDENBERG, S., (1980), 'Instigation of and Participation in Revolts and Revolutions'. Paper presented at the 'Studiedag van de Werkgemeenschap Verklarende Sociologie', Utrecht.

LINDENBERG, S., (1981), 'Erklärung als Modellbau: Zur soziologische Nutzung von Nutzentheorien', pp. 20-35 in W. Schulte (ed.), Soziologie in der Gesellschaft. Bremen: Zentraldruckerei der Universität.

MOORE, B., (1966), Social Origins of Dictatorship and Democracy. Boston: Beacon.

MOORE, B., (1978), Injustice. The Social Bases of Obedience and Revolt. White Plains, N.Y.: M.E. Sharpe.

OLSON, M., (1965), The Logic of Collective Action. Cambridge, Mass.: Harvard University Press.

PORTES, A., (1971), 'On the Logic of Post-Factum Explanations: The Hypothesis of Lower-Class Frustration as the Cause of Leftist Redicalism', Social Forces 50: 26-44.

RUDE, G., (1959), The Crowd in the French Revolution. Oxford: University Press.

RUDE, G., (1964), The Crowd in History, 1730-1848. New York: Wiley.

SALERT, B., (1976), Revolutions and Revolutionaries. New York: Elsevier.

SCHWARZ, D., (1971), 'A Theory of Revolutionary Behavior', pp. 109-132 in J.C. Davies (ed.), When Men Revolt and Why. New York: Free Press.

SKOCPOL, T., (1976), 'Explaining Revolutions: In Quest of a Social-Structural Approach', pp. 155-175 in L.A. Coser and O.N. Larsen (eds.), The Uses of Controversy in Sociology. New York: Free Press.

SKOCPOL, T., (1979), States and Social Revolutions. Cambridge: University Press.

SKOCPOL, T., (1979a), 'State and Revolution', Theory and Society 7: 7-95.

TANTER, R. and M. MIDLARSKY (1967), 'A Theory of Revolution', Journal of Conflict Resolution 11: 264-280.

TILLY, Ch., (1975), 'Revolutions and Collective Violence', pp. 483-555 in F.I. Greenstein and N.W. Polsby (eds.), Macropolitical Theory. Reading, Mass.: Addison-Wesley.

TILLY, Ch., (1978), From Mobilization to Revolution. Reading, Mass.: Addison-Wesley.

TILLY, Ch., L. TILLY and R. TILLY, (1975), The Rebellious Century. Cambridge, Mass.: Harvard University Press.

TULLOCK, G., (1975), The Social Dilemma. Blacksburg, Virg.: University Publications.

ZIMMERMANN, E., (1981), Krisen, Staatsstreiche und Revolutionen. Opladen: Westdeutscher Verlag.

Thomas Voss

RATIONAL ACTORS AND SOCIAL INSTITUTIONS: THE CASE OF THE ORGANIC EMERGENCE OF NORMS

Introduction

One of the most promising branches of the structural-individualistic program in sociology is the economic approach to social phenomena. It rests on the idea that individual behavior under social conditions and its collective consequences should be explained with explicit recourse to the behavioral assumption of rational action [1] (as elaborated in utility and game theory). The success of this approach largely stems from the insight that the social institutions which can be dealt with by such an approach are by no means exhausted by competitive markets of transferable physical commodities. On the contrary, it has been widely recognized that markets tend to fail under certain conditions and that in these cases an efficient allocation of resources can only be achieved if markets are supplemented, or replaced by other institutional arrangements consisting of norms, social networks of various kinds, or of hierarchies.

The task of this essay is to investigate whether the economic approach might contribute to a solution to one of the most important problems in theoretical sociology, viz. the problem of order in society. To this end I shall first (Part I) present a short and highly stylized reconstruction of the Durkheimian criticism of the market-conception of order proposed by the British Moralists and the Utilitarians (including Spencer). It will be argued that it has to be conceded to Durkheim and his followers that exchange relations are not sufficient to create stability in society, since markets presuppose social institutions. On the other hand, and contrary to the assertions in the traditions of Durkheim and Parsons, the evolution and functions of social institutions can be determined endogeneously within the framework of an economic approach. The purpose of the next sections is to give first (Part 2) a selective survey of some general principles of this approach and then (Part 3) to discuss some contributions to a problem especially relevant in this context, viz. the explanation of the emergence of order and of social norms from an anarchistic state of nature without making use of assumptions about altruistic preferences or an external enforcing agency.

1. Durkheim's challenge: the exchange solution to the problem of order and its difficulties

The importance of answering the Hobbesian question -how can there a society be established in which force and fraud are not routinely used for the provision of commodities satisfying individual wants?- has been widely acknowledged as being a touchstone for an adequate social theory. According to Parsons (1937: 91), this problem 'constitutes the most fundamental empirical difficulty of utilitarian thought'. Aside from Hobbes' own answer -usually termed the 'coercive' solution -the utilitarian tradition has proposed a solution of this problem known as the exchange or market-conception of order. Roughly stated, it is argued here that self-interested actors under the condition of a complementary control of resources (including individual capacities and human capital) and a certain diversity of demands (not necessarily of tastes) will have incentives to develop a division of labor and to engage voluntarily in mutually beneficial transactions. Under competitive conditions, these exchanges will be facilitated by market prices indicating the whole means-ends-structure of the economy (so-to-speak providing solutions of Walrasian simultaneous equations in a highly condensed form) and serving as institutions enabling quick adjustments to changing market conditions. Prices are in this view costless informational devices guiding individual actors in a decentralized, 'organic' (Menger) manner to the achievement of efficient allocations of scarce resources (cf. Hayek, 1945). Since in equilibrium these allocations are optimal in the Pareto sense, no rational actor has an opportunity to deviate from the attained order, holding constant the institutional (market) framework, resources and tastes. There results a highly stabilized state of society contraintuitively due to the diversity and (non-strategic) interdependency, not the similarity of individual actors pursuing their selfish wants and thereby guided by the invisible hand of the price system.

An antecedent to this exchange solution to the problem of order was proposed by Spencer and criticized in a well-known chapter of Durkheim's De la division du travail social (1973: 177-209; cf. also Parsons, 1937: 311-317). According to Durkheim, this approach can explain the fact that individuals are motivated to voluntarily enter into contractual relations. But it neglects the fact that these contracts concerning transactional relations are based on 'precontractual' binding rules: the institution of contract which helps to enforce these voluntary agreements. Durkheim especially argues that every explicit agreement between exchange partners is based on an agreement of a higher order which functions as an enforcing agency (law of contract and legal institutions), and that due to a high degree of uncertainty not all possible future states of the world affecting the enactment of a contract can be the object of an explicit agreement. Consequently, contractual relations are possible only if there exist certain legal institutions and conventions (cf. e.g. Durkheim, 1973: 192-193), but these institutions cannot be explained by the principle of self-interest. With the help of game theoretical concepts, we may state one main aspect of the Durkheimian argument [2] more precisely. A sector of our society of actors involved in a situation possibly leading to bilaterally beneficial exchange may be represented as a Coordination-Prisoners' dilemma game[3]:

FIGURE-1: Bilateral exchange as a Coordination-Prisoners' dilemma game

		Actor B		
		transfer at competitive price	non-competitive transfer	withhold commodity
Actor A	transfer at competitive price	10,10	2,8	-5,20
	non-competitive transfer	8,2	4,4	-3,10
	withhold commodity	20,-5	10,-3	0,0

First, suppose we have to deal with the upper left 2x2 submatrix of exchange strategies only. In this case, the market mechanism could coordinate the actions towards the efficient equilibrium point [3a] of exchanging the commodities at an exchange rate dictated by competitive prices. If the game is not played in a strictly noncooperative manner, i.e. if communication is possible between the players, there would be no problem in reaching the outcome at the upper left corner at all. If -due to the information contained in competitive prices- there exists coorientation among the actors, this outcome would even be realized in the absence of prior communication. But -this would be a version of Durkheim's argument- the game is not simply this coordination game solved by the market, it really is a Prisoners' dilemma which prevents the invisible hand from coming into action. The two actors will inevitably reach the suboptimal equilibrium point of dominant strategies which represents the situation of no exchange at all.

The next question we might pose concerns the conditions under which a social situation such as represented by the above game matrix emerges, vanishes or is 'solved'. To the end of answering this question, it is useful to take a look first at the properties of the transactions. A first dimension which is important in this respect is whether the commodities exchanged are physically alienable. If they are, it may be possible that the resulting transfers are spot transactions. Here, the act of exchange takes place at a point at which all goods are exchanged simultaneously. One might say that in this case A gives his commodities to B only on the condition that B transfers to A his goods and vice versa. There may result a state in which the alternative of unilaterally withholding the commodity is not feasible, so that we do not have a Prisoners' dilemma (Hardin, 1982: 252-253).

Even if we are dealing with resources which are physically alienable, there may be a considerable time-lag between A's and B's acts of transferring their goods and services. Under this condition of high transaction costs, explicit contracting and its legal enforcement through state power and a set of informal norms seem to be ways leading out of the Prisoners' dilemma. These are the kinds of transactions considered by Durkheim.

Continuing along the dimensions of transactions we can find on the other extreme those kinds of transfers from which so-called social exchanges[4] are built up. The essential fact about social exchange is that it entails unspecified obligations about some future return (Blau, 1964: 93) which cannot be explicitly contracted. The situation becomes even more intricate if we consider so-called 'indirect' exchange relations (Blau, 1964: 259-263), i.e. exchange not between pairs of actors, but taking place in the structural configuration of a chain, for instance: A does a favor to B, B to C, C to A, etc. In these cases of direct and indirect social exchange it may be expected that the development of mutual trust, of a norm of reciprocity (Gouldner) and of other norms, e.g. (in some cases of indirect exchange) norms of solidarity, could enable the initiation and continuation of social exchange relations. Further hints for explaining the attachment of a cooperative solution of the Prisoners' dilemma may be found in the fact that social exchange markets are clearly imperfect in a number of respects (cf. Blau, 1964: 190-194 for some of these points). First, the number of participants is quite small. Secondly, neither the actors nor the commodities exchanged are homogeneous (in the sense of micro-economics). Social exchange takes place as a set of long-term recurrent interactions within the same pairs or networks of actors. These conditions are similar to a supergame setting (as reviewed in Part 3), making possible the evolution of cooperative conventions of behavior and of norms. Furthermore, it is relevant here that under these conditions explicit competitive prices will not emerge. Consequently actors do not have costless information about exchange rates satisfying the equal value condition and thereby guiding the way to an efficient solution of the coordination problem. In social exchange theory it is hypothesized that special kinds of norms fulfill the functions of shadow prices: norms of fairness, distributive justice or equity.

Our considerations above concerning the role of institutions in the attainment of an orderly society through the invisible hand of the market can be summarized in the following table:

TABLE-1

	competitive economic markets	markets of social exchange
information solving the coordination problem	competitive prices: equal value condition	social norms as shadow prices: fairness, equity, distributive justice
solution of the prisoner's dilemma	.conditional (spot-) exchange .property rights .. laws, legal institutiond .. informal norms	.conventions .informal norms (reciprocity, solidarity)

We are now led to the conclusion that Durkheim's challenge to the economic approach has to be taken seriously. It has to be conceded to Durkheim, Parsons and their epigones that there may be institutional deficits in exchange-theoretical explanations of order in society which become even more severe when the problem is to explain social exchange structures and their integrative consequences. But this challenge could be answered effectively if it were possible to supply endogeneous explanations of this normative-institutional framework. In fact, as early as in Hume and other Scottish moralists we find attempts to explain rules norms and laws with the help of principles of rational action. In what follows, some hints will be given about the general theoretical arguments of some current rational-choice explanations of social institutions and some problems connected with them.

2. The economic approach to social institutions: some general principles and problems

The purpose of this part is not to give an exhaustive survey and evaluation of the vast and rapidly growing literature on economic explanations of institutions. We merely want to present a sample of arguments serving mainly illustrative purposes and leading to a more systematic discussion.

2.1. Social exchange theory

Within the realm of social exchange theory, which is interpreted here as a rational-choice approach (cf. Heath, 1975) some hypotheses concerning the emergence and functions of institutions have been presented which, although somewhat rudimentary, fit well into approaches from economics which will be discussed later on. Firstly, it must be recognized that in social exchange theory a model of man is proposed which must be sharply contrasted with the long prevailing over-socialized conception of man, who is simply seen as being propelled to fulfill certain role expectations and has no freedom of choosing among alternatives at all. According to Blau (1964: 13, 254) man does not act in a norm-directed, but rather in a self-interested manner, and is thereby constrained by norms and values, which are by no means the only constraints on action.

There is not much to be found in the work of Blau concerning the problem of the emergence of norms. Using quasi-functionalistic kinds of arguments, Blau frequently states that norms are necessary to perform certain functions in social exchange (cf. also our discussion above). For instance, with reference to problems created by a situation of interdependencies representable as a Prisoners' dilemma (Blau, 1964: 255-257), he argues: 'social norms are necessary to prohibit actions through which individuals can gain advantages at the expense of the common sense interests of the collectivity' (p. 257). As was already pointed out above, norms may help in establishing and stabilizing networks of indirect exchange (cf. Blau, 1964: 255-257). Similarly, the 'main function of common values is (...) to broaden the scope of social associations and transactions of various kinds' (Blau, 1964: 264). Summarizing Blau's arguments in a sentence, we might suggest that norms tend to emerge if they tend to fulfill certain functions in the interests of the collectivity as a whole (i.e., converting the situation in the direction of some Pareto- or other social optimum and if -an obvious premise not stated by Blau- these functions cannot be fulfilled by exchange mechanisms in the narrower sense or by other mechanisms. A more elaborate approach, though restricted to small-scale social relationships, was advanced within the exchange theory framework by Thibaut and Kelley (1959). These authors too emphasize the function of norms in attaining more efficient social situations: 'norms improve the reward-cost positions attained by the members of a dyad and thus increase the cohesiveness of the dyad' (Thibaut and Kelley, 1959: 138-139).

Norms may be especially suited to serve this end because they may cut costs in that they substitute or replace more costly informal influence processes (1959: 126). According to Thibaut and Kelley (1959: 131) both members of a group, the weaker and the more powerful one, gain from the establishment of mutually acceptable rules which introduce regularity and control into the relationship without recourse to direct interpersonal influence. Thus, norms improve the situation in the Pareto sense. Thibaut and Kelley (1959: 138-139 et passim) not only state what kinds of costs norms may reduce, thereby improving the situation (communication costs, costs due to interference -some of these costs increase with size-, lack of cognitive coordination and others), they also detect social conditions and processes leading to the formation of norms. Among the conditions, the most important obviously is that the actors are locked into a recurrent situation of interdependence in which there is some 'need' for norms. The process

of norm creation itself may either be an explicit bargaining process or -more
frequently- results from some trial-and-error-process which filters out an
adequate (not necessarily optimal) solution to the problems generated by
interdependency (Thibaut and Kelley, 1959: 138-141).

2.2. Law and economics

Under the heading 'Law and economics' (named after the journal with this title)
there has emerged, mainly within economics, a large number of -not always
entirely coherent- approaches and concepts which can by no means be described
adequately here. However, we may characterize these approaches by the common idea
that the function of institutional arrangements (norms, institutions and laws)
which arise voluntarily -either organically or by design- lies in an altering of
incentives and thus a regulation of behavior in such a way that societal output
is directed towards efficiency.

The most important of these approaches seems to be the property rights paradigm
(cf. Furubotn and Pejovich (eds.), 1974 for a collection of major papers). Here
we find in the first place analyses about effects of various institutional
arrangements on resources which actors have at their disposal in this social
context [5] (e.g. forms of managerial discretion vs. profit maximization as
managerial objectives in capitalist firms; budget or waste maximization in public
bureaucracies). More importantly, hypotheses have been developed concerning social
conditions leading to the emergence or change of property rights institutions.
One of these conditions is that the market significantly fails in efficiently
allocating resources because there exist externalities. Leaving aside the
empirically insignificant cases of zero transaction costs where Coase's (1960)
theorem has to be applied, these social costs arising from externalities may be
privatized by changes in the system of property rights (cf. Demsetz, 1967 and
North and Thomas, 1973 for empirical examples) [6]. Thus, the emergence of
institutions is explained by their function of enhancing the aggregate welfare
of some group of actors as measured by the Pareto criterion: the (anticipated)
economizing properties of institutions in these cases generate incentives to
bring about a change in the institutional structure. These kinds of arguments
need not be restricted to property rights in the narrower sense of the term,
i.e. rights to use, transform and transfer tangible resources. For instance, with

help of this approach we can analyze the allocation of property rights to perform
certain actions in situations of social interdependency of a strategic kind
(coordination games) via rules. Wittman (1982) presents an investigation of
various rules of thumb in certain traffic situations and comes to the conclusion
that only the most efficient rules will be used. From the set of institutional
alternatives the least efficient rules are prices due to high transaction costs
and externalities. The others have evolved such that two types of costs are
optimized: 'costs associated with monitoring the rule of thumb, and inappropriate
incentives created by the rule' (Wittman, 1982: 78).

Another approach in this realm has been called the 'transaction cost approach'
(Williamson, 1975, 1981) in order to suggest the idea that the choice or
emergence of alternative institutional arrangements should be explained by their
economizing properties with primary regard to transaction costs. This approach
has major implications within the area of formal organizations which will not
be reviewed here (cf. Williamson and Ouchi, 1981). It also seems to have
implications, which have not been worked out to date, in the domain of informal
organizations and network structures. Following a social exchange framework, one
may begin with the premise that 'in the beginning' there were markets of bilateral
social exchange relations. Obviously, each actor's resources, consisting of time,
rewards to be provided to a potential exchange partner and the like, are scarce.
Some of these resources are needed to maintain a contact with another actor who
may be a possible partner in some future transaction, so they clearly can be
conceptualized in terms of transaction costs. The emergence of indirect structures
of exchange as well as of persons functioning as mediators, middlemen, brokers
and the like, who have access to 'second order resources' (Boissevain, 1974), i.e.
a large personal network of contact relations, may be interpreted as a result
of economizing activities with respect to transaction costs. Another direction
of investigations may be the analysis of economizing properties of social ties
along the dimension of their weakness or strength (Granovetter, 1973). One
example of a rigorous analysis of this kind focuses on the efficiency- and
equilibrium-properties of weak versus strong contacts in terms of the trade-off
between time costs (of maintaining the respective ties) and value of supplied
information (about job opportunities) through the maintained ties (Boorman, 1975).

2.3. General principles and problems

The sketches of explanations given above have in common the fact that institutions are explained by their desirable consequences for certain groups of actors [7]. Most natural among possible criteria of desirability is the concept of efficiency in the Pareto sense, and it is widely used in this domain. But efficiency clearly is not the only measure for aggregate welfare. Another plausible criterion is that of a stable equilibrium in the noncooperative or Nash point sense, which gives expression to the fact that no individual will be motivated to change his mode of behavior, taking everyone else's behavior as parametric. In game theoretical contexts -where it does make sense to speak of Nash equilibria- the most desirable state of affairs in terms of the actors' utilities is obviously the one in which these two criteria are fulfilled simultaneously, and the least desirable one is realized when they are not, as in the case of the Prisoners' dilemma. We shall not discuss additional concepts of this kind here, since these two are the most familiar ones in the noncooperative game-context.

A distinct class of criteria of desirability may be represented by those indicating efficiency in the presence of risk, i.e. some degree of insurance, reduction of uncertainty or risk-shifting for a group of actors (cf. Arrow, 1965), which may be inter alia important in explanations of certain norms and institutions in primitive societies (Posner, 1980: 10-28). Under certain conditions it may even be possible to consider (in empirical analyses) ethical or moral criteria such as (rule) utilitarianism or Rawlsian maximin justice, e.g. when we are dealing with consciously designed institutions. It should be noted here that in contrast to certain forms of functional reasoning in sociology, we have here rather precise criteria -formulated in terms of individual preferences- indicating the directions in which the system may be drifting under certain conditions, thereby realizing some equilibrium state. Furthermore, these criteria make it possible to identify those classes of social situations which are prone to generate norms and institutions [8]. Here we may especially point out those problematic noncooperative game situations which are not only suboptimal, because there exists a deficient equilibrium (Prisoners' dilemma) or because there exist multiple (efficient) equilibria requiring some coordination of expectations and actions in order to realize one of them (coordination games), but which can also in principle be altered by creating norms and institutions. Within a micro economic framework, we might mention here cases of externalities in the presence of transaction costs. For heuristic purposes, it may prove useful to distinguish these norm-generating situations from conditions of norm formation, since obviously not every norm generating situation leads to the emergence of a new institution. Some interaction problems may not be solved at all and in general it may take time to reach a solution. Furthermore solutions achieved may not represent global but rather local maxima of some desirability variable -or even less then that [9]. Another point to be made here is that there may exist functional alternatives to norms which might transform the norm-generating situation. For instance, we may have to take into account the development of altruistic preferences [10]. This issue must be distinguished from the possibility that solutions in some cases are not unique in that there exist various equally valuable (in terms of efficiency or Nash equilibria) solutions via norms. Among the conditions which seem to be most important for the generation of norms is the recurrence of the problematic situation (cf. inter alia Schotter, 1981). Intuitively this can be made clear by considering that

(i) today's societal losses due to inefficient problematic allocations of resources increase with the number of occurences of these allocations, assuming the existence of some form of long-term rationality.

(ii) Processes of creating and enforcing institutions are costly.

Consequently, norms may emerge only if a certain treshold of societal loss (social costs in cases of externalities) is transgressed [11], because appropriate incentives to initiate processes of norm creation may exist only in these cases. With regard to conditions of norm formation, we shall not go into greater details here, since these depend to a great extent upon the circumstances of the situation. Another dimension of importance is represented by the actual methods or processes of norm generation. With respect to this dimension one must distinguish mainly between 'organic' and 'artificial' or 'designed' methods (Schotter, 1981). As an intermediate case we may speak of semi-organic processes. The extension of these may consist of problems of interdependency within a cooperative game context. In these cases a pre-existing institutional framework provides the cooperative context for enforcing some agreement. The process may nevertheless include elements of evolutionary indeterminateness with respect to the agreement itself.

3. The organic emergence of norms from Prisoner's dilemma situations

In what follows we shall review some formal game-theoretical reasoning which may give hints for generating testable predictions about social conditions of the evolution of cooperation and norms out of Prisoners' dilemma situations. We thereby apply the state-of-nature-method (Nozick, 1974) in that we do not assume the existence of some enforcing agent. Consequently, the reported results refute the frequently uttered assertions in the tradition of Durkheim and Parsons that an economic approach cannot supply potential explanations of the emergence of cooperation and norms out of the original situation of mankind such as Hobbesian anarchy (cf. for a recent statement of this thesis Münch, 1980: 37). Another task of this part will be to provide hints for an explication of the concept of a norm within a rational-choice approach.

3.1. The ordinary Prisoner's dilemma

In order to introduce concepts needed for the further analysis, it seems necessary to begin with the ordinary Prisoners' dilemma (PD) game situation as represented by the matrix in figure 1. What makes it a PD is that for each player: $y>x>w>z$.

FIGURE-2

	C_2	D_2
C_1	x,x	z,y
D_1	y,z	w,w

Player 2 (columns); Player 1 (rows)

In this game, D_1 and D_2 (read D as 'defection') are strictly dominant strategies for each player resulting in an equilibrium outcome (w,w) which is the only inefficient one in this game. The dilemma results from the fact that outcome (x,x) dominates the stable equilibrium outcome (w,w). Unless the PD is not played strictly cooperatively there is no way out of this dilemma. Even in the presence of preplay communication possibilities without enforceable agreements the situation remains the same.

3.2. Iterated Prisoner's dilemmas

An idea leading to a more efficient solution of the PD is that the ordinary game above may be iterated a number of times, say T times. The repeated play of this game by the same players clearly corresponds to what can be observed in social life. We only have to assume actors as being rational for more than one period, that is that payoffs received in period T affect utilities of actions in period 0 (today) in some positive way, which seems quite reasonable in most cases (but may not hold true for corporate actors such as capitalist firms).
Disappointingly, an investigation of such a situation leads to the conclusion that even here rational actors will constantly choose D, as long as it can be determined in advance what the last game T is. This is so (cf. Luce and Raiffa, 1957: 99), because in that last game D is a dominant strategy for player i (i=1,2) since there is no way for player j (j=1,2;i≠j) to 'punish' i for deviating from cooperation in T+1. In view of the fact that now T-1 becomes the last game, we can by backward induction come to the conclusion that for all other iterations it is rational to defect.

What is required is the assumption that the number of iterations is indefinite (formally infinite) [12]. Furthermore, it must be assumed that we in fact have a new kind of game which is no longer a PD, but a supergame consisting of ordinary PD's as constituent games. The strategies available for the players now become supergame strategies which are 'modes of behavior' (Schotter, 1981) for the entire infinite horizon of the game. Most importantly, the strategy set of each player consists of conditional strategies. One of them is the cooperative mode of behavior (s^{coop}) dictating ego's cooperation as long as alter cooperates. This type of supergame strategy may be stated more precisely as follows:

$$s_i^{coop} = s_i(C_i/C_j) = \begin{cases} a_{i_1} = C_i \\ a_{i_t} = C_i & \text{if } a_{j_\tau} = C_j \quad \tau = 1,2,\ldots,t-1 \\ a_{i_t} = D_i & \text{otherwise} \quad t = 2,3,\ldots. \end{cases}$$
$$i = 1,2$$
$$j = 1,2$$
$$i \neq j$$

Here a_i and a_j index the moves of the players in each period of the game. We may note here that this is a rather extreme form of a punishing strategy involving eternal damnation for just one faux pas (cf. for less extreme types of policing mechanisms Taylor, 1976: 31-32). The payoffs for such supergame strategies have to be conceptualized as infinite sums of the payoffs in each ordinary game weighted with the degree of negative time preference. For example, we can define the payoff to player i received today (period 0) when both i and j play their cooperative modes of behavior as

$$\pi_i(s_i^{coop}, s_j^{coop}) = \lim_{T \to \infty} \sum_{\tau=1}^{T} \alpha_i^{\tau-1} x = \frac{x}{1-\alpha_i}$$

where α_i is player i's discount rate with $0 < \alpha_i < 1$. Aside from various other conditional strategies, there are the obvious unconditional strategies of defecting in each period (s_i^D) and of unconditionally cooperating forever (s_i^C). Analysing the strategic properties of such strategies and their combinations (cf. Taylor, 1976; Schotter, 1981), one comes to the conclusion that there do not exist dominant strategies. Furthermore, there can exist multiple equilibria within the set of pure supergame strategies (which are the only ones we shall deal with).

(i) It can easily be seen that the strategy pair (s_i^D, s_j^D) is always a Nash equilibrium of the supergame. Consider actor i whose supergame payoff is

$$\pi_i(s_i^D, s_j^D) = \sum_{\tau=1}^{\infty} \alpha_i^{\tau-1} w = \frac{w}{1-\alpha_i}$$

Unilateral deviation of i from s_i^D consists in choosing C_i in at least one ordinary game yielding a payoff of $z < w$ from that move. For example, the resulting supergame payoff from one deviation in the period $\tau = n$ is

$$\frac{w}{1-\alpha_i} + \alpha_i^{n-1}(z-w) < \frac{w}{1-\alpha_i}$$

Each such deviation diminishes the resulting payoff to i.

(ii) It can also very easily be shown that (s_i^C, s_j^C) is never an equilibrium since each deviation leads to a payoff higher than $\pi_i(s_i^C, s_j^C)$ to the quantity of $\alpha_i^{n-1}(y-x) > 0$.

In light of the fact that according to Parsons norms involve generalized, 'categorical' commitments to cooperate (cf. Münch, 1980: 37 et passim) this is an important result. Such unconditional cooperation will never be a stable regularity of behavior, even if there exists mutual trust in the sense that expectations about the occurence of this unconditional cooperation fully converge.

(iii) The pair $s^{coop} = (s_i^{coop}, s_j^{coop})$ may be an equilibrium point, but here some qualifications must be made. The supergame payoff of s^{coop} to i is

$$\pi_i(s^{coop}) = \sum_{\tau=1}^{\infty} \alpha_i^{\tau-1} x = \frac{x}{1-\alpha_i}$$

It suffices to explore the consequences of deviating from s_i^{coop} in choosing D_i in at least one ordinary game for the first period, since the game is homogeneous with respect to time (Schotter, 1981: 59). The payoff resulting from such a deviation is

$$\pi_i^* = y + \sum_{t=2}^{\infty} \alpha_i^{t-1} w = y + \frac{\alpha_i w}{1-\alpha_i}$$

The condition $\pi_i(s^{coop}) \geq \pi_i^*$ holds true,

iff (T) $\alpha_i \geq \alpha_i^* = \frac{y-x}{y-w}$.

Consequently, the strategy pair s^{coop} is an equilibrium point if condition (T) - the right-hand term of which may be termed 'temptation' (Taylor, 1976) is fulfilled. This means that the value of future payoffs should not be too low in order to reduce incentives from trade-offs between gaining in the present due to defection and loosing in the future. Another aspect of temptation should be made clear: the higher the differences between x (payoff resulting from mutual cooperation in the ordinary game) and w (payoff resulting from mutual defection), the lower will be c.p. the temptation to deviate (strictly speaking: the lower are the requirements the discount parameters have to fulfill). Aside from time preferences, a second factor influencing the likelihood of cooperation is therefore the quantity of mutual externalities in the ordinary game [13].

Before going further in the analysis of strategy possibilities, it should be said that the 2-person supergame just described can be generalized to the n-person case (cf. Taylor, 1976: 47; Schotter, 1981: 82-84). Consider as the most simple generalization a constituent ordinary n-person PD with the following characteristics:

(1) For each player i it holds: i has two pure strategies D_i, C_i.
(2) Denote by x the payoff to i when he chooses C_i and all n-1 other players $\gamma \in \{1,2,\ldots,i-1,i+1,\ldots,n\}$ choose C_γ.
(3) Denote by y the payoff to i when he chooses D_i and at least one other player chooses C_γ.
(4) Denote by w the payoff to i when he chooses D_i and all other D_γ.
(5) Denote by z the payoff when he chooses C_i and at least one other D_γ
(6) For each i it holds $y > x > w > z$.

A n-person analogue to the cooperative mode of behavior mentioned above would be a supergame strategy dictating that player i choose C_i as long as all n-1 other players play C_γ. Assuming that all players i choose a strategy s_i^{coop}, it can be seen that the resulting n-tuple of strategies $s^{coop}=(s_1^{coop},\ldots,s_i^{coop},\ldots,s_n^{coop})$ is an equilibrium if supergame payoffs are defined analoguously to the 2-person case and if the discount parameters of all n players fulfill the above stated condition (T) of exceeding the 'temptation'.

3.3. Conditions of cooperation and social norms

Notice the restrictive conditions of cooperation in a PD-supergame setting:

(1) Every player i's strategy set contains conditional supergame strategies such as s_i^{coop}.
(2) Every player i's time preference exceeds the value α_i^*, i.e. fulfills condition (T).
(3) Furthermore, it must be assumed -as in any classical game theoretical analysis- that the condition of complete information is fulfilled.

Notice the requirements of complete information in the case of supergames. Since supergame payoffs depend decisively on individual time preferences, players must have some hints about them.

(4) It must be kept in mind that concerning the execution of supergame strategies some perfection of information is required.

In order to apply the accurate moves in each period t of the game, each player has to be informed about the past moves in t-1 executed by every other player (who may remain anonymous, see below). This is a crucial condition, since some non-perfection will create incentives for defecting.

Consequently, cooperative equilibrium points seem to occur most likely within a small and stable (completely connected) population of actors homogeneous with respect to preferences, in which there also exists some knowledge of this homogeneity. But there still is no rationale for the conclusion that in such a group cooperation actually occurs and persists, since aside from s^{coop} there exist various other equilibria within the set of n-tuples of pure supergame strategies. Taylor (1976) seems to suggest an investigation of the relation of joint dominance between equilibria. Applying this criterion, one comes to the conclusion that the n-tuples of equilibrium strategies containing only cooperative modes of behavior, e.g. s^{coop} (and some other conditional strategies dictating the same behavior under certain conditions), rank highest within the set of all equilibrium points (Taylor, 1976). On the assumption that the actors choose their strategies such that they represent best replies to the (n-1) other components of this efficient equilibrium point, it can be concluded that the cooperative outcome of the game occurs and persists as long as the players do not cease to execute their supergame strategies. This conclusion rests on the rather strong assumption that each player expects that each other player will choose his best reply to the cooperative equilibrium strategy. We are now led to the tentative conclusion

(5)   that there must in addition exist some coorientation in the group, i.e. reciprocal expectations concerning the execution of cooperative equilibrium strategies. In summary, a group which has established such anarchistic cooperative conventions of behavior may be imagined as a community of actors who are rationally tied together on the basis of some pre-existing amount of 'mechanical solidarity' (Durkheim).

A slightly different image of the situation results from a dynamic perspective advanced by Schotter (1981) considering only certain types of conditional supergame strategies, which focuses on processes of developing and changing expectations about each other's mode of behavior. These expectations are used in each period of the game to decide anew in Bayesian fashion about the supergame strategy to be followed. The result may be a game consisting of player i's (i=1, ..., n) moves which are the first steps of different supergame strategies.

The game theoretical rationale of this approach is Harsanyi's 'tracing procedure' (Harsanyi, 1975). This solution process is defined in two steps. First, there is assumed a prior probability distribution p_i over the set of pure strategies of each player i (i=1, ..., n), i.e. a probability vector $p=(p_1, p_2, \ldots p_n)$. Formally, introducing these expectations leads to mixed strategies. The second step is defined by a solution process which consists of gradual modifications of expectations and strategy choices until both players' expectations and strategy choices converge to equilibrium strategies corresponding to an equilibrium point solution. This process of gradual modifications is necessary, because assuming every actor i to choose just his best reply to the probability vector $\tilde{p}_i = (p_1, \ldots, p_{i-1}, p_{i+1}, \ldots p_n)$ and the corresponding mixed strategies does not generally lead to equilibrium solutions.

The process is modeled by Schotter (1981) such that it may be represented by a stationary (time-homogeneous) Markov chain which reaches absorbing states when according to convergent mutual expectations each player executes the same mode of behavior. The model is constructed in such a way that an absorbing state of societal stability cannot be reached if the modes of behavior are not equilibrium strategies, even if each player's expectations have converged with subjective probability p=1 to one mode of behavior (cf. the Bayesian best-response satisfactory static Bayesian solution procedure (SBSP), Schotter, 1981: 68). In this view, the emergence of anarchistic cooperation as described above may result. But this depends upon the history of the process, especially the initial distribution of subjective expectations concerning each other's behavior and upon certain chance events included into the process.

If a stationary absorbing state has been reached in the stochastic-dynamic supergame a regularity of behavior has emerged which can be called convention (Lewis, 1969) or social institution (Schotter, 1981). In fact, in each occurrence of the PD actors conform to this regularity, since

(1)   it is an equilibrium of the supergame,
(2)   everyone expects everyone else to conform to it, i.e. everyone's expectations concerning each other's behavior fully converge,
(3)   it is known to each player that deviations from the regularity will lead to deviations by other actors in each period following that deviation, with the result of a decrease in the longrun payoffs of the deviator (cf. Schotter, 1981: 78).

Schotter (1981) proposes to call reciprocal expectations concerning the existence of such regularities norms, which in fact corresponds to sociological conceptualizations. Note that these norms not only contain the belief that others act in a particular way, but also -since these acts are supergame strategies- that sanctions from others' acts may result. This concept of norms differs from those dominating in sociology in one decisive aspect: the stability of these reciprocal expectations across time and individuals is based on the fact that the regularity is an equilibrium solution of an iterated game. The theory advanced by Schotter predicts that only such regularities will be stable (in the Nash sense that no actor has an incentive to deviate). In the case of a PD-norm this equilibrium property of the regularity rests on threats of sanctioning, where sanctions are moves prescribed by supergame- and consequently ordinary PD-strategies. This sanctioning mechanism is a rather indirect and impersonal one. Firstly, deviators need not be detected personally. What must be known is that someone (or a particular proportion of actors in some cases of n-person PD supergames) has defected. Furthermore, sanctions are applied by each member of the group, changing outcomes for each member of the group. They do not consist in exhortations applied to the defector alone. Another limitation of this conception seems to be that these norms and institutions having evolved by such processes are restricted in the range of their applicability to just one concrete PD situation, whereas most kinds of norms seem to apply to multiple PD situations (cf. Lindenberg, 1979). This seems to be not only not in accord with common sociological reasoning, but furthermore quite inefficient for the society of actors.

Assuming a society of actors simultaneously involved in multiple PD supergames, some of them exerting large externalities, one can offer hypotheses concerning the evolution of generalized norms (e.g., golden rule, norm of reciprocity, solidarity, etc.). These institutions may be conceptualized as being equilibrium solutions of PD supergames of a higher order. Cooperative acting in the constituent games of such supergames may be imagined as involving the conformity to this norm in the multiple PDs and the direct application of (costly) sanctions via threats, exhortations etc. to those persons who deviate in one of the multiple PDs. The evolution of such generalized norms may lead to solutions (or changes in the situation) of the multiple PDs even in those cases where these social dilemmas would not be solved seperately because the highly restrictive conditions of the emergence of cooperation as stated above are not fulfilled.

4. Conclusions

In this essay we have attempted to investigate what a rational action approach might contribute to an explanation of the emergence of order in society. The most natural idea in this context is that order derives from market institutions involving various kinds of exchange transactions, e.g. 'social' exchange. Such a conception was shown to be not wholly satisfactory in that it presupposes the existence of certain non-market institutions. On the other hand, there already exist some elements of an economic theory of non-market institutions predicting the emergence of such institutions if

(1) actors are involved in a norm-generating situation which can be identified with help of certain standards of social inefficiency;

(2) certain conditions of norm formation are fulfilled, including the condition of an iteration of the situation and the existence of some particular amount of externalities. Processes and conditions of norm formation were then studied in the course of an investigation of the case of an organic or evolutionary process of norm creation out of Hobbesian anarchy.

A final remark should emphasize that in the rational choice approaches reviewed, norms are not conceptualized via changing preferences but via constraints including expectations (this is contrary to Opp, 1982, for example). This is extremely important with respect to the fact that changing preferences cannot (yet) be explained with help of rational action approaches.

Notes

(1) In this essay we will use the terms 'utilitarian', 'economic', 'rational-choice theoretic' etc. interchangeably. With respect to the notions of 'norms' and 'institutions' too, there will be no semantical rigidity. An attempt to clarify the concept of 'norms' will not be made until Part 3, since the topics covered in the earlier sections are too diverse and heterogeneous to present a coherent explication of the explananda.

(2) Usually such an attempt at an exegesis of a classical text is called

'rational reconstruction' by modern historians of ideas. It may be conceded here that our argument is even more than such a reconstruction and has lost all immediate contact with Durkheim's writings. I can only apologize by the fact that a similar reconstruction of Durkheim's arguments as involving a Prisoners' dilemma situation is undertaken in Collins and Makowsky (1978: 99-101).

(3) Since we assume here a competitive market of price takers, the actors are not involved in a bargaining game setting. Efficient exchange rates are provided by the price mechanism, and these prices are taken as parametric. Naturally, it may be feasible for the actors to engage in a suboptimal exchange. The resulting exchange rate may -as we assume here- be the outcome of a -noncompetitive- bilateral bargaining game and will be -as is also assumed here- dominated by the market solution. Although they result from a bargaining game, the payoffs become entries of a noncooperative game matrix.

(3a) Throughout this essay game theoretical terminology is used in accordance with Harsanyi's definitions (Harsanyi, 1977).

(4) A market representing indirect social exchanges of a particular kind and leading under certain conditions (supergame setting) to an 'altruistic equilibrium' as contrasted to a competitive equilibrium is modeled in Kurz (1977). Walrasian social exchange markets are modeled with rather distinct objectives and conceptual tools in Coleman (1973), but here all exchanges are treated as if they were undertaken by price takers trading homogeneous goods in a perfect market.

(5) This type of theoretical argument is stated here in a manner strongly influenced by Becker's household production function approach (cf. Becker, 1976) in order to indicate that effects of norms and institutions should be conceptualized via constraints and not preferences. This has many theory-strategic advantages, e.g. it allows us to avoid problems connected with the determination of utility functions if we want to undertake comparative-static (or even dynamic) analyses. More generally, this approach may lead to a solution of a problem which might be taken to be crucial for an economic approach to social phenomena, viz. changes of preferences (cf. Raub and Voss, 1981: 47-54).

(6) In sociology, some of the few attempts to discuss the property rights paradigm as an approach to the explanation of social norms have been presented by Opp (1979, 1981).

(7) The problem of inequality and power cannot be discussed here. Frequently one finds in this context the assertion that within an economic approach power

cannot be adequately conceptualized, and that in cases of power differentials emerging institutions tend to be desirable only for those actors which are more powerful. But we must be very careful in distinguishing
1. the obvious fact that in situations of inequality there are differences in the potential of actors to determine the processes and results of norm creations, from the fact
2. that these resulting norms contribute in building up socially efficient states, e.g. in the Pareto sense - even if they stabilize large inequalities.

(8) What follows owes much to the works of Ullmann-Margalit (1977) and Schotter (1981).

(9) This terminology was introduced into this context by Simon (1978). He seems to draw an analogy between optimizing behavior on the individual and the collective level. From this bold jump he gets an argument for the idea that one may work with conceptions of rational behavior much weaker than neoclassical marginalism implies. This is so because what is chosen is a small number of discrete institutional alternatives, not quantities of divisible goods (Simon, 1978: 6-8). On the other hand, it must be said that choosers are not omniscient and benevolent collective actors acting in the interest of the system as a whole, but individuals pursuing their own self-interest. If this kind of aggregation problem is included in the analysis -which need not be fruitful in most cases- it may become important to utilize highly quantitative analysis.

(10) Strictly speaking, altruism should not be seen as a functionally equivalent solution of a problem due to interdependency of actors, but as a change of that situation via changing preferences. A rational choice approach does not have much to say about these processes of changing preferences.

(11) Similar theses have been advanced within the property rights approach (cf. e.g. Demsetz, 1967).

(12) Alternatively, we may get similar results by assuming that a stochastic stop rule is at work, leaving it indeterminate when $\tau = T$ (cf. Shubik, 1970).

(13) Cf. also Lindenberg (1979), who alludes to the same aspect, but with another justification.

References

ARROW, K.J., (1965), Insurance, Risk and Resource Allocation, pp. 45-56 in Aspects of The Theory of Risk-Bearing. Helsinki: Yrjö Jahnssonin Säätiö.

BECKER, G.S., (1976), The Economic Approach to Human Behavior. Chicago: University of Chicago Press.

BLAU, P.M., (1964), Exchange and Power in Social Life. New York: Wiley.

BOISSEVAIN, J., (1974), Friends of Friends. Oxford: Blackwell.

BOORMAN, S.A., (1975), A Combinatorial Optimization Model for Transmission of Job Information through Contact Networks', Bell Journal of Economics 6: 216-249.

COASE, R.H., (1960), The Problem of Social Cost, Journal of Law and Economics 3: 1-44.

COLEMAN, J., (1973), The Mathematics of Collective Action. London: Heinemann.

COLLINS, R. and M. MAKOWSKY, (1978), The Discovery of Society. New York: Random House.

DEMSETZ, H., (1967), Toward a Theory of Property Rights, American Economic Review 57: 347-359.

DURKHEIM, R., (1973), De la division du travail social. 9th ed., Paris: Presses Universitaire de France.

FURUBOTN, E.G. and S. PEJOVICH, (eds.), (1974), The Economics of Property Rights. Cambridge, Mass.: Ballinger.

GRANOVETTER, M.S., (1973), The Strength of Weak Ties, American Journal of Sociology 78: 1360-1380.

HARDIN, R., (1982), Exchange Theory on Strategic Bases, Social Science Information 21: 251-272.

HARSANYI, J.C., (1975), The Tracing Procedure: A Bayesian Approach to Defining a Solution for n-Person Noncooperative Games, International Journal of Game Theory 4: 61-94.

HARSANYI, J.C., (1977), Rational Behavior and Bargaining Equilibrium in Games and Social Situations. Cambridge: University Press.

HAYEK, F.A., (1945), The Use of Knowledge in Society, American Economic Review 35: 519-530.

HEATH, A., (1975), Rational Choice and Social Exchange. Cambridge: University Press.

KURZ, M., (1977), Altruistic Equilibrium, pp. 177-200 in B. Belassa and R. Nelson (eds.), Economic Progress, Private Values and Public Policy. Amsterdam: North-Holland

LEWIS, D., (1969), Convention. Cambridge, Mass.: Harvard University Press.

LINDENBERG, S., (1979), Solidaritätsnormen und soziale Struktur, paper presented at the annual meeting of the Section for Theoretical Sociology of the Deutsche Gesellschaft für Soziologie, mimeo.

LUCE, R.D. and H. RAIFFA, (1957), Games and Decisions. New York: Wiley

MÜNCH, R., (1980), Über Parsons zu Weber: Von der Theorie der Rationalisierung zur Theorie der Interpenetration, Zeitschrift für Soziologie 9: 18-53.

NORTH, D.C. and R.P. THOMAS, (1973), The Rise of the Western World, Cambridge: University Press.

NOZICK, R., (1974), Anarchy, State, and Utopia. Oxford: Clarendon.

OPP, K.-D, (1979), The Emergence and Effects of Social Norms, Kyklos 32: 775-801.

OPP, K.-D, (1981), The Economic Theory of Social Norms (Property Rights) and the Role of Social Structures and Institutions, Archiv für Rechts- und Sozialphilosophie 67: 344-360.

OPP, K.-D, (1982), The Evolutionary Emergence of Norms, British Journal of Social Psychology 21: 139-149.

PARSONS, T., (1937), The Structure of Social Action. Glencoe, Ill.: Free Press.

POSNER, R.A., (1980), A Theory of Primitive Society with Special Reference to Law, Journal of Law and Economics 23: 1-53.

RAUB, W. and T. VOSS, (1981), Individuelles Handeln und gesellschaftliche Folgen. Darmstadt: Luchterhand.

SCHOTTER, A., (1981), The Economic Theory of Social Institutions. Cambridge: University Press.

SHUBIK, M., (1970), Game Theory, Behavior, and the Paradox of the Prisoners' Dilemma, Journal of Conflict Resolution 14: 181-194.

SIMON, H.A., (1978), Rationality as Process and as Product of Thought, American Economic Review 68: 1-16.

TAYLOR, M., (1976), Anarchy and Cooperation. London: Wiley.

THIBAUT, J.W. and H.H. KELLEY, (1959), The Social Psychology of Groups. New York: Wiley.

ULLMANN-MARGALIT, E., (1977), The Emergence of Norms. Oxford: Clarendon.

WILLIAMSON, O.E., (1975), Markets and Hierarchies. New York: Free Press.

WILLIAMSON, O.E., (1981), The Economics of Organization: The Transaction Cost Approach, <u>American Journal of Sociology</u> 87: 548-577.

WILLIAMSON, O.E. and W.G. OUCHI, (1981), The Markets and Hierarchies Program of Research, pp. 371-386 in A. van der Ven and W.F. Joyce (eds.), <u>Perspectives on Organization Design and Behavior</u>. New York: Wiley.

WITTMAN, D., (1982), Efficient Rules in Highway Safety and Sports Activity, <u>American Economic Review</u> 72: 78-90.

Frits Tazelaar

FROM A CLASSICAL ATTITUDE-BEHAVIOR HYPOTHESIS TO A GENERAL MODEL OF BEHAVIOR VIA THE THEORY OF MENTAL INCONGRUITY

1. Attitudes and behavior

Not only in the past, but also today in ongoing social-scientific research, investigators have been tempted to make room for attitude variables through the -at first glance- conceptual simplicity of the notion of attitudes and the even simpler underlying classical hypothesis that in a particular situation individuals always act according to their attitudes. One could even say that for some time it has been quite common in research to attach great importance to attitudes as a starting point in predicting behavior. However, in retrospect, after a systematic consideration of research in which the attitude-behavior relation is central, one must admit that this assumption has seldom met with succes: the classical hypothesis that people (always) behave according to their attitudes is usually refuted [1].

The interesting question which arises here is: can this refutation of the classical hypothesis be explained? I am of the opinion that the answer to this question is affirmative, not only when one refers to research-technical shortcomings in the practice of social-scientific investigation [2], but also when referring to theoretical solutions. Some of the simpler theoretical suggestions are worth mentioning here. In the first place, the conditional statement has been formulated whereby the consistency in the relationship between attitude and behavior is greater when the aim of the attitude is in line with the predicted behavior (the so-called 'suggestion of specifity' [3]). Furthermore, it has been stated that this consistency is greater when the attitude is 'embedded' in a system of 'related' attitudes (the so-called 'suggestion of embedding' [4]). Under the title 'multi-component suggestion', which will later prove to be of extreme importance, we find the theoretical solution that the consistency between attitude and behavior is greater when attitudes are operationally defined with the help of evaluation stimuli and behavior-intentional stimuli and not with the help of cognitive stimuli [5]. Finally, it has often been stated that the relation between attitude and behavior would be stronger when the attitude of the individual in fact corresponds with the attitude of significant others in relation to the same object (the so-called 'similarity-suggestion' [6] and when the attitude of the individual corresponds with the perception of that individual of the attitude of other significant individuals in relation to the same object (the so-called 'perceived similarity-suggestion' [7]).

These simple theoretical solutions have remained fragmented for a long time and have not been integrated into a general behavior-tendency theory. Even less can be said of a combined testing of the five separate hypotheses in empirical research. I will return to this later.

With regard to the development of the theoretical solutions the work of the so-called 'Yale-school' (Rosenberg, Hovland, Abelson, McGuire, Brehm) and the work of Fishbein & Ajzen, Cook & Selltiz, Insko & Schopler and Newcomb c.s. cannot go unmentioned (for a more detailed discussion, see Tazelaar, 1980). A particularly fruitfull theoretical attempt is that of Münch, 1972. A reconstruction shows that the already-mentioned separate hypotheses which assume that:

1. the more the objective of the attitude corresponds with the objective of the predicted behavior, the greater the consistency in the relationship between attitude and behavior;
2. the more the attitude is 'embedded' in a system of related attitudes and underlying motives, the greater the consistency in the relationship between attitude and behavior;
3. the more the attitude is operationally defined with the help of stimuli which refer to attitude components, the greater the consistency in the relationship between attitude and behavior;
4. the more the attitude actually corresponds with the attitude of other significant individuals with regard to the same object, the greater the consistency in the relationship between attitude and behavior.
5. the more the attitude corresponds with the perceived attitude of other significant individuals with regard to the same object, the greater the consistency in the relationship between the attitude and behavior.

can be incorporated into the theory of mental incongruity [8].

The theoretical step-for-step process becomes much clearer since in one investigation not only the classical attitude-behavior hypothesis is tested, but also the five separate conditional hypotheses and also the predictions derived from the theory of mental incongruity. This theory enables us not only to arrange the central statements under investigation in such a way that instead of a list of statements, a system is employed whereby an arrangement can be introduced according to the level of generality (from general theoretical statements, to problem-specific statements and finally to specific operational predictions), but above all offers us assistance in relating different statements concerning social-structural conditions and mental dispositions to each other and is useful for solving the same problem of explanation.

Two types of conditions are explicitly used in the explanation and prediction of behavior and the changes in that behavior, i.e. a) the objective possibilities the individual has to behave in a particular way (i.e. his 'activity arena') and b) the individuals' disposition to carry out a particular action [9]. Given this starting point, it is clear that the existence of a minimal activity arena as much as the existence of a minimal disposition form the necessary, but not sufficient conditions for the behavior of the individual. If the individual finds himself in surroundings in which it is impossible for him to behave in a particular way, the likelihood of that behavior taking place is zero. If the circumstances are less restrictive and the individual is 'permitted' to act in a particular way, it does not necessarily follow that the individual will act in such a way. Therefore a minimum inclination to act is a necessary condition. This inclination or disposition should not be described in terms of a single attitude as is usually the case in social and social-psychological literature, but is formed by a connected complex of mental characteristics.

In our disposition theory, a distinction is made between 'what people think is desirable' or 'what people think should be' on the one hand and 'what people actually experience' on the other hand. This distinction between two elements of different modus, between 'standards' and 'cognitions', forms the decisive difference between the so-called 'consistency theory' and the 'incongruity theory' in its first and later versions. In the consistency theories as well as in the incongruity theory, the stress reducing postulate is central, but the stress or 'incongruity' in the incongruity theory is related only to the, qua modus different, elements of the mental system. Only the 'dissonance' between two elements of different modus is behavior-determined and even then only when both elements are related to the same point of reference or field of reality [10].

Mental elements in the theory of mental incongruity are: primary and secondary standards and their related cognitions, as well as connected and corresponding auxiliary-cognitions.

FIGURE-1: Mental elements in the theory of mental incongruity.

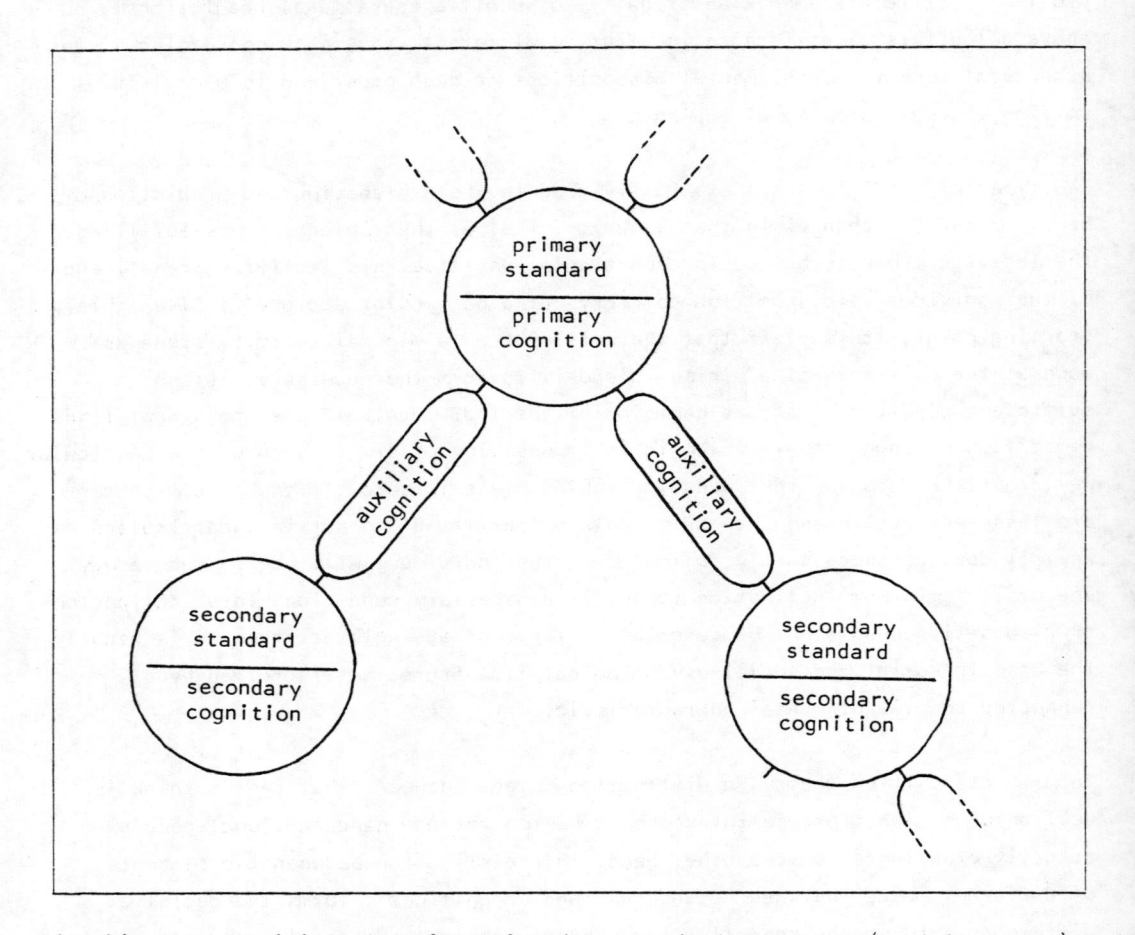

In this way, cognitions are also related to standard agreement (social support) and to the restrictiveness of the performance situation elements of the theory. The actual activity arena and the actual social support or pressure form the most important boundary conditions of the disposition theory [11]. The theory of mental incongruity can not only help in the explanation of behavior and behavior change, but also in the explanation of mental changes such as changes in standards and changes in cognitions through illusion or deception ('cognitive trucage' or wishful thinking) Finally the theory can be used to demonstrate when a discrepancy between actual experienced and desired behavior (mental incongruity) is not being reduced, but is being maintained.

In a second and to some extent modified and expanded version of the mental incongruity theory [12], the conditions for different means of incongruity reduction are clearly given. The predictions resulting from this disposition theory appear to stand up to initial testing rather well. In a following, further expanded (third) version, the disposition theory becomes a general behavioral theory. In this version, the incongruity theory is no longer a calculus or 'empty' theory, but a meaningful complex of statements. Hypotheses are related to 'fixed' elements such as the previously mentioned perceived activity arena and the percieved standard agreement (with other significant individuals) or social support, except for the primary elements to be determined always by the researcher, depending on the chosen problem of explanation. Also, the secondary standards and cognitions related to the areas of 'time', 'status/prestige', 'money' and 'social contacts' which, by means of related auxiliary-conditions, are combined with the primary area, can be labelled as 'fixed' elements because of their repeated central role in each of the investigations in the research programme [13]. In addition, the theory leaves room for some problem specific and also secondary standards and cognitions to be completed on the basis of literature study or on the basis of investigation. The possibilities of immunizing the theory, such that one can later, in case of a rebuttal, refer to 'forgotten' secondary mental elements, no longer play a role. In recent versions of the theory of mental incongruity, it has been stated how different primary, 'fixed' secondary and problem specific secondary elements relate to each other. The hypothesis is: that in the explanation of behavior change and mental change of an individual it holds: the greater the actual 'activity arena', the fewer mental elements, and moreover, the fewer 'loose' or problem specific secondary elements are included. This statement offers the researchers the opportunity for retesting, within subgroups, according to the actual activity arena. By refuting the predictions derived from the theory about people who find themselves in favorable and therefore less restrictive surroundings, one cannot easily call upon the 'forgotten' problem specific mental elements. Under the given conditions, these elements may not play a decisive role in the explanation of behavior or mental states. Their significance is, on the other hand, greater in the explanation of behavior of people who must direct their actions in restrictive surroundings. An earlier research-finding [14] has thus been incorporated in the newer version of the theory [15]. Here an explanation is given for the discovery [16] that the consistency in the relationship between attitude and behavior is smaller -and the simpler classical hypothesis is therefore less acceptable- the more the activity arena is limited: the less favorable the circumstances in which one must act and the less the social support for the activity, the more complex and the more element-based is the explanation of the behavior. The answer to the question as to why the classical hypothesis that people act according to their attitudes is sometimes refuted [17] can thus be found in the theory of mental incongruity.

A simple, but too often unsatisfactory classical attitude-behavior hypothesis has been replaced by a complex theory. This theory, in the third version with four postulates and eight hypotheses, will be outlined here briefly (for a detailed description, see Tazelaar and Wippler, 1981). Less attention will be paid to the related modification and expansion (see Tazelaar and Verbeek, 1982).

2. The theory of mental incongruity

The first and central postulate of the theory of mental incongruity (TMI) relates to the mechanism which determines the results of the problematized mental processes:

P_1 Mental systems have a tendency to reduce the total incongruity (TI) as much as possible.

The total incongruity (TI) is the sum of all incongruities in the various areas. In view of the fact that usually only one explanation problem is assumed when applying the theory of mental incongruity and that therefore certain dimensions which are irrelevant to the problem are placed between brackets (the so-called 'tertiary areas'), total incongruity can be considered as

(1) $TI = PI + \Sigma SI$

i.e., the same as the primary incongruity (PI) plus the sum of all secondary incongruities (ΣSI). The total incongruity TI' is equivalent to the expected primary incongruity after reduction (PI') plus the sum of all secondary incongruities after reduction of the primary incongruity ($\Sigma SI'$):

(2) $TI' = PI' + \Sigma SI'$

The second postulate is:

P_2 Under the condition that the net-primary incongruity (NPI) and the total net incongruity (NI) are negative, it holds: the smaller the net-secondary incongruity (NSI), the stronger the tendency towards reduction of the primary incongruity (PI).

Net-primary incongruity is the same as the difference between the primary (in)congruity which is expected as a result of a reduction and the original primary incongruity:

(3) $NPI = PI' - PI$

While the net-secondary incongruity in a mental system is the same as the difference between the combined secondary incongruities which are expected as a result of a reduction (in a particular way) of the primary incongruity, and the sum of all secondary incongruities before such a reduction of primary incongruity:

(4) $NSI = \Sigma SI' - \Sigma SI$

The total net incongruity (NI) is the same as the difference between the total incongruity (TI') which is expected as a result of a reduction and the original total incongruity (TI):

(5) $NI = TI' - TI$
      $= (PI' + \Sigma SI') - (PI + \Sigma SI)$ ((1), (2))
      $= (PI' - PI) + (\Sigma SI' - \Sigma SI)$
      $= NPI + NSI$ ((3), (4))

Which concrete expectations about the effects of a reducation are available, is determined by the nature of the combined auxiliary-cognitions, which give a causal relationship between the primary and secondary areas [18]. It is clear that:

- I -   A reduction in PI occurs if NSI $\leq$ 0 as a result of that reduction alongside this,

- II -   If a reduction in PI leads to NSI > 0, the difference between NSI and NPI determines if the reduction of PI takes place such that
   a. if NI = NPI + NSI $\geq$ 0, no reduction takes place, and
   b. if NI = NPI + NSI < 0, a reduction in primary incongruity takes place despite the production of incongruity in the secondary area.

The size of an incongruity is determined by two factors, in terms of which two hypotheses have been formulated:

H_1 Given an incongruity in a mental dimension, the greater the dominance of a standard, the greater the incongruity.

H_2 Given an incongruity in a mental dimension, the more the standard relates solely to the holder of that standard, the greater the incongruity.

The first postulate of the TMI concerns only the question as to what extent mental incongruity is reduced. The question as to the means by which incongruity is reduced, is not yet answered. The third postulate relates to this:

P_3 If incongruity reduction occurs then the means of reduction which appear are those which lead to the most reduction of incongruity and the least production of incongruity.

Reduction of incongruity involves change of standards on the one hand and change of cognitions (with or without changes in reality) on the other hand. So for each incongruity, there are three possible means for reduction:
1) the standard is adapted to the cognition;
2) the cognition is brought into line with the standard as a result of a change in reality (one's own doing or externally induced) and
3) the cognition is brought into line with the standard through cognitive 'trucage' without a change taking place in reality.

Hypotheses three to six of the theory of mental incongruity relate to the occurrence of these various means of reduction:

H_3 If a given incongruity is reduced it holds: the less the perceived (= auxiliary-cognition) agreement between one's own standard and that of significant others, the stronger the tendency to adapt this standard to the related cognition, and the stronger this tendency when the surroundings are perceived (= auxiliary-cognition) as being unfavorable and/or the more the cognition is central.

H_4 If a given incongruity is reduced it holds: the more favorable the surroundings are perceived (= auxiliary-cognition), the stronger the tendency to change reality by means of behavior (i.e. the behavior-tendency is stronger) and it is even stronger, the more the perceived (= auxiliary-cognition) agreement between one's own standard and that of significant others, in relation to the same area, and/or the more the cognition is central.

H_5 If a given incongruity is reduced and if a given constellation of mental characteristics is characterized by
   a. a greater percieved standard agreement, and
   b. a perception of unfavorable surroundings then it holds:
   the less the centrality of the (primary) cognition, the stronger the tendency to adapt the cognition to the related (primary) standard by means of cognitive trucage.

With a similar mental constellation, it can be shown, with the help of the sixth hypothesis, that given a central (primary) cognition, which is firmly fixed in the mental system, no incongruity takes place and that the mental state is characterized by stress:

H_6 If a given incongruity is reduced and if a given constellation of mental characteristics is characterized by
   a. a greater perceived standard agreement, and
   b. surroundings are perceived to be unfavorable then it holds:
   the more central the (primary) cognition is, the stronger the tendency towards psycho-somatic complaints.

Not only the content of secondary mental dimensions is important in the context of TMI, but also the number of secondary dimensions. The seventh hypothesis refers to this point:

H_7 The fewer opportunities an arena offers to carry out a particular activity, the greater the extent to which mental constellations in the secondary area determine the means of reduction of primary incongruity.

Apart from the perceived arena, the actual arena is introduced here into the hypothesis. By introducing another postulate and an eighth hypothesis, the theory can be used not only as a behavior-tendency or disposition theory, but also as a general theory of behavior. Postulate four relates to the conditions under which a disposition leads to actual behavior:

P_4 Given a disposition to a certain behavior it holds: the greater the opportunities the arena allows for performing, the greater the probability that the disposition will manifest itself in behavior.

The characteristics of the structure which increase or decrease the restrictiveness of the arena for carrying out the activity can only be determined in the context of a specific problem of explanation. The characteristics of the context of interaction, however, form an exception. The eighth hypothesis of the theory of mental incongruity relates to this:

H_8 The more agreement exists between the tendency to act with regard to a particular activity and the actual standard and performance of significant others, the greater the probability that the disposition will manifest itself in behavior and this probability is even greater, if these significant others find themselves in as restrictive or more restrictive surroundings in which to carry out the activity.

The latter addition to the eighth hypothesis, concerning the comparison of the activity arena in which other significant individuals find themselves is new and has not yet appeared in the third version of the theory [19]. It can be remarked that in testing this expanded version of the theory in empirical research it has not been refuted [20].

In the fourth version of the theory of mental incongruity, the dynamic system-character of the theory is emphasized. With the help of the theory, it can not only be shown when an incongruity is retained and not reduced, but also - in conjunction with the previously given sixth hypothesis -when maintenance of incongruity (i.e. non-reduction) indicates a relatively stable mental state and when it indicates an unstable mental state. In the constellation of mental characteristics whereby (see H_6) there is a large primary incongruity, a small net-secondary incongruity, large perceived standard agreement, perceived unfavorable surroundings and a central primary cognition, stress induced by psycho-somatic complaints was predicted. Now the hypothesis is added that such a mental state (stress, no reduction) is of a temporary nature: via changes in the mental system, predicted with the help of the theory, it becomes merged into a more stable mental state of maintenance of incongruity without stress, or reduction of incongruity by means of behavior change, standard change or cognitive trucage. The fact that this hypothesis is more informative than it at first appears to be, becomes clearer when one transfers the theory into an incongruity model.

3. The incongruity model

The mental incongruity model consists of a collection of non-linear equations. With the help of these equations it can be shown how great, given a combination of mental characteristics, the chance is that behavior change, cognitive trucage or standard change will occur within a particular activity arena. At the same time, it can be shown with the help of the equations how great the chance is of maintenance of an existing congruent or incongruent mental state. Finally, with the help of the model, it can be shown how stable such a mental state is and how great the chance is that continued maintenance of incongruity (i.e. continued non-reduction by any means) will produce stress induced by psycho-somatic complaints.

The core of the incongruity model is formed by a combination of primary and secondary elements:

$$\beta_1 \cdot (PSt_i - PCo_i) + \beta_2 \cdot \left[\sum_j ACo_{ij} \cdot (SSt_{ij} - SCo_{ij}) + \sum_j ACo_{ij} \cdot (SSt_{ij} - SCo_{ij}) \right]$$

$$\text{group } 2_a \qquad \qquad \text{group } 2_b$$

| effect of primary (in)congruity | sum-effect of secondary (in)congruities by which group 2_a concerns the 'fixed' secondary mental elements (the areas: time, status, money and social contacts) and by which 2_b concerns the problem-specific secondary mental elements |

where:

(symbol)	(mental element)	(operational form)	(range)
PSt_i	primary standard	'I (don't) find it desirable to perform activity X' (or 'I (don't) find it desirable to operate in situation X')	[0,1]
PCo_i	primary cognition	'I (do not) perform activity X' (or 'I (do not) operate in situation X')	0,1
SSt_{ij}	secondary standard	'I (don't) find it desirable to operate in situation Y_j' (or: 'I (don't) find it desirable to perform activity Y_j')	[0,1]
SCo_{ij}	secondary cognition	'I (do not) operate in situation Y_j' (or: 'I (do not) perform activity Y_j')	[0,1]
ACo_{ij}	connected auxiliary-cognition	'If I perform activity X, then the chance that I will operate in situation Y_j is greater/more (or less)'	[-1,1]

and where:

i = individual i (i=1,2,...)
j = secondary area (j=1,2,....)
β_1 = weight-factor 1
β_2 = weight-factor 2

Assuming for the sake of simplicity, that

$$I_{1i} = (PSt_i - PCo_i)$$

and

$$I_{2i} = \left[\sum_j ACo_{ij} \cdot (SSt_{ij} - SCo_{ij}) + \sum_j ACo_{ij} \cdot (SSt_{ij} - SCo_{ij}) \right]$$
$$\quad\quad\quad \text{group } 2_a \quad\quad\quad\quad\quad\quad\quad \text{group } 2_b$$

the core of the model can be shown as follows:

$$\beta_1 \cdot I_{1i} + \beta_2 \cdot I_{2i}$$

The means of incongruity reduction are, except for the above-mentioned elements, mainly dependent upon the perceived restrictiveness of the activity arena (how the individual views the opportunities of performing in a particular way in a particular situation), the perceived standard agreement with other significant individuals (how the individual thinks others think he should behave, and to what extent the individual takes account of what concerns others) and the extent of the certainty of the primary cognition. With regard to the latter, it is important to know how firmly the primary cognition is 'anchored' in the mental system. The second series of variables is given as follows:

(symbol)	(mental element)	(operational form)	(range)
$SCCo_{ik}$	social-comparative auxiliary-cognition	'Other individual k finds it (un)desirable that I perform activity X (or, operate in situation X')'	$[0,1]$
$SCSt_{ik}$	secondary standard with regard to conforming behavior	'I find it (un)desirable to operate according to the wishes of other individual k'	$[0,1]$

where:

k = other significant individual (k=1,2,...)

and where the total perceived social support can be written as follows:

$$pSP_i = (SCCo_{i1})^{SCSt_{i1}} \cdot (SCCo_{i2})^{SCSt_{i2}} \cdot \ldots = \pi_k (SSCc_{ik})^{SCSt_{ik}}$$

After the introduction of

| pAA_i | auxiliary cognition with regard to the restrictiveness of the activity arena (= perceived activity arena) | 'The possibilities of performing activity X are (for me) (un)favorable' | $[0,1]$ |

and

c_i = centrality of the primary cognition (= the extent to which the primary cognition is 'fixed' or 'anchored' in the mental system of individual i)

the five equations can be shown as follows

$$T_{BCh'} = \text{EXP}\left[\beta_0 + \beta_1 \cdot I_{1i} + \beta_2 \cdot I_{2i} + \beta_3 \cdot pSP_i\right] \cdot pAA_i$$

$$= \text{EXP}\left[\beta_0 + \beta_1 \cdot (PSt_i - PCo_i) + \beta_2 \cdot \left(\sum_{\substack{j \\ \text{group } 2_a}} ACo_{ij} \cdot (SSt_{ij} - SCo_{ij})\right) + \beta_3 \cdot pSP_i\right] \cdot pAA_i$$

$$T_{Stress} = \text{EXP}\left[\beta_0 + \beta_1 \cdot I_{1i} + \beta_2 \cdot I_{2i} + \beta_3 \cdot pSP_i\right] \cdot (1 - pAA_i)$$

$$= \text{EXP}\left[\beta_0 + \beta_1 \cdot (PSt_i - PCo_i) + \beta_2 \cdot \left(\sum_{\substack{j \\ \text{group } 2_a}} ACo_{ij} \cdot (SSt_{ij} - SCo_{ij})\right) + \beta_3 \cdot \pi_k (SCCo_{ik})^{SCSt_{ik}}\right] \cdot (1 - pAA_i)$$

$$T_{CTruc} = \text{EXP}\left[\beta_4 + \beta_5 \cdot I_{1i} + \beta_6 \cdot I_{2i} + \beta_7 \cdot pSP_i\right] \cdot (1 - c_i)$$

$$= \text{EXP}\left[\beta_4 + \beta_5 \cdot (PSt_i - PCo_i) + \beta_6 \cdot \left(\sum_{\substack{j \\ \text{group } 2_a}} ACo_{ij} \cdot (SSt_{ij} - SCo_{ij})\right) + \beta_7 \cdot \pi_k SCCo_{ik}^{SCSt_{ik}}\right] \cdot (1 - c_i)$$

$$T_{StCh} = \text{EXP}\left[\beta_8 + \beta_9 \cdot I_{1i} - \beta_{10} \cdot I_{2i}\right] \cdot (1 - pSP_i)$$

$$= \text{EXP}\left[\beta_8 + \beta_9 \cdot (PSt_i - PCo_i) - \beta_{10} \cdot \left(\sum_{\substack{j \\ \text{group } 2_a}} ACo_{ij} \cdot (SSt_{ij} - SCo_{ij})\right)\right] \cdot (1 - \pi_k (SCCo_{ik})^{SCSt_{ik}})$$

$$T_{Zero} = \text{EXP}\left[\beta_{11} - \beta_{12} \cdot \left[I_{1i} + \text{ABS } I_{2i}\right]\right]$$

$$= \text{EXP}\left[\beta_{11} - \beta_{12} \cdot \left[(PSt_i - PCo_i) + \text{ABS}\left(\left(\sum_{\substack{j \\ \text{group } 2_a}} ACo_{ij} \cdot (SSt_{ij} - SCo_{ij})\right) + \sum_{\substack{j \\ \text{group } 2_b}} ACo_{ij} \cdot (SSt_{ij} - SCo_{ij})\right)\right]\right]$$

where:

EXP = exponential function
ABS = absolute value

and where:

$T_{BCh'}$ = tendency towards incongruity reduction by adapting the primary cognition to the primary standard by means of behavior change;

T_{Stress} = tendency towards temporary non-reduction paired with stress (induced by expression of psycho-somatic complaints);

T_{CTruc} = tendency towards incongruity reduction by adapting primary cognition to primary standard, by means of cognitive trucage (wishful thinking);

T_{StCh} = tendency towards incongruity reduction by adapting primary standard to the primary cognition (standard change);

T_{Zero} = tendency towards non-reduction, without stress.

The sum of these five 'tendencies' varies according to the size of the primary and secondary incongruities, the perceived social pressure or support, the percieved opportunities for behavior change and the degree of centrality of the primary cognition.

$$SUM = T_{BCh'} + T_{Stress} + T_{CTruc} + T_{StCh} + T_{Zero}$$

By dividing the separate tendencies it can be shown, in percentages or proportions, how great the probability is that reduction of primary incongruity will occur, either through behavior change or through cognitive trucage or through standard change:

$Pr_{BCh'} = T_{BCh'}/SUM$

$Pr_{CTruc} = T_{CTruc}/SUM$

$Pr_{StCh} = T_{StCh}/SUM$

The probability of incongruity reduction occurring is the same as the sum of the probabilities of reduction by the proposed means:

$$Pr_{Reduction} = Pr_{BCh'} + Pr_{CTruc} + Pr_{StCh}$$

$$= (T_{BCh'} + T_{CTruc} + T_{StCh})/SUM$$

Since

$$Pr_{Stress} = T_{Stress}/SUM$$

$$Pr_{Zero} = T_{Zero}/SUM$$

and

$$Pr_{BCh'} + Pr_{CTruc} + Pr_{StCh} + Pr_{Stress} + Pr_{Zero} = 1$$

it is also evident that the probability that reduction of primary incongruity will not occur, is:

$$Pr_{\overline{Reduction}} = 1 - (Pr_{BCh'} + Pr_{CTruc} + Pr_{StCh})$$

$$= Pr_{Zero} + Pr_{Stress}$$

$$(= (T_{Zero} + T_{Stress})/SUM)$$

A stable mental state (in which the probability of non-reduction without stress is great) can therefore be distinguished from an unstable mental state. Such an unstable mental state exists not only if the probability of incongruity reduction by means of behavior change, standard change or cognitive trucage is great, but also if the probability of stress occurring is great. The latter demands some comments. If the probability of stress occurring is great and greater than the probability of incongruity reduction occurring, we predict that this mental state is of a temporary nature and that eventually via changes in the mental system, the reduction means will occur or the stable state will develop, which has the second best chance according to the previous results of the model. Thus, it is predicted that as long as the probability of stress occurring is greater than the probability of a particular means of incongruity reduction, those changes in the mental system occur which increase the probability of that one means of incongruity reduction, and to the extent that eventually the probability of that one means of incongruity reduction will be greater than the probability of non-reduction with stress.

4. The model adapted in empirical research

These rather abstract theoretical statements are most simply clarified by means of a concrete example from one of the investigations of the programme in which the incongruity theory is tested and the model is adapted [21]. It concerns a longitudinal investigation of the effects of long term unemployment among older married men. This investigation, which took place during the period 1978-1982 with the support of the Netherlands Organization for the Advancement of Pure Research (ZWO), covers three measuring points; one directly after retrenchment, one approximately 5 months after the first, and one approximately 10 months after the first. From the collected data it appears that there are unemployed men who in a period of one year display three different reactions to their retrenchment: first, intensive jobapplication (= search)behavior, followed by a period of stress, with considerably more psycho-somatic complaints and finally a change in attitude towards work status (= change in the primary standard: 'Initially I said I wanted nothing other than to immediately find other employment, but that's no longer the case with me. Consider me now as being retired early').

How can these different reactions within one year be explained? It is clear that we won't get too far with the classical attitude-behavior hypothesis. Also, the previously mentioned 'loose' conditional hypotheses don't offer much assistance here. The last version of the theory of mental incongruity and the incongruity model offer greater scope for a satisfactory explanation, as I shall now demonstrate.

Let us assume that the β-coefficients in the five model equations have the following values:

$\beta_0 = \beta_4 = \beta_8 = 0$
$\beta_1 = \beta_3 = \beta_5 = \beta_6 = \beta_7 = \beta_9 = \beta_{10} = \beta_{12} = 1$
$\beta_2 = 2.\beta_1 = 2$
$\beta_{11} = 3$

We know that men with such a reaction pattern initially display, at measuring point 1, a very dominant primary standard in relation to re-entering the labor market ('It is extremely desirable that I again participate in the labor market as soon as possible'). The vast majority possesses a central primary cognition which is not in agreement with that standard ('At present I am unemployed, that can't be denied'). Most of them have a strong primary incongruity (assume: $I_{1i}=0.9$). Moreover, it is clear that most of them initially attach more disadvantages than advantages to unemployment, which relates to the second dimension (assume: $I_{2i}=0.5$). Directly after retrenchment, most consider themselves to be supported by direct family members, friends, ex-colleagues, etc: they believe that these other significant individuals hold the same opinion (e.g. 'As long as you haven't reached 60, you ought to work'). We assume $t_1:pSP_i = 0.8$. Moreover it is evident that the vast majority displays some optimism directly following retrenchment: 'There are surely possibilities for re-employment in the immediate future' (assume: $pAA_i = 0.6$). The primary cognition is, as previously stated, firmly anchored in the mental system: $c_i = 0.9$.

If one starts with this constellation of mental characteristics, the model results reveal that the probability of behavior change ($Pr_{BCh'}$) in this case of job-application behavior, is greater than the probability of no reduction of primary incongruity (Pr_{Zero}). The probability of stress (Pr_{Stress}) occurring is much smaller, while the probability of cognitive trucage (Pr_{Truc}) and standard change (Pr_{StCh}) occurring is zero.

If we therefore assume that the value of I_{1i}, I_{2i}, c_i and pSP_i remains unchanged, and only the perceived activity arena becomes increasingly limited, in view of the many disappointed applicants and applications (pAA_i decreases from e.g. 0.6 to 0.2), we see that the model results present another picture: now the probability of stress occurrring (Pr_{Stress}) is by far the greatest, the probability of behavior change (job-application behavior) occurring has sharply decreased and the other probabilities (Pr_{CTruc}, Pr_{StCh} and Pr_{Zero}) remain small.

Which changes in the mental process must now occur if the probability of stress appearing, as is predicted in the theory, is to decline? With the help of the model we can show that the probability of behavior change occurring at the expense of stress increases if -at first- pAA_i increases. Moreover, the probability of behavior change increases slightly if:
a) I_{1i} becomes greater, b) I_{2i} becomes greater, c) c_i becomes greater and d) pSP_i becomes greater. Considering that in the given example most of these variables have almost reached their ceiling values, the possibilities of increasing the probability of behavior change at the expense of stress by this means is small. If the actual labor market situation and also the associated perceived activity arena do not improve, the chance of (once again) job-application behavior

occurring remains small.

The probability of cognitive trucage can only increase at the cost of stress if the centrality of the primary cognition, in relation to being unemployed, decreases.

The probability of standard change occurring at the cost of stress increases, in the first place, according to whether the value of pSP_i decreases and in the second place, the value of I_{2i} decreases. If, for example, perceived social support decreases through social isolation, or rather through retreating from particular social relationships, and if, for some reason, one minimizes the advantages of participating in the labo market, whereby pSP_i declines from 0.8 to 0.2 and where I_{2i} declines from 0.5 to -0.6, the model results (by otherwise unchanged c_i, I_{1i} and pAA_i) will appear to be totally different.

In the latter case it can be said that the probability of standard change occurring is greatest while not only the probability of stress, but also cognitive trucage, behavior change and non-reduction occurring, is smallest. With the help of the incongruity model, it can also be shown why, after retrenchment, some unemployed and not others, actively seek new employment; why it is that some unemployed, and not others, display psycho-somatic complaints after a period of time, and why therefore some unemployed retreat from their social relationships.

Finally, the question remains why, after some time, some unemployed find work and others do not. Up till now, with the help of the model, we could only show the probability of the tendency towards behavior change (Pr_{Bch^i}) which, in the example, is really the probability of job-application or search behavior occurring. Whether that search behavior eventually leads to work is not yet shown. Thereto, we must, analogous to the expansion of the incongruity theory, expand the incongruity model. That expansion from a disposition model to a general model of behavior occurs by adding two variables. Apart from the perceived activity arena (pAA_i) and the perceived support (pSP_i) we can now also distinguish:

AA_i = the actual activity arena in which individual i finds himself $[0,1]$

and

SP_i = the actual social support or pressure that individual i experiences $[0,1]$

where SP_i, except for the behavior and standards of other significant individuals, is dependent upon the activity arena in which others find themselves, in comparison with the activity arena in which the individual finds himself:

$$SP_i = \frac{\sum_{k}^{n} (B_k \cdot PSt_k) \left[\frac{1}{(1-AA_k)((1+AA_i - AA_k)/2)} \right]}{N}$$

where:

B_k = the behavior of significant other individual k (primary area) [0,1]

PSt_k = the standard of significant other individual k related to the primary area [0,1]

AA_k = the actual activity arena in which significant other individual k finds himself [0,1]

Actual social pressure is greater the more people among the significant others carry out the intended activity, the more they possess a dominant standard in relation to the same area, and the more they absolutely and in comparison with individual i display that behavior and that standard in activity arenas which hinder the carrying out of the activity. The probability of behavior change is then a function of the probability of the tendency towards behavior change $Pr_{BCh'}$, the actual activity arena and the actual social support or pressure:

$$Pr_{BCh} = (AA_i^{\beta_{13}} \cdot SP_i^{\beta_{14}}) \cdot (Pr_{BCh'})$$

5. Conclusion

Here therefore, the behavior model has been presented, although in the briefest possible way. For a more detailed presentation, the reader is referred to Tazelaar and Verbeek (1982). The value which, in the end, is attributed to the model depends of course on the degree of consistency of the test results.

Notes

(1) See among others: Kiesler et al. (1969), Wicker (1969), Lauer (1971), Wicker (1971), Fishbein and Ajzen (1972), Benninghaus (1973), Deutscher (1973), Meinefeld (1977).
(2) See among others: Ehrlich (1969), Wicker (1969), Lauer (1971), Benninghaus (1973), Liska (1974), Gross and Niman (1975), Tazelaar (1976), Meinefeld (1977), Tazelaar (1980).
(3) The so-called 'suggestion of specifity': Chein (1949), Kendler and Kendler (1949), Cook and Selltiz (1964), Fishbein (1966), Wicker and Pomazal (1971), Weigel et al. (1974), Heberlein and Black (1976).
(4) The so-called 'suggestion of embedding': Corey (1937), Deutsch (1949), Hyman (1949), Kendler and Kendler (1949), Newcomb et al. (1952), Campbell et al. (1960), Cook and Selltiz (1964), Insko and Schopler (1967), Wicker (1969), Jeffries and Bansford (1972), Schuman (1972), Griffith and Garcia (1979).
(5) Katz and Stotland (1959), Mann (1959), Rosenberg and Hovland (1960), Krech et al. (1962), Fishbein (1965), Triandis (1967), Woodmansee and Cook (1967), Ostrom (1969), Waldo and Hall (1970), Brigham (1971), Buffalo and Rogers (1971), Kothandapani (1971), Ewens and Ehrlich (1972), Albrecht and Carpenter (1976).
(6) See among others: Newcomb and Svehla (1937), Precker (1952), Cohen (1960), Rosenbaum and Franc (1960), Cohen (1968), Woelfel and Haller (1971), Gasson et al. (1972), Benninghaus (1973), Liska (1974a and c), Magura (1974).
(7) See among others: Chowdry and Newcomb (1952), Newcomb (1953), Monk and Newcomb (1956), Clark and Gibbs (1965), Laing et al. (1966), Fendrich (1967), Scheff (1967), Defriese and Ford (1969), Acock and Defleur (1972), Ewens and Ehrlich (1972), Brannon et al. (1973), Sample and Warland (1973), Newcomb (1978), Andrews and Kandel (1979).
(8) See Tazelaar (1980: 76-78)
(9) See Tazelaar (1980: 37-39).
(10) See Tazelaar (1980: 53).
(11) See Tazelaar (1980: 229),Tazelaar and Wippler (1981: 3 ff).
(12) See Tazelaar (1980: 53-67).
(13) See Tazelaar and Wippler (1981) and Tazelaar and Verbeek (1982).
(14) See Tazelaar (1980: 139-151).
(15) See Tazelaar and Wippler (1981: 12).
(16) Cf. Meinefeld (1977: 158).

(17) Cf. Lapiere (1934), Corey (1937), Saenger and Gilbert (1950), Bernberg (1952), Kutner et al. (1952), Vroom (1962), Himelstein and Moore (1963), Linn (1965), Defriese and Ford (1969), with (among others) Stouffer et al. (1949), Defleure and Westie (1958), Frost (1961), Poppleton and Pilkington (1963), Fendrich (1967), Reiss (1967), Ajzen and Fishbein (1970), Frideres et al. (1971), Brannon et al. (1973), Bonfield (1974), Harrell and Benneth (1974), Kelman (1974), Speare (1974), Hagan (1975), Steffensmeier (1975), Kahle and Berman (1979).

(18) See further: Tazelaar and Wippler (1981: 6).

(19) See Tazelaar and Wippler (1981).

(20) See Tazelaar and Gerats (1982).

(21) See Tazelaar and Verbeek (1982).

(22) See Tazelaar (1978, 1979), Wippler (1980), Tazelaar and Wippler (1982).

References

ACOCK, A.C. & M.L. DEFLEUR, (1972), 'A configurational approach to contingent consistency in the attitude-behavior relationship', American Sociological Review 37: 714-726.

AJZEN, I., R.K. DARROCH, M. FISHBEIN & J.A. HORNIK, (1970), 'Looking backward revisited: A Reply to Deutscher', American Sociologist 5: 267-273.

AJZEN, I. & M. FISHBEIN, (1970), 'The prediction of behavior from attitudinal and normative variables', Journal of Experimental Social Psychology 6: 466-487.

AJZEN, I. & M. FISHBEIN, (1973), 'Attitudinal and Normative Variables as Predictors of Specific Behaviors', Journal of Personality and Social Psychology 27: 41-57.

ALBRECHT, S.L. & K.E. CARPENTER, (1976), 'Attitudes as predictors of behavior versus behavior intentions: A convergence of research traditions', Sociometry 39: 1-10.

ANDREWS, K.H. & D.B. KANDEL, (1979), 'Attitude and behavior: a specification of the contingent consistency hypothesis', American Sociological Review 44: 298-310.

BENNINGHAUS, H., (1973), 'Soziale Einstellungen und soziales Verhalten. Zur Kritik des Attitüdenkonzepts', pp 671-707 in: Albrecht, G., H. Daheim & F. Sack, (eds.) Soziologie - Sprache, Bezug zur Praxis, Verhältnis zu anderen Wissenschaften, Opladen: Westdeutscher Verlag.

BERNBERG, R.E., (1952), 'Socio-Psychological Factors in Industrial Morale: a) The Prediction of Specific Indicators', The Journal of Social Psychology, 36: 73-82.

BONFELD, E.H., (1974), 'Attitude, Social Influence, Personal Norm, and Intention Interactions as related to Brand Purchase Behavior', *Journal of Marketing Research*, 11: 379-389.

BRANNON, R., G. CYPHERS, S. HESSE, S. HESSELBART, R. KEANE, H. SCHUMAN, T. VICARRO & D. WRIGHT, (1973), 'Attitude and Action: A Field Experiment joined to a General Population Survey', *American Sociological Review* 38: 625-636.

BRIGHAM, J.C., (1971), 'Racial Stereotypes, Attitudes and Evaluations of and Behavioral Intentions towards Negroes and Whites', *Sociometry* 34: 360-380.

BUFFALO, M.D. & J.W. ROGERS, (1971), 'Behavioral norms, moral norms, and attachment - problems of deviance and conformity', *Social Problems* 19: 101-113.

CAMPBELL, A., Ph.E. CONVERSE, W.E. MILLER & D.E. STOKES, *The American Voter*, New York: Wiley.

CHEIN, I., (1948), 'Behavior theory and the behavior of attitudes: Some critical comments', *Psychological Review* 55: 175-188.

CHEIN, I., (1949), 'The problems of inconsistency: A restatement', *Journal of Social Issues* 5: 52-61.

CHOWDRY, K. & Th.M. NEWCOMB, (1952), 'The relative abilities of leaders and non-leaders to estimate opinions of their own groups', *Journal of Abnormal and Social Psychology* 47: 51-57.

CLARK, A.L. & J.P. GIBBS, (1965), 'Social Control: a Reformulation', *Social Problems* 12: 398-414.

COHEN, A.R., (1960), 'Attitudinal consequences of induced discrepancies between cognitions and behavior', *Public Opinion Quarterly* 24: 297-318.

COHEN, A.R., (1964a), *Attitude Change and Social Influence*, New York: Basic Books.

COHEN, A.R., (1964b), 'The influence of the group', pp 100-120 in: Cohen, A.R. *Attitude Change and Social Influence*, New York: Basic Books.

COOK, S.W. & C. SELLTIZ, (1964), 'A multiple-indicator approach to attitude measurement', *Psychological Bulletin* 62: 36-55.

COREY, S.M., (1937), 'Professed attitudes and actual behavior', *Journal of Educational Psychology* 28: 271-280.

DEFRIESE, G.H. & W.S. FORD, (1969), 'Verbal attitudes, overt acts and the influence of social constraint in interracial behavior', *Social Problems* 16: 483-505.

DEFLEUR, M.L. & F.R. WESTIE, (1958), 'Verbal attitudes on overt acts', *American Sociological Review* 23: 667-673.

DEFLEUR, M.L. & F.R. WESTIE, (1963), 'Attitude as a scientific concept', *Social Forces* 42: 17-31.

DEUTSCH, M., (1949), 'The direction of behavior. A field-theoretical approach to the understanding of inconsistencies', *Journal of Social Issues* 5: 43-49.

DEUTSCHER, I., (1973), *What we say/what we do. Sentiments and acts*. Glenview, Ill.: Scott & Foresman.

EHRLICH, H.J., (1969), 'Attitudes, behavior and the intervening variables', *American Sociologist* 4: 29-34.

EWENS, W.L. & H.J. EHRLICH, (1972), 'Reference-Other Support and Ethnic Attitudes as Predictors of Intergroup Behavior', *Sociological Quarterly* 3: 348-360.

FENDRICH, J.M., (1967a), 'A study of the association among verbal attitudes, commitment and overt behavior in different experimental situations', *Social Forces* 45: 347-355.

FENDRICH, J.M., (1967b), 'Perceived reference group support: Racial attitudes and overt behavior', *American Sociological Review* 32: 960-970.

FESTINGER, L., (1957), *A Theory of Cognitive Dissonance*, New York: Row, Peterson.

FISHBEIN, M., (1965), 'A consideration of beliefs, attitudes and their relationships', in: Steiner, I.D. & M. Fishbein, (eds), *Current Studies in social psychology*, New York: Holt, Rinehart & Winston.

FISHBEIN, M., (1966), 'The relationship between beliefs, attitudes and behavior', p. 199-233 in: Feldman, S. (ed.), *Cognitive Consistency*, New York: Academic Press.

FISHBEIN, M., (1967), 'Attitude and the prediction of behavior', in: Fishbein, M., (ed.), *Readings in Attitude Theory and Measurement*, New York: Wiley.

FISHBEIN, M. & I. AJZEN, (1972), 'Attitudes and Opinions', *Annual Review of Psychology* 23: 487-544.

FRIDERES, J.S., L.G. WARNER & S.L. ALBRECHT, (1971), 'The impact of social constraints on the relationship between attitudes and behavior', *Social Forces* 50: 102-112.

FROST, R.T., (1961), 'Stability and change in local party politics', *Public Opinion Quarterly* 25: 221-235.

GASSON, R.M., A.O. HALLER & W.H. SEWELL, (1972), 'Attitudes and Facilitations in the Attainment of Status', *Caroline Rose Monograph Series*, American Sociological Association, Washington.

GRIFFITH, W. & L. GARCIA, (1979), 'Reversing Authoritarian Punitiveness: The Impact of Verbal Conditioning', *Social Psychology* 42: 55-61.

GROSS, S.J. & C.M. NIMAN, (1975), 'Attitude-behavior-consistency. A Review', *Public Opinion Quarterly* 39: 358-368.

HAGAN, J., (1975), 'Law, Order and Sentencing: A Study of Attitude of Action', *Sociometry* 38: 374-384.

HARRELL, G.D. & P.D. BENNETT, (1974), 'An Evaluation of the Expectancy Value Model of Attitude Measurement for Physician Prescribing Behavior', *Journal of Marketing Research* 11: 269-278.

HEBERLEIN, T.A. & J.S. BLACK, (1976), 'Attitudinal Specificity and the Prediction of Behavior in a Field Setting', *Journal of Personality and Social Psychology* 33: 474-479.

HIMELSTEIN, Ph. & J.C. MOORE, (1973), 'Racial Attitudes and the action of negro- and white-background figures as factors in petitionsigning', Journal of English Psychology 61: 267-272.

HYMAN, H., (1949), 'Inconsistencies as a problem in attitude measurement', Journal of Social Issues 5: 38-42.

INSKO, Ch.A., (1967), Theories of Attitude Change, Englewood Cliffs, New Jersey: Prentice Hall.

INSKO, Ch.A. & J. SCHOPLER, (1967), 'Triadic consistency: A statement of affective-cognitive-conative consistency', Psychological Review 74: 361-376.

JEFFRIES, V. & H.E. RANSFORD, (1972), 'Ideology, social-structure, and Yorty-Bradley Mayoral Election', Social Problems 19: 358-372.

KAHLE, L.R. & J.J. BERMAN, (1979), 'Attitudes cause behaviors: a cross-lagged panel analysis', Journal of Personality and Social Psychology 37: 315-321.

KATZ, D. & E. STOTLAND (1959), 'A preliminary statement to a theory of attitude structure and change', pp. 423-475 in: Koch, S., (ed.), Psychology: a study of science Vol. 3, New York.

KELMAN, H.C., (1974), 'Attitudes are alive and well and gainfully employed in the sphere of action', American Psychologist 29: 310-324.

KENDLER, H.H. & T.S. KENDLER, (1949), 'A methodological analysis of the research area of inconsistent behavior', Journal of Social Issues 5: 27-31.

KIESLER, C.A., B.E. COLLINS & N. MILLER, (1969), Attitude Change: A critical Analysis of Theoretical Approaches, New York: Wiley.

KRECH, D., R.A. CRUTCHFIELD & E.L. BALLACHEY, (1962), 'The nature and measurement of attitudes', pp. 138-179, Ch. 5 in: Krech, D., R.A. Crutchfield & E.L. Ballachy, Individual in Society, New York: McGraw-Hill.

KOTHANDAPANI, V., (1971), 'Validation of Feeling, Belief and Intention to Act as three components of Attitude and their Contribution to prediction of contraceptive behavior', Journal of Personality and Social Psychology 19: 321-333.

KUTNER, B., C. WILKINS & P.R. YARROW, (1952), 'Verbal attitudes and overt behavior involving racial prejudice', Journal of Abnormal and Social Psychology 47: 649-652.

LAING, R.D., H. PHILLIPSON & A.R. LEE, (1966), Interpersonal Perception. A Theory and a Method of Research. New York: Springer Publishing Co.

LAPIERE, R.T., (1934), 'Attitudes versus actions', Social Forces, 13: 230-237.

LAUER, R.H., (1971), 'The problems and values of attitude research', Sociological Quarterly 12: 247-252.

LINN, L.S., (1965), 'Verbal attitudes and overt behavior. A study of racial discrimination', pp. 76-104 in: Deutscher, I., (ed.), What we say/what we do, Glenview, Ill.: Scott & Foresman.

LISKA, A.E., (1974), 'Emergent issues in the attitude-behavior consistency controversy', American Sociological Review 39: 261-272.

LISKA, A.E., (1974), 'Attitude-behavior consistency: reply to Magura', American Sociological Review 39: 762-763.

LISKA, A.E., (1974), 'The impact of attitude on behavior: attitude-social support interaction', Pacific Sociological Review 17: 83-97.

MAGURA, S., (1974), 'A comment on 'attitude-behavior consistency' ....', American Sociological Review 39: 761-762.

MANN, J.H., (1959), 'The relationship between cognitive, affective and behavioral aspects of racial prejudice', Journal of Social Psychology 21: 223-228.

McGUIRE, W.J., (1966), 'The current status of cognitive consistency theories', pp 1-46 in: Feldman, S., Cognitive Consistency, New York.

MEINEFELD, W., (1977), Einstellung und soziales Handeln, Reinbek bei Hamburg: Rowohlt

MONK, M. & Th.M. NEWCOMB, (1956), 'Perceived consensus within and among occupational classes', American Sociological Review 21: 71-79.

MÜNCH, R., (1972), Mentales System und Verhalten, Tübingen: J.C.B. Mohr (Paul Siebeck).

NEWCOMB, Th.M., (1953), 'An approach to the study of communicative acts', Psychological Review 60: 393-494.

NEWCOMB, Th.M., (1956), 'The prediction of interpersonal attraction', American Psychologist 11: 575-580.

NEWCOMB, Th.M., (1959), 'The Study of Consensus', p. 277-292 in: Merton, Broom & Cottrell, (eds.), Sociology Today, New York: Rinehart & Winston.

NEWCOMB, Th.M., (1961), The acquaintance process, New York: Holt.

NEWCOMB, Th.M., (1968), 'Interpersonal Balance', in: Abelson, R.P. a.o. (eds.), Theories of cognitive consistency, Chicago

NEWCOMB, Th.M., (1978), 'The acquaintance process: Looking mainly backward', Journal of Personality and Social Psychology 36: 1075-1083.

NEWCOMB, Th.M. & G. SVEHLA, (1937), 'Intra-family relationships in attitude', Sociometry 1: 180-205.

OSTROM, T.M., (1969), 'The Relationship between the Affective, Behavioral and Cognitive Components of Attitude', Journal of Experimental Social Psychology 5: 12-30.

POPPLETON, P. & G.W. PILKINGTON, (1963), 'The measurement of religious attitudes in an university population', British Journal of Social and Clinical Psychology 2: 20-36.

PRECKER, J.A., (1952), 'Similarity of valuings as a factor in selection of peers and need-authority figures', Journal of Abnormal and Social Psychology 47: 406-414.

REISS, I.L., (1967), The social contest of premarital sexual permissiveness, New York: Holt, Rinehart & Winston.

ROSENBAUM, M.E. & D.E. FRANC, (1960), 'Opinion change as a function of external commitment and amount of discrepancy from the opinion of another', Journal of Abnormal and Social Psychology 61: 15-20.

ROSENBERG, M.J. & C.I. HOVLAND, (1960), 'Cognitive, Affective and Behavioral Components of Attitudes', pp. 1-14 in: Rosenberg, Hovland, McGuire, Abelson, Brehm, Attitude Organization and Change, New Haven: Yale University Press.

ROSENBERG, M.J., C.I. HOVLAND, W.J. McGUIRE, R.P. ABELSON & J.W. BREHM, (1960), Attitude Organization and Change, New Haven: Yale University Press.

SAENGER, G. & E. GILBERT, (1950), 'Customer reactions to the integration of negro sales personnel', International Journal of Opinion and Attitude Research 57-76.

SAMPLE, J. & R. WARLAND, (1973), 'Attitude and Prediction of Behavior', Social Forces 51: 292-304.

SCHEFF, Th.J., (1967), 'Toward a sociological model of consensus', American Sociological Review 32: 32-46.

SCHUMAN, H., (1972), 'Attitude vs. Action versus Attitudes vs. Attitudes', Public Opinion Quarterly 36: 347-354.

SPEARE, A., (1974), 'Residential satisfaction as an intervening variable in residential mobility', Demography 11: 173-188.

STEFFENSMEIER, R.H. & D.J. STEFFENSMEIER, (1975), 'Attitudes and Behavior toward Hippies: A Field Experiment accompanied by Home Interviews', Sociological Quarterly 16: 393-400.

STOUFFER, S.A., E.A. SUCHMAN, L.C. DEVINNEY, S.A. STAR & R.M. WILLIAMS jr., (1949) 'The American soldier: adjustment during army life (studies in social psychology in world war II), Vol. 1, Princeton, New Jersey: Wiley.

TAZELAAR, F., (1976), Onderzoeksproject mentale incongruentie en klassieke attituden: een theoretisch alternatief voor het verklaren van gedrag, Vakgroep Theorie en Methodologie van de Sociologie-publication, Utrecht University.

TAZELAAR, F., (1978), Mentale incongruenties en de gevolgen van werkloosheid, First Interim Report for ZWO, Vakgroep TMS, Utrecht University.

TAZELAAR, F., (1979), Statusinconsistentie en de gevolgen van werkloosheid, Second Interim Report for ZWO, Vakgroep TMS, Utrecht University.

TAZELAAR, F., (1980), Mentale incongruenties-sociale restricties-gedrag; een onderzoek naar beroepsparticipatie van gehuwde vrouwelijke academici, diss., Utrecht.

TAZELAAR, F. & G.E. GERATS, (1982), Hygiëne en hygiënegedrag in Nederlandse Varkensslachterijen, Vakgroep TMS and Vakgroep VVDO-publication, Utrecht University.

TAZELAAR, F. & A. VERBEEK, (1982), The mental incongruity model, Utrecht (forthcoming)

TAZELAAR, F. & R. WIPPLER (1981), Die Theorie mentaler Inkongruenzen und ihre Anwendung in der empirischen Sozialforschung, paper for the Congress 'Soziologische Theorien' of the Deutsche Gesellschaft für Soziologie, Utrecht, november 21-22.

TAZELAAR, F. & R. WIPPLER (1982), Mentale incongruentie en statusinconsistentie, een onderzoek naar de gevolgen van werkloosheid. Stand van het onderzoek april 1982, Fourth Interim Report for ZWO, Vakgroep TMS, Utrecht University.

TRIANDIS, H.C., (1967), 'Toward an Analysis of the Components of Interpersonal Attitudes', p. 227-270 in: Sherif, C.W. & M.S. Sherif, (eds.), Attitude, Ego-Involvement and Change, New York: Wiley.

VROOM, V.H., (1962), 'Ego-Involvement, job satisfaction and job performance', Personnel Psychology 15: 159-177.

WALDO, G.P. & N.E. HALL, (19), 'Delinquency potential and attitudes toward the criminal justice system', Social Forces 49: 291-298.

WEIGEL, R.H., D.I.A. VERNON & L.N. TOGNACCI, (1969), 'Specifity of the Attitude as a Determinant of Attitude-Behavior Congruence', Journal of Personality and Social Psychology 30: 724-728.

WICKER, A.W., (1969), 'Attitude versus actions: The relationship of verbal and overt behavioral responses to attitude objects', Journal of Social Issues 25: 41-78.

WICKER, A.W., (1971), 'An examination of the 'other variables' explanation of attitude-behavior inconsistency', Journal of Personality and Social Psychology 19: 18-30.

WIPPLER, R., (1980), Mentale incongruentie, statusinconsistentie en de gevolgen van werkloosheid, Third Interim Report for ZWO, Vakgroep TMS-publication, Utrecht University, paper for Symposium 'Verklarende Sociologie en grote Maatschappijproblemen', Werkgemeenschap Verklarende Sociologie.

WOELFEL, J. & A.O. HALLER, (1971), 'Significant others, the self-reflexive act and the attitude formation process', American Sociological Review 36: 74-87.

WOODMANSEE, J.J. & S.W. COOK, (1967), 'Dimensions of verbal racial attitudes: their identification and measurement', Journal of Personality and Social Psychology, 7: 240-250.

Part II

EMPIRICAL ANALYSES

Hartmut Esser

ON THE EXPLANATION OF CONTEXTUAL EFFECTS ON INDIVIDUAL BEHAVIOR: THE CASE OF LANGUAGE ACQUISITION BY MIGRANT WORKERS

Introduction

This paper has two goals. On the one hand, a substantial explanandum - the acquisition of linguistic skills by migrant workers in the Federal Republic of Germany - is to be investigated empirically. In addition to the 'individual' explanatory variables which are normally taken into account in this context, we shall explicitly investigate the relative significance of the influence of the 'environment' of the migrant workers. This will be done in section 1 to 3 with the aid of techniques of multi-level analysis (cf. e.g. Boyd and Iversen, 1979). The second goal is methodological. On the basis of the established effects and the theoretical arguments, which will remain rather implicit in the empirical investigation, for a possible relevance of environmental variables, section 4 will offer some considerations aiming at remedying the theoretical deficit of most multi-level-and contextual analyses. The background of these considerations is on the one hand the assumption that statistically discovered 'effects' by no means constitute a theoretical explanation, but must be taken themselves as the point of departure for a more general explanation. Specifically, we shall attempt to interpret environmental effects as the result of a general mechanism: of the rational and interest-guided action and adaptive behavior of persons. The background of these considerations is in addition the attempt to use the methodological procedures and theoretical approaches of multi-level analysis in providing a (partial) solution of the so-called problem of coordination. The problem of coordination is the question concerning the explanatory coordination of social-structural conditions and individual behavior (as distinguished from the problem of transformation, which concerns the derivation of social-structural effects and processes from individual effects, cf. Lindenberg and Wippler, 1978). This problem is by no means new; it is one of the basic problems of classical sociology. Relatively new, however, is the special idea that one can give an adequate explanation of the influence of social structures on individual action only by means of a general theory of action. And attention to the problem raised by the fact that established environmental effects are themselves in need of explanation is relatively new in empirical sociology. Thus, attempts at providing solutions of these problems are at the present time rather disparate and preliminary. But it is surely a step forward that we become aware of the need for an explanation of the empirically discovered relations between social structures and the action of individuals, refusing to be satisfied with 'explained variance' by means of context variables or with the dictum that all action is conditioned by social structures.

1. Social conditions of language acquisition by migrant workers

The acquisition of linguistic skills by migrant workers as well as by migrants in general can be regarded as the most essential prerequisite to any further absorption. Without language capabilities, orientation is more difficult and contacts with the indigenious population are hardly possible. Status assignments are significantly dependent upon language capabilities. Apart from this, a change of orientation and identification is only to be expected within the framework of language competence and linguistic 'Welterschliessung'.

This has already been discussed in the general Sociology of Language literature (cf. Luckmann, 1979: 60 ff). The significance of language for social absorption is especially emphasized in studies concerned with the assimilation of migrant workers. One usually assumes that language skills relate more or less clearly to education, length of residence, contact with the indigenous population, and other associated factors (cf. for example Hoffmann-Nowotny, 1973: 288; Mehrländer et al., 1981: 483 ff).

Although the significance of linguistic skills might be recognized in most studies, knowledge concerning the exact determinants of different language skills of migrant workers is diffuse. This is because conventionally three-dimensional tables have already exhausted the potential of empirical analysis (with the result that multivariate processes cannot be identified).
Furthermore, this situation is also to be viewed in the light of the fact that

the explanation of the acquisition of language and its consequences is hardly theoretically satisfactory when one works with simple 'variables' such as length of residence and education without making their theoretical significance more explicit.

In these studies a variety of factors is striking: since as a rule data are gathered by individual survey questionnaires, 'individual' variables are almost exclusively used to explain language acquisition. Usually any existing influences from the 'surroundings' are investigated in these analyses only on the basis of estimates given by the individuals questioned (for example, about the extent of ethnic concentration in the residence environment). However, the problem cannot be solved in this manner. Individuals are hardly qualified to act as informants concerning their own environment, so the corresponding analyses (naturally, also multivariate analyses) must always remain subject to the flaw of 'subjectivity'.

Thus, the following investigation deals with four general problems which can be only pointed at without going into detail: first, theoretical considerations about the process of integration will have to be founded empirically (for more details see below). By taking the context into account, we can make it sure, secondly, that neither of the two central factors determining social processes of any kind ('person' and 'environment') is neglected. On the basis of the results, interpretations of the established effects will, thirdly, contribute to the explanation of microeffects (language acquisition of persons) from macro-conditions (contextual criteria). Finally, it would be possible to base political measures to improve the situation of foreign workers (here concerning language acquisition) more specifically on person- respectively context-related variables. There are, however, a number of complex methodological problems usually underlying such multi-level analyses; as satisfactory solutions could not always be found, the results must be treated carefully - especially the ones concerning the issues mentioned above. Therefore, the considerations and results should be understood rather as a first exploratory step toward a more detailed inquiry into a previously often neglected but central factor of social processes: the social context of acting and learning persons.

2. Language acquisition and the absorption of migrants

If the term 'absorption' of migrants is divided into the two central dimensions of 'assimilation' and 'integration', the acquisition of the language of the receiving system belongs to the cognitive assimilation which itself is the prerequisite of all further levels of assimilation and the establishment of a personal and relational balance.

Assimilation can refer to different dimensions. If assimilation is related to personal criteria, it can be divided into cognitive assimilation (referring to instrumental abilities) and identificational assimilation (referring to cathectic evaluations); since changes of values can only occur after changes of 'knowledge', cognitive assimilation is to be regarded as the prerequisite to any change of identification. Assimilation in relational criteria can occur either vertically (structural assimilation) or horizontally (social assimilation). Again, cognitive assimilation is a prerequisite to both - to status acquisition resp. status mobility as well as to establishing interethnic contacts (for the theoretical conception cf. Esser, 1980: 21 ff, 231 ff). The so-called causal significance of cognitive assimilation - such as language acquisition - has been well established empirically (cf. Esser, 1981). The significance of personal integration, however, was not considered; furthermore, the causal sequence of cognitive, structural, social and identificational assimilation can only be tested in the following by non-panel-data.

Basically, assimilation (and integration) is theoretically explained by an argument in terms of the theory of action. 'Assimilation' (like acting and learning in general, where 'learning' is interpreted as a kind of 'acting') takes place when the respective 'actions' (e.g. learning German, establishing contacts with Germans, accepting a value etc.) are possible as far as skills are concerned, when other motives make it seem 'necessary', when the 'costs' are not too high and when these actions are encouraged resp. not discouraged by the environment. Thus assimilation is - as any other action resp. result of action - the joint product of 'person' and 'environment'.

Thus this approach (cf. Esser, 1980: 209 ff.) includes other conceptions: interactionistic explanations (e.g. Rose and Warshay, 1957) based on correct estimations of situations and anticipations of actions resp. the existence of common symbols; reference group theories that state that integration is only possible after removing ties that are obstructive to assimilation (cf. Eisenstadt, 1954); dissonance theoretical conceptions that presuppose that assimilation is only possible when dissonances have been solved: 'dissonances' can be interpreted as 'costs' which have to be reduced to realize assimilative acts that are generally possible. The reduction of such dissonances can also be explained in terms of the theory of action. Relations of an unbalanced relation system regarded as 'unpleasant' are only revalued if the total consequences of this revaluation are positive resp. not too negative; or, in case, only that relation is revalued the revaluation of which has the relatively greatest positive consequences (e.g. the greatest total reduction of dissonances). Cognitive assimilation generally also includes such processes of 'reorientation' and re-establishment of an ordered 'relevance system' of everyday knowledge. The increasing command of linguistic codes is an important part of this process of cognitive acculturation (as a process leading to cognitive assimilation).

Assimilation is understood as the result of a process in which the respective results of one phase are pre-conditions of the next phase. Generally, four phases of different conditions of assimilation can be distinguished: sending situation, arrival situation, a number of intermediate situations -increasing with the length of stay- and present situation. It is assumed that assimilation is determined by the migrant's cognitive skills and his motives for assimilation right at the beginning of his stay. Status acquisition and interethnic contacts at the beginning of the stay are the consequences of assignments of positions (e.g. according to qualifications) resp. of interactions that are not discouraged by ties opposed to them. Cognitive skills and motivations for migration are dependent on certain conditions in the sending country: living in urbanized developed regions of the sending country causes - at least comparatively - higher school qualifications and a higher motivational affinity to staying in an industrialized receiving area.

Based on these considerations, a causal model of assimilation was developed that combines in the way described above sending situation, school qualification (to measure cognitive skills acquired in the sending country), motivations for migration (for staying resp. returning), and the initial structural and social assimilation. Due to the lack of detailed investigations and empirical data, the intermediate situation was covered by the variable 'length of stay' mediating between arrival and present situation. Then cognitive, structural, social and identificative assimilation was explained by sending, arrival and intermediate situations (measured by 'length of stay'). The causal arrangement of these four dimensions of assimilation has already been established above. Considering that changes of values (toward identification with the receiving country) occur only when the general situation is regarded as cognitively ordered, 'pleasant' and satisfying, idenficational assimilation was explained by personal integration (measured as 'satisfaction').

On the basis of these considerations, a causal model of the whole process was formulated and tested empirically. The data are taken from a survey on the integration of migrant workers that also includes conditions in the sending country and conditions at the time of arrival. The model is over-identified, but as it shows a relatively close approximation, the causal structure can be regarded as congruent with the survey data (cf. Diagram 1 and Table 1; the broken arrow between INTRODUCTORY CONTACTS and LENGTH OF STAY is to indicate that there is a direct relation that is not easy to interpret theoretically although it is empirically valid in the model.

TABLE-1: Causal model: 'Absorption of Migrant Workers'(without environmental variables)

Means and Distributions

Variables	∅	s	N
Region (1)	4.36	1.497	464
Education (2)	2.90	1.215	465
Motivation (3)	5.02	2.211	454
Beginning Social Status (4)	1.36	.672	374
Introductory Contacts (5)	1.57	.495	465
Length of Stay (6)	9.68	4.546	462
Language (7)	3.52	.947	465
Professional Status (8)	1.59	.769	385
Contacts (9)	2.32	.913	465
Satisfaction (10)	5.26	1.388	461
Willingness to be Assimilated (11)	3.67	1.382	417

Inter-Correlations of Variables

Variables	(1)	(2)	(3)	(4)	(5)	(6)	(7)	(8)	(9)	(10)
(2)	.343									
(3)	.049	.155								
(4)	.224	.383	.199							
(5)	-.047	.046	.126	.088						
(6)	.085	-.001	-.056	.046	.271					
(7)	.202	.397	.152	.280	.318	.403				
(8)	.179	.357	.265	.710	.208	.168	.381			
(9)	.072	.222	.231	.141	.333	.228	.452	.245		
(10)	.071	.154	.132	.129	.198	.252	.265	.184	.241	
(11)	.024	.085	.210	.161	.263	.229	.275	.246	.244	.361

DIAGRAM-1: Causal model: 'Absorption of Migrant Workers' (without environmental variables)

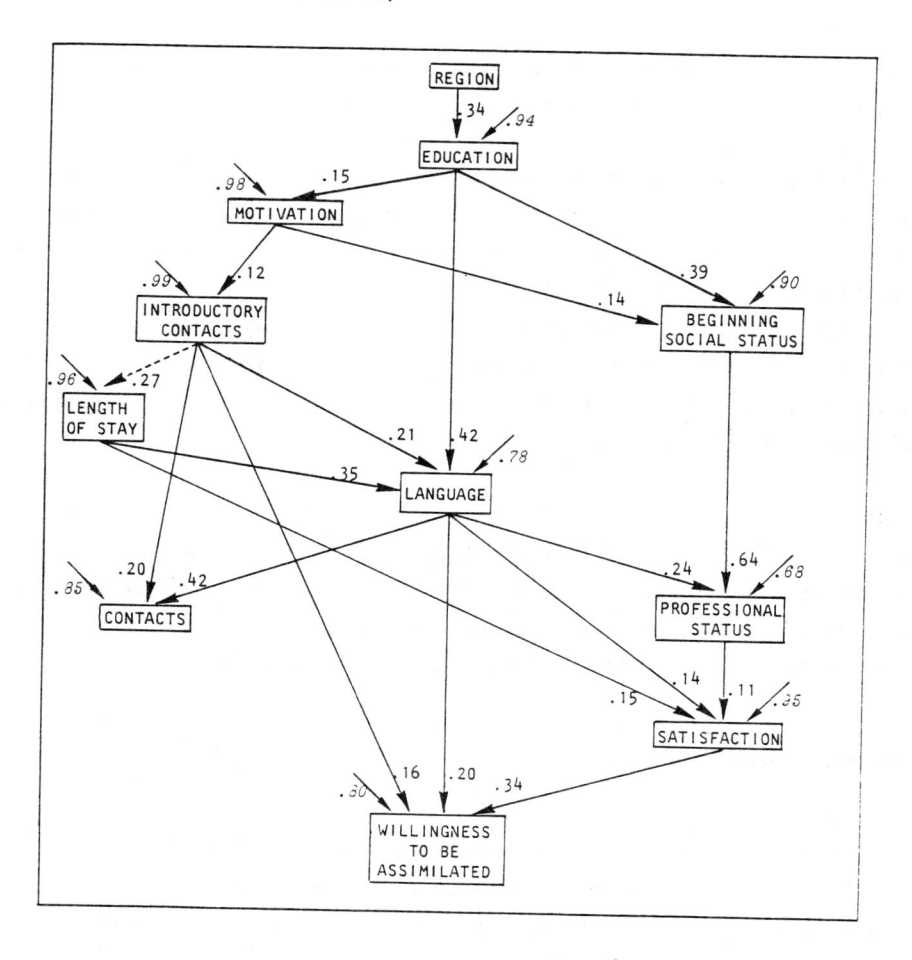

In this context we are especially interested in the significance of language as a measure of cognitive assimilation. On the one hand, language acquisition is relatively easy to explain in the model: the decisive factors of language acquisition are education, length of stay and contacts with Germans at the beginning of the stay. On the other hand, the command of language is important to all aspects of integration: status assignment, interethnic contacts and ethnic identification, as well as personal integration are to a high degree determined directly or indirectly by linguistic skills. To summarize, it is confirmed once more that linguistic competences are the most important mediating variable in the general process of absorption; without linguistic-cognitive assimilation, structural, social, and identificational assimilation, as well as personal integration, are hardly possible.

Up to this point, language acquisition was explained in the survey without explicitly referring to the conditions of the respective 'social environment'. Relevant to the explanation were the criteria 'education' (as general individual learning ability), individual contacts with the German population at the beginning of the stay and individual length of stay. Variables of the social environment such as ethnic structure, social controls, existence of learning opportunities etc. either were not or only implicitly taken into account. The 'individual' variables 'length of stay' and 'contacts at the beginning', however, imply environmental variables as well: length of stay can also be regarded as relating to the environment if education is considered as the result of characteristic conditions in the sending system.

The following investigation is based on the attempt to take into account such environmental effects explicitly and establish their influence under control of the respective 'individual' variables. Only then it is possible to meet the requirements of the theoretical statement that social processes have to be explained as the joint result of personal and environmental factors.

3. Research approach and data basis

The starting point of the following inquiry is the idea that, besides 'individual' characteristics, the relational absorption of a person - whatever the social psychological mechanisms may be - is important to his actions. 'Relational

absorption' means, in a narrow sense, that a person is part of a social network and
that his actions are (also) determined by the characteristics of the other persons
belonging to the respective network. In a broader sense, it means that a person
is a member of a collective - to be determined more closely - which has certain
characteristics ('social context') and that the actions of the person can (also)
be explained by the characteristics of the collective. Since the latter - broader -
sense of 'relational absorption' requires a much simpler approach, it was taken
as the basis of the exploratory investigation reported here. The 'social context'
of the migrant workers investigated was understood as their residence in a
district, defined mainly administratively (and partly social-ecologically). In
order to keep the efforts of the exploratory inquiry within limits, the respective
contexts were defined within the administrative limits of a West German city
(Cologne). This definition itself was based on two hypotheses concerning the
effect of contextual criteria on the absorption of migrant workers: it was
assumed on the one hand that the (infrastructurally bad) innter-city situation
and the (infrastructurally good) situation in the city outskirts influenced
absorption and that - independent of that - the ethnic structure of the
residential environment was important to assimilative acting and learning.

On the basis of the data of the municipal statistics (census of residences and
houses of 1968; register of inhabitants of the City of Cologne), four districts
were selected, two in the centre and two in the outskirts, that differed on each
level in the extent of ethnic concentration. The districts thus defined were
Kalk, Humboldt-Gremberg, Chorweiler and Bocklemünd. Kalk and Humboldt-Gremberg
are part of the centre, Chorweiler and Bocklemünd are sattellites on the outskirts.
Kalk shows a higher ethnic concentration than Humboldt-Gremberg, whereas the
infrastructure is similar. Chorweiler has a higher ethnic concentration than
Bocklemünd, while the infrastructure of both is also similar.

Then the addresses of foreigners (Italians and Turks over 18 years) were selected
from these four districts initially defined only administratively. In the course
of the investigation, however, special attention was paid to include persons in
buildings close to one other in order to make sure that - in contrast to a mere
random sample- the 'context' was operationalized as far as possible within the
frame of existing social relations. Second, it was intended to divide the four
districts further into sub-contexts which should encompass areas belonging
together. The resulting lack of representativeness of the established data was
accepted in view of the considerations mentioned above.

As the results of intensive inspections in the districts and the results of the individual investigations, each district was further subdivided into four quarters. Since the investigated sub-districts should be handled as one unit, the respondents in the random sample, who were not part of the intended clusters, were left out of the further analysis. Thus the number of respondents was reduced from 465 to 338.

The result of this operation was the establishment of three corresponding context levels:

(1) the level of differentiation between center and outskirts ('area')
(2) two 'districts' within each of these districts (Kalk and Humboldt as sub-districts of the center area; Chorweiler and Bocklemündt as sub-districts of the outskirts).
(3) four sub-contexts ('quarters') within each district. Thus the level of the quarter context consists of 16 different small contexts each integrated in a specific district resp. area context.

This approach should answer two different empirical questions: first, can context effects on language acquisition be proved at all, in so far as differences in the language acquisition of persons belonging to different contexts can be established after controlling for relevant 'individual' criteria? This should answer the question whether there are - besides the selective migration of persons with certain individual criteria into certain contexts- any independent effects. Secondly: on which context level - area, district, or quarter - can the most significant effects on language acquisition be established? Settling this issue will certainly presuppose that the contexts are not only to be differentiated 'qualitatively' but that the context effects are also to be specified quantitatively and substantially. This leads, finally, to the interesting theoretical question: which social psychological mechanisms can explain observed effects of contextual affiliation?

These questions will be approached by two methods: by analysis of covariance and by a multi-stage multi-level analysis. With the help of the analysis of covariance between-group-differences can be established for each context level and their stability can be tested by controlling for individual variables. By this method we can acquire enough information to offer a first solution to the problem whether or not there are any context effects at all and whether or not they can be completely explained by selective migration into contexts. It is certainly neither possible to establish the respective isolated significance of each of the three context levels nor to obtain indicators of the relevant substantial context variables. A solution of these two problems requires a multi-level regression approach (for more details see below). Each theoretical interpretation will have to be based on this approach because of the complexity of information; in this context, analyses of covariance are to be understood rather as exploratory pre-investigations.

4. Results

Having suggested the approach, we will now present the results of the empirical survey in the following order. First, the three context levels are described with regard to the dependent variable (language acquisition) and 'individual' variables that are presumably relevant. These individual variables were selected according to the result of the path analysis sketched above: they are the variables 'education' and 'lenght of stay', which are causally directly relevant to language acquisition; the variable 'contacts at the beginning' was not taken into account as an individual variable because, on the one hand, it showed a relatively small direct influence, and, on the other hand, which is more important, it is more likely to be affected by 'environmental effects' of past contexts than by 'individual' criteria and skills. Nevertheless, with regard to the further analysis a 'genuine' environmental variable was included to specify the contexts: the 'residential segregation' of the respondents as stated in the municipal statistics. Then the respective bivariate relations between the individual variables and language acquisition are presented. With the help of the analysis of covariance, first general indications of context effects under control of the individual variables will be established. Finally, the results of the multi-stage multi-level analysis are reported.

4.1. Description of the contexts

The description of the contexts (by the means of the variables examined) shows that there are systematic and significant differences between the level of 'area' and the level of 'district' concerning the characteristics of the persons living in them. It is remarkable that in the district of Bocklemünd there is - compared to other variables - a relatively small number of persons with higher levels of education. It also turns out that the segregation data of the municipal statistics could not be established in the expected extent. Although Chorweiler shows a relatively high ethnic concentration on the level of the total district, the average ethnic concentration on the residential level (of the respondents) is relatively low. It differs insignificantly from the ethnic concentration in the district of Bocklemünd. On the quarter level, significant variations can partly be established within the respective district contexts; yet no immediately evident covariation of certain characteristics in a specific area could be observed. Since the quarters of the city differ significantly from each other by being part of a certain district resp. area, the question has to be answered to what extent the quarters maintain their influence on knowledge of German when one investigates their affiliation to the larger contexts of district resp. area.

TABLE-2a: Context Description of the 'Area' for the Variables Analyzed (Means)

Area		Knowledge of German	Education	Length of Stay	Segregated Residence	N
1		2.96	2.48	9.12	27.3	25
2		3.14	2.57	9.43	31.0	14
3		3.36	2.64	8.00	34.5	14
4	(KALK)	3.37	2.47	8.77	36.6	30
5		3.15	2.42	8.38	42.1	26
6		3.45	2.76	8.63	42.5	38
7		3.57	3.00	10.00	85.3	14
8	(HUMB)	3.73	3.40	9.47	59.1	15
9		3.45	3.22	9.95	75.8	22
10		3.63	2.79	12.68	78.6	19
11		3.70	3.45	9.00	70.9	20
12	(CHOR)	3.84	3.47	10.39	68.2	19
13		3.70	2.99	12.10	67.2	27
14		3.93	3.20	10.67	83.2	15
15		3.95	2.85	12.75	88.4	20
16	(BOCK)	4.00	3.65	10.70	84.1	20

TABLE-2b: Context Description of the 'District' for the Variables Analyzed (Means)

City District	Knowledge of German	Education	Length of Stay	Segregated Residence	N
1 KALK	3.20	2.52	8.86	32.5	83
2 HUMB	3.43	2.81	8.90	51.6	93
3 CHOR	3.65	3.24	10.47	73.4	80
4 BOCK	3.89	2.93	11.67	79.4	82

TABLE-2c: Context Description of the 'Quarter' for the Variables Analyzed (Means)

Quarter	Knowledge of German	Education	Length of Stay	Segregated Residence	N
1 Inner-City	3.32	2.67	8.88	42.6	176
2 Outskirts	3.76	3.08	11.08	76.5	162

Explanation: The 'areas' are so arranged, that they include in each case groups of four 'districts'; the 'districts include by analogy in each case groups of two 'quarters'. Therefore, number 1 represents the city district KALK, number 2 the city district Humboldt, number 3 the city district Chorweiler and number 4 the city district Bocklemünd. In Table 2c number 1 indicates the Inner-City and number 2 the City Outskirts.

The enumerated means of Knowledge of German and Education are based on a scale with values from 1-5; the Length of Stay is indicated by the appropriate number of years the respondent has resided in the Federal Republic; Segregated Residence is the proportion of German families residing in the same apartment house as the foreign respondent.

4.2. The influence of the individual variables on language acquisition

Before further approaching the question as to what extent context variables explain language acquisition, we shall discuss the bivariate relations between the individual variables and the acquisition of linguistic skills (Table 3). It turns out - as was to be expected from the results of the path analysis on the data basis of all 465 original respondents - that both individual variables are closely connected with language acquisition. Both variables combined explain 31% of the variance of linguistic attainments (R = .557), each variable accounting for about the same part of the explanation (β = 388 for education, β = .410 for length of stay, cf. Table 4).

TABLE-3a: Language Acquisition as a Dependent of Individual Attributes: Education in Country of Origin.

	Education in Country of Origin					
	(1)	(2)	(3)	(4)	(5)	N
Proportion German 'good'	28.2	47.0	66.6	83.9	88.2	
n	39	100	117	31	51	338

C = .430   (1) No Schooling
r = .377   (2) School Attendance without Diploma
Sig = .007   (3) 'O'-levels
                (4) Continuing Education without Degree
                (5) Continuing Education, Degree.

TABLE-3b: Language Acquisition as a Dependent of Individual Attributes: Length of Stay in Receiving Country

	Length of Stay in Years				
	1-5	6-8	9-11	12 and more	N
Proportion German 'good'	25.0	53.7	69.7	77.5	
n	44	110	72	111	338

C   = .418
r   = .400
Sig = .000

TABLE-4: Multiple regression of individual variables (education and lenght of stay) on language acquisition

Means distributions and inter-correlations

	∅	s	N	Y	x_1
Y	3.53	.926	337		
x_1	2.87	1.201	337	.337	
x_2	9.93	4.47	337	.400	-.026

Regression equation

$Y = 1.847 + .299\ x_1 + .084\ x_2$ (unstandardized)
$Y = .388\ x_1 + .410\ x_2$ (standardized)
$R = .577$
$R^2 = .311$

Explanation

Y = Language acquisition (scale knowledge of German)
x_1 = Scale education
x_2 = Length of stay in years
∅ = Means
s = Standard deviation

Stating the extent to which the linear regression model explains the established connection between both individual variables and language acquisiticn does obviously not explain the phenomenon theoretically. In this context, a short outline may suffice to supplement the considerations in part 1. Linguistic competence is acquired by 'learning'. Such changes of the structure of the organism are, on the one hand, dependent on a general capacity for receiving and restructuring environmental influences. This general capacity is indicated resp. encouraged by education. On the other hand, learning requires certain stimulations and -time-consuming- feedbacks. The longer the stay, the greater the chance that such processes occur accidentally. In that respect, length of stay can also be regarded as an indicator of past environmental influences on individuals. According to the linear regression model, both variables obviously have an additive effect. The verification of a - theoretically more adequate - multiplicative model cannot be provided in this context.

3.3. The stability of context influences controlling for individual variables

Having outlined the contexts and the significance of the individual variables for language acquisition, the question has to be answered whether or not the context differences in linguistic skills persist when we take into account the fact that persons with different education and different length of stay choose to remain in the different contexts. A plausible alternative hypothesis woulc be that the differences in linguistic skills in the quarters, districts and areas can be explained exclusively in terms of the fact that the respective persons living there differ systematically in education and length of stay and that the context differences in linguistic skills can be explained exclusively by differences in the individual attributes of the members of the population. The 'stability' of the context influences in regard to such effects of selective migration can principally be tested by analysis of covariance. At first the mean differences (in language acquisition) between the contexts are established and characterized quantitatively by the eta-coefficient (column 1 in Table 5 a-c). Then these differences are re-calculated by assuming an equal distribution of the individual variables in the contexts. The beta-coefficient indicates - controlling for the individual variables - the remaining degree of context differences.

TABLE-5a: Stability of the Context Differences on Context Level 'Area' (Deviation from the Mean, Knowledge of Language)

Area	(1)	(2)	(3)	(4)	n
1	-.58	-.47	-.51	-.40	25
2	-.39	-.31	-.35	-.27	14
3	-.18	-.12	-.03	.04	14
4	-.17	-.06	-.08	.04	30
5	-.38	-.26	-.26	-.13	26
6	-.09	-.06	.01	.05	38
7	.04	.00	.03	-.01	14
8	.20	.06	.23	.09	15
9	-.08	-.18	-.08	-.18	22
10	.10	.12	-.11	-.10	19
11	.16	.01	.24	.08	20
12	.31	.14	.26	.09	18
13	.17	.32	.00	.14	27
14	.40	.31	.34	.25	15
15	.41	.42	.20	.20	20
16	.46	.25	.41	.19	20
eta/beta	.32	.26	.26	.19	337
R		.458	.478	.587	

TABLE-5b: Stability of the Context Differences on Context Level 'District') (Deviation from the Mean, Knowledge of Language)

City District	(1)	(2)	(3)	(4)	n
1	-.33	-.24	-.25	-.14	83
2	-.11	-.09	-.03	-.01	93
3	.11	.01	.07	-.04	79
4	.34	.33	.22	.19	82
eta/beta	.27	.22	.18	.13	337
R		.437	.438	.572	

TABLE-5c: Stability of the Context Differences on the Context Level 'Quarter' (Deviation from the Mean, Knowledge of Language).

Quarter	(1)	(2)	(3)	(4)	n
1	-.21	-.16	-.13	-.07	176
2	.23	.17	.14	.08	161
eta/beta	.24	.18	.15	.08	337
R		.417	.426	.563	

Such analyses of covariance were carried out for all three context levels (cf. table 5). First the individual variable 'education' (column 2 in table 5 a-c), then the variable 'length of stay' (column 3 in table 5 a-c), and finally both individual variables together (column 4 in table 5 a-c) were put in as controlling variables. These operations show which of the two individual variables has stronger correcting effects.

The data prove that the corrected as well as the uncorrected context differences become smaller when the size of the context increases. Education and length of stay reduce the context differences by about the same degree, although partly significant differences and special effects (also disclosed suppressions) are established. On the level of the quarters the differences can be significantly but not completely explained by the individual variables (from eta = .32 to beta = .19).

On the level of the districts, the length of stay seems to have a slightly greater individual influence. Here the differences can be reduced as well, yet a certain context effect persists. It is remarkable that after the correction concerning the individual variables, the district of Chorweiler (as a satellite with a good infrastructure yet a high percentage of foreigners) loses the relatively good position it initially had: the context advantages of the uncorrected differences disappear with the control of the individual variables. Thus - at least on this descriptive level - the relatively good image of the satellite of Chorweiler has to be corrected: the relatively good assimilation situation (concerning language acquisition) that initially appeared is exclusively caused by the (self- or extraneous) selection of migrant workers who

are already prone to assimilation because of their good education and long stay.
Controlling for these variables, Chorweiler is actually 'below average' as far
as the 'mere' context effect is concerned. The overproportional decline of
language acquisition in Kalk and the overproportional effect in Bocklemünd are
still significant; according to this result, the 'context effect' seems to be
caused by the cumulation of favorable resp. unfavorable context criteria
(infrastructure and ethnic structure).

On the level of the areas, the differences almost disappear when the distribution
of the individual variables is controlled. Here - as on the level of the districts -
the length of stay proves to have the greatest correcting influence.

This analysis may lead to the conclusion that above all the individual variables
'education' and 'length of stay' are responsible for language acquisition.
Context effects are obviously striking only on the level of small units (quarters).
This result may be plausible when it is assumed that language acquisition is
primarily determined by interethnic contacts and everyday feedbacks.

Yet this interpretation raises two problems: first, the increase of effects on
the level of the quarter could have been caused by the fact that the analysis
of all 16 quarters was - in addition to the differences between quarters within
the districts - implicitly affected by the differences on the level of the
districts and areas. In other words: the quarter differences are really the
combined result of differences on all three context levels. Second, analysis of
covariance only takes into account differences between variables not specified
otherwise. That means: if the context units could somehow be characterized
'quantitatively', the context effects would perhaps show up in a different way.
This, however, demands a different process of analysis than analysis of
covariance, and it requires a decision concerning the variables in terms of
which the contexts should be quantified. Such an approach - including the
corresponding analysis - would give, in addition to a simple description of the
differences of the contexts, the first indications which specific criteria of
the contexts cause effects and which are not significant for a theoretical
explanation of the effects of contexts on language acquisition.

4.3. The effect of context variables on different context levels for language acquisition

Analysis of covariance is not suited to dealing with the question which specific criteria of context affect language acquisition and to which extent each context level, isolated from the other context levels, contributes to it. Instead, a regression approach which is known as multi-level analysis was chosen. In addition to stating individual variables that are presumably relevant, the contexts must first be specified by quantitative variables. In this case the contexts are specified in three ways: first, the contexts (quarters, districts, areas) are specified by the means of the 'residential segregation' of the respondents. By means of this operation, the eventual influence of segregation on language acquisition is to be analysed.

Second and third, according to the common approach of multi-level analysis, the contexts are specified by the respective means of the individual variables 'education' and 'length of stay'. This is done mainly for exploratory reasons, since at present specific substantial hypotheses concerning relevant context variables are completely lacking: this must be considered when evaluating the results.

A special problem occurs when the contexts are specified by the means of the respective individual variables that are controlled simultaneously: Since the means of the contexts are linearly dependent on the individual variables, there is a high multicollinearity of these variables used exogenously. This problem can be solved by a centering procedure for the variables (cf. Boyd and Iversen, 1979: 65 ff.): the individual variables are transformed as deviations from the respective context mean, and the context means are transformed as deviations from the total mean.

Now all contexts have the same mean (namely zero), the slope and the intercept of the respective regression line remaining unchanged. Technically this means (after a corresponding transformation of the dependent variable) that the exogenous variables belonging to different aggregation levels are now orthogonalized, i.e.: that their respective, completely isolated, contribution to the total effect can be derived from the estimated regression coefficient.

Variables of the same aggregation level, however, cannot be orthogonalized, i.e. if any individual variables are multicollinear, only their jointly explained variance, not the isolated contribution of each, can be estimated. Fortunately, this is no problem in this analysis since both relevant individual variables are orthogonal to each other; their correlation is -.026 (cf. Table 4).

The consideration of three seperate levels is unproblematic: each of the contexts (quarters, districts, areas) is specified by the corresponding mean and then centered with regard to the specific larger context. By this means one establishes an orthogonalization of the context variables to each other, which shows that all context means are equal to 0 and that there are no connections between the context variables themselves, and between them and the individual variables (with the exception of rounding mistakes).

The analysis starts with the specification of the contexts by the segregation variables listed above. In general a regression model is read:

$$y = b_0 x_{i1} + b_2 x_{i2} + b_3 X_g + b_4 X_s + b_5 X_q$$

with: Y as index linguistic skills
X_{i1} as individual variable education
X_{i2} as individual variable length of stay
X_g as mean segregation on the level of quarters
X_s as mean segregation on the level of districts
X_q as mean segregation on the level of areas

Since the contexts in this case are not characterized by any of the individual variables used before, only the context variables must be centered to one other. For this case the equation is:

$$y = b_0 + b_1 x_{i1} + b_2 x_{i2} + b_3 (X_g - X_s)$$
$$+ b_4 (X_s - X_q)$$
$$+ b_5 (X_q - X)$$

with X as total mean.

The expressions are abbreviated here (and in the following):

$$s_g = (X_g - X_s)$$
$$s_s = (X_s - X_q)$$
$$s_q = (X_q - X)$$

with 's' indicating that it is a segregation variable specifying the contexts. Thus the regression model with the centered context variables reads:

$$y = b_o + b_1 x_{i1} + b_2 x_{i2} + b_3 s_g + b_4 s_s + b_5 s_q$$

The result of the empirical estimation of the regression coefficients of the individual and context variables is stated in Table 6.

TABLE-6: Multi-level Analysis with two Individual Variables and three Context Levels for 'Average Segregated Residence'.

Means, Distributions and Inter-Correlations

	$\emptyset$	s	N	Y	x_{i1}	x_{i2}	s_g	s_s
Y	3.53	.926	337					
x_{i1}	2.87	1.201	337	.377				
x_{i2}	9.93	4.547	337	.400	-.026			
s_g	.00	.962	337	.093	.121	.061		
s_s	.00	.721	337	.109	.056	.029	-.003	
s_q	.00	1.696	337	.238	.171	.242	.006	-.002

Regression Equation

$$Y = 1.945 + .282 x_{i1} + .079 x_{i2} + .023 s_g + .099 s_s + .045 s_q$$
$$Y = .366 x_{i1} + .386 x_{i2} + .024 s_g + .076 s_s + .081 s_q$$

Multiple Correlation and Explained Variance (stepwise)

Variables	R	R^2
x_{i1}	.377	.142
x_{i2}	.557	.310
s_g	.558	.311
s_s	.563	.317
s_q	.568	.323

Here we can see that the operationalization of the contexts by the segregation variable controlling the individual influences and sep rating the context effects establishes almost no independent context effect. This means (at least) that 'segregation' cannot be considered to be a relevant attribute of the environment - on all aggregation levels - influencing language acquisition. With regard to segregation, language acquisition is almost exclusively determined by individual criteria. With regard to the question of other environmental criteria that might prove to be effective, the contexts were characterized by the first individual variable (education). 'Average education' could be an indicator itself e.g. of the infrastructure in the quarter, variety of stimuli or a 'better' climate of interaction in the interethnic field. These questions of the theoretical relevance of such context specifications cannot be further clarified within this frame.

Since education also appears as an individual variable, this variable must be centered with relation to the contexts. Then the dependent variable must be centered with education according to its context regression (cf. Boyd and Iversen, 1979: 66). The regression equation is:

$$\begin{aligned} y' &= y - (b_{1g} X_{1g}) \\ &= b_o + b_1 (X_{i1g} - X_{1g}) + b_2 X_{i2} \\ &\quad + b_3 (X_{1g} - X_{1s}) \\ &\quad + b_4 (X_{1s} - X_{1q}) \\ &\quad + b_5 (X_{1q} - X_1) \end{aligned}$$

with:
- b_{1g} as the slope of the regression line for X_1 in the quarter g
- X_{i1g} as the individual value of X_1 in the quarter g
- X_{1g} as the mean of X_1 in the quarter g
- X_{1s} as the mean of X_1 in the district s
- X_{1q} as the mean of X_1 in the area q
- X as total mean of X_1

After introducing the symbol 'e' for the centered variable 'education', it follows, simplified:

$$y' = b_0 + b_1 e_i + b_2 x_{i2} + b_3 \bar{e}_g + b_4 \bar{e}_s + b_5 \bar{e}_q$$

The results of the estimation of coefficients are listed in table 7.

TABLE-7: Multi-level Analysis with two Individual Variables and three Context Levels for 'Average Education'.

Means, Distributions, and Inter-Correlations

	∅	s	N	Y'	e_i	x_{i2}	$\bar{e}_g$	$\bar{e}_s$
Y'	2.78	1.108	337					
e_i	.00	1.124	337					
x_{i2}	9.93	4.546	337	.425	-.039			
$\bar{e}_g$	-.01	.339	337	-.044	.000	-.091		
$\bar{e}_s$	.01	.141	337	.134	.002	-.041	.021	
$\bar{e}_q$	.00	.205	337	.378	.001	.242	-.033	.068

Regression Equation

$$Y' = 1.868 + .283 e_i + .091 x_{i2} - .014 \bar{e}_g + 1.022 \bar{e}_s + 1.503 \bar{e}_q$$
$$Y' = .287 e_i + .374 x_{i2} - .004 \bar{e}_g + .130 \bar{e}_s + .278 \bar{e}_q$$

Multiple Correlations and Explained Variance (stepwise).

Variables	R	R^2
e_i	.273	.075
x_{i2}	.515	.265
$\bar{e}_g$	.515	.265
$\bar{e}_s$	.536	.288
$\bar{e}_q$	.600	.360

It must be added that the correlation between the centered dependent and the centered independent variable drops by the centration (cf. table 7). This is caused by the fact that now the context effects -which were implicitly included before- are eliminated from the correlation of the individual variable 'education' with the variable 'linguistic skills'. But the two individual variables together still explain a significant portion of the variance in linguistic skills: 26.5%. In contrast to previous results, the corresponding contexts prove to be significant. With the contexts included -operationalized by context means of the variable 'education'- the explained variance rises to 36%. It seems most interesting that in this view the larger context 'area' is more significant and that the smaller environment (as the 'climate of education') becomes less significant for language acquisition. This means that the result of the analysis of covariance is almost reversed. This, however, can be easily explained by the fact that in the analysis of covariance the effects on the quarter level implicitly included all other effects.

In the last step of the analysis, the same procudure was carried out with 'length of stay' as a variable. Now the contexts were specified by the means of 'length of stay'. 'Education' was included in the model as an individual variable. The individual length of stay had to be centered within the quarters (to achieve orthogonality of X_{i2} with the means of the quarters); the other contexts were centered analogously with respect to the respective higher context mean. After abbreviating the centered variables (with 'l' for 'length of stay') the model reads as follows:

$$y' = b_o + b_1 x_{i1} + b_2 l_i + b_3 l_g + b_4 l_s + b_5 l_q$$

TABLE-8: Multi-Level-Analysis with two Individual Variables and three Context Levels for 'Average Length of Stay'.

Means, Distributions, and Inter-Correlations

	$\emptyset$	s	N	Y'	x_{i1}	l_i	l_g	l_s
Y'	2.79	1.066	388					
x_{i1}	2.87	1.199	388	.360				
l_i	-.03	4.335	388	.295	-.039			
l_g	.00	.867	388	-.086	-.116	.001		
l_s	.00	.416	388	.169	-.087	.010	.001	
l_q	.00	1.101	388	.360	.171	-.007	-.001	-.004

Regression Equation

$Y' = 1.874 + .320 x_{i1} + .076 l_i - .054 l_g + .339 l_s + .106 l_q$

$Y' = .360 x_{i1} + .308 l_i - .044 l_g + .133 l_s + .110 l_q$

Multiple Correlations and Explained Variance (Stepwise)

Variables	R	R^2
l_i	.295	.087
x_{i1}	.475	.225
l_g	.476	.227
l_s	.495	.245
l_q	.507	.257

Again the individual variables show a stable significance although their effects seem to be reduced by the centration - which was necessary for the reasons mentioned above. Once more, the small and even slightly negative effect of the 'climate of length of stay' in the small quarters (with control of the individual variables and other effects of the quarters) is significant. This phenomenon could perhaps result from a certain 'apathisation' of the residents in the 'ghettos' after a longer stay. In contrast to the 'climate of education', the average length of stay seems especially to have an effect at the level of the districts; in any case, the effect of the quarters proves to be much smaller than in the analysis of the contexts of education.

These results can be summarized as follows: The multi-stage context analysis on the basis of quantified context variables established a result significantly different from that of the analysis of covariance. The effects of the context depend on the respective substantial specification of context variables. The ethnic concentration within the contexts proves to be almost unimportant to language acquisition, whereas the 'climate of education' has a highly significant effect and the 'environment of length of stay' is at least worth taking into account. In any case, the individual variables 'education' and 'length of stay' maintain their high degree of independent influence. When the significance of each of the three context levels are compared, the context of the quarters is of only subordinate importance. On the narrower level even negative effects of the environment of education and length of stay on language acquisition can be established. The wider level of the area, however, has more significance for the educational 'climate'. The 'climate' of length of stay seems to be mainly effective on the level of the districts. Additional theoretical interpretations of the established results cannot be pursued here, in view of the highly exploratory character of the study. Nevertheless, the established insignificance of the ethnic concentration may be of some use for further approaches. It may be that this result - and the significance of the 'educational' environment - confirms the assumption that the absorption of foreign workers (measured by language acquisition) is primarily a matter of structural conditions rather than a problem of ethnic and cultural differences.

5. The problem of the theoretical interpretation and empirical investigation of context levels

The most important results of the preceding empirical analysis were as follows: there were only relatively minor effects in the 'individual' dependent variables which could be traced by the contexts. The largest amount by far of 'explained variance' was tied to individual variables. In the case of the context effects which were discovered, language acquisition could be relatively clearly explained on the one hand in terms of 'educational climate', measured in terms of the average school education in the country of origin. On the other hand, it could be observed that only rather large units had significant effects - an observation that contradicts our normal understanding of the process of language acquisition, which is after all closely tied to interactions and continual corrections and reinforcements in everyday contacts.

This result is - though perhaps rather curious - unsatisfying for a variety of reasons. It can at most be taken to be only a hint that in addition to the individual variables there are also effects of environmental variables. But the question concerning the manner in which the observed effects come about remains completely unanswered. This question may sound a bit unusual in the context of the presentation of an empirical investigation. It is true that the empirical sociology of 'variables' only rarely poses the question of the theoretical explanation of the statistical relations it discovers. At this point the problem of the explanation of the mechanism in terms of which the statistically identified effects can be explained raises the question mentioned in the introduction concerning the theoretical explanation of individual effects in terms of structural conditions. And the question concerning the specification of the general mechanisms and the specific initial conditions which are hidden behind the statistical 'variables' is precisely the question concerning the explication of so-called implicit explanations. To this extent, neither the coordination problem nor the question concerning the explanation of statistical relations in general poses a new problem. It is merely the application of a demand which Boudon (1980: 181 ff.) directed at 'empirical social research' in general to a special case. Boudon demands that a 'plausible explanation of Y ... is actually only achieved when one is in a position to interpret this phenomenon as the result of actions which are carried out by agents who find themselves in a certain institutional and social context. If one is in a position to describe the logic of these actions with sufficient accuracy, then one can derive from it the structure of the statistical relations between the variables and thus explain this structure!

So far, at least two things have remained unclear: In the first place, the mechanisms and intermediate processes in terms of which the relevance of the context variables and especially of the context means for action can be understood. In the second place, we do not yet have a general explanation of social action - as a general background theory - in terms of which the specific mechanisms are not merely plausible but identifiable as special cases of the application of a general theory. The 'practical' goal of this discussion is - in addition to its general methodological significance - the search for possibilities of an adequate consideration and modelling of contextual variables; it is quite possible that the relations we have discovered are so small not because of a negligible significance of the social environment but rather because neither were the relevant variables taken into account nor were the models adequately specified for these variables.

With regard to the question concerning the 'mechanisms' by means of which the context variables influence individual behavior or in terms of which contextual differences in individual behavior are to be explained, we must distinguish between at least four processes. First, the selective migration of persons, who differ from one another with respect to the dependent and independent variables, into specific areas. Here there is no 'effect' of the areas, unless one were to interpret the varying attraction of areas as such an effect. The general explanatory mechanism would be in principle the same mechanism in terms of which one explains migrations in general: persons take advantage of opportunities for realizing their goals in specific areas, assume that these goals can also be realized after the immigration, perceive no insurmountable barriers and have the resources and abilities to undertake the immigration. Statistically it is relatively easy - as we have seen - to distinguish this case from that of 'genuine' context effects: if the corresponding regional differences in the dependent variables disappear following the adjustment for relevant individual independent variables.

Only if regional differences remain after the adjustment do we confront the question concerning other mechanisms. Such mechanisms are the assumption that regions offer differing opportunities for actions or learning processes. One can also assume that social influences and controls take place in different ways in various regions, that there are differing conversions and sanctions with respect to specific modes of conduct. Finally, different regions can become objects of symbolic identification in different manners, even if there is no social influence and even in the absence of specific opportunities: specific characteristics of a region (e.g. the 'reputation' of a city quarter) may well change the life style of the immigrant without his being directly influenced by other persons.

In traditional contextual analysis the regions are often characterized by the means of the independent variables. This procedure rarely makes explicit reference to one of these mechanisms: Erbring and Young (1980: 24 ff.) have demonstrated in a rather impressing manner the absurd implications such a procedure can produce. Let us assume the simple basic equation of context analysis:

(1) $\quad Y_{ij} = a + b_1 x_{ij} + b_2 \bar{x}_j + e_{ij}$

Rewriting the average score $\bar{x}_j$ explicitly as the mean of individual scores, we get:

(2) $\quad Y_{ij} = a + b_1 x_{ij} + (b_2/n_j)(x_{1j} + x_{2j} + \ldots + x_{n_j j}) + e_{ij}$

By collecting terms equation (2) becomes

(3) $\quad Y_{ij} = a + (b_1 + b_2/n_j) x_{ij} + (b_2/n_j) \sum_{i' \neq i} x_{i'j} + e_{ij}$

where $x_{i'j}$ is referring to all persons in the context except ij. Equation (3) may be simplified to

(4) $\quad Y_{ij} = a + b_1^* x_{ij} + b_2 \bar{x}_{i'j} + e_{ij}$

where $b_1^* = b_1 + b_2/n_j$
$\quad \bar{x}_{i'j} = (1/n_j) \sum_{i' \neq i} x_{i'j}$

This signifies substantially that the y-values of the persons under consideration
are influenced by their 'individual' x-values and the x-values of every other
person in the context in question; in contrast, the y-values are not influenced
by the y-values of the other persons. In the context the question concerning the
mechanism by means of which the x-values of all other persons exercise their
influence remains open. If, for example, x is the formal education of the
immigrant workers, then we must clarify the manner in which the formal education
of other persons influences the linguistic behavior of the person in question.
Erbring and Young ironically name 'social telepathy' as the relevant process, to
the extent that, as is generally the case, no other mechanism is specified.

However, area means can indeed be plausible indicators for the mechanisms in
question. Most investigators have referred to opportunities for interactions
and the resulting conversions (as successful influence) in this context. Thus,
for example, the proportion of natives in a context -on the assumption of
random mixing- could yield the probability with which a foreign worker would
come into contact with a native in everyday situations. The probabilities that
such an interaction would produce a linguistic reinforcement would be expressed
in the regression coefficients of the context variables. The more practical
problem is the assumption of random mixing: if -which is surely probable-
immigrant workers tend to move in their own social networks, then the proportion
of natives is unlikely to be a valid measure for the probability of interethnic
interactions.

A third interpretation of the theoretical significance of area means makes
direct use of the mechanism of opportunities. According to this approach, a
specific mean is an indicator that a context determines specific initial
conditions in terms of which all members of the context must orient themselves
or which are available to them as opportunities for acting: educational
institutions, social infrastructure, special attention of the community admini
administration, etc. But the identification hypothesis is just as plausible:
persons identify themselves with well endowed regions rather than with poorly
endowed regions, and this can give rise to an increased motivation toward
linguistic assimilation - even if the existing opportunities are not taken
advantage of and even in te absence of interactions and linguistic reinforcement.

The problem is obvious: area means are indicators for hidden properties of the contexts which become relevant for action by the actors' perceptions and for hidden processes in which the persons who constitute the context reciprocally influences one another, processes which converge toward specific regularities. The problem of the theoretical explanation of context effects which is posed in this connection is very similar to the problem concerning inference from empirical indicators to latent variables or latent processes in general. In both cases we encounter two related problems: since the latent variables in question can only be measured very indirectly, one must expect a high degree of error variance in the empirical relations. And in view of the multiplicity of possible alternative theoretical explanations in the given case and the low number of empirically discovered relations, inferences to the latent processes are hardly possible: the models are generally underidentified with respect to hypothesized latent variables and processes.

There is still another problem. If one is interested in a 'general explanation' of the specified 'mechanisms' as well, one must make reference to a general explanation of actions. In this connection Blalock and Wilken (1979: 292 ff.) have made an explicit suggestion. Their point of departure is the fact that every action is the result of subjectively expected utilities for specific courses of action. The two decisive parameters for decisions concerning actions are thus the utilities U_i of the expected result of action i and the (subjective) probability p_i with which action i is expected to yield the goal in question. Context variables can -according to these authors- only be 'effective' within these multiplicatively connected two parameters U_i and p_i. In other words: there are no direct effects of the context variables on the behavioral variables in question; the context variables influence the utilities and expectations which in turn determine the resulting behavior.

According to this interpretation, context variables can enter into a statistical model in two ways: First, as explanatory factors for U_i and p_i. This is also implicitly the case when contexts are interpreted as e.g. opportunity structures: Depending on the context to which they belong, persons differ with regard to their perceptions of opportunities for attaining specific goals by specific courses of action, and correspondingly make decisions concerning existing or perceived opportunities . Secondly, context variables serve as indirect measurements for the 'genuinely' relevant, immediate determinants of action U_i and p_i. Accordingly, context variables would only be indicators for the latent variables U_i and p_i. Both interpretations accept only an indirect relation to the variables of the model of action and for this reason only a small correlation between these variables is to be expected even if the influence of the context variables is high or the indicator function is good.

Blalock and Wilken's suggestion has the advantage, that it does not merely refer the effect of the context variables to certain 'mechanisms' but rather to a general explanation of action. To this extent their interpretation is an important initial clarification of the question concerning the general basis of a theoretical explanation of context effects and a step toward a solution of the coordination problem we have been dealing with. However, the suggestion neglects the 'dynamic' character of certain context effects which comes to expression in e.g. the conversion assumption (in the sequence of interactions): the 'effect' of the contexts is sometimes the consequence of - more or less time consuming - processes of adapting to environmental conditions and is not restricted to guiding actual decisions. The mechanism of influence and control often rather vaguely expressed as the 'climate' of a context, can only be made action-theoretically explicit if it is taken to be dynamic: persons make decisions concerning actions in a context - whose properties they are not completely familiar with. This action has - depending on the context conditions - different consequences. These consequences are perceived by the person in question. On the basis of these perceptions the utility estimates and expectations eventually change and this is the basis for a further action, etc. Only when this process converges to a typical and stable result for a group of persons in typical contexts is it possible to detect empirically significant context effects. With regard to the specification of context models, however, this means that they must be dynamized and that there must be measurements both of the context variables as well as of the latent parameters of the action decisions of other persons in a context (cf. also Erbring and Young, 1980: 37 ff.).

The result of these considerations is that the small amount of context effects - also according to the present investigation - by no means necessarily indicates the insignificance of context membership for individual actors. In addition, we have the usual problems of the specification of genuinely action-relevant 'natural boundaries' and the identification of action-relevant interaction-network. In view of the fact that we have here - as is generally the case and is often unavoidable - worked within the framework of administratively determined aggregations and with the assumption of random mixing, the notoriously weak statistical amount of context effects can hardly be surprising. This problem can only be overcome, as is necessary if we are to avoid false conclusions of the insignificance of 'social structures', by means of the further theoretical explication of possible 'effects' of contexts (on the basis of a general explanation of action). Here we will have to distinguish - as the preceding discussion has already made clear - between a variety of different special processes. There is no unitary solution to the coordination problem, just as there is no unitary solution to the transformation problem in the explanation of social structures on the basis of individual action - although the general background theory of rational and interest guided action and the fundamental logic of explanation are the same in both cases.

References

BLALOCK, M. Jr. and H. WILKEN, (1979), Intergroup Processes. A Micro-Macro Perspective. New York: Free Press.

BOUDON, R., (1980), Die Logik gesellschaftlichen Handelns. Eine Einführung in die soziologische Denk- und Arbeitsweise. Darmstadt: Luchterhand.

BOYD, H. Jr and R. IVERSEN, (1979), Contextual Analysis: Concepts and Statistical Techniques. Belmont, Cal.: Wadsworth.

EISENSTADT, S.N., (1954), 'Reference Group Behavior and Social Integration', American Sociological Review 19: 175-185.

ERBRING, L. and A.A. YOUNG (1980), 'Individuals and Social Structure. Contextual Effects as Endogeneous Feedback', pp. 25-95 in E. Borgatta and D.J. Jackson, (eds.), Aggregate Data. Analysis and Interpretation. Beverly Hills: Sage.

ESSER, H., (1979), 'Räumliche Segregation, ethnische Schichtung und die Assimilation von Wanderern', pp. 48-74 in B. Hamm (ed.), Lebensraum Stadt. Beiträge zur Sozialökologie deutscher Städte. Frankfurt a.M.: Campus.

ESSER, H., (1980), Aspekte der Wanderungssoziologie. Darmstadt: Luchterhand.

ESSER, H., (1981), 'Aufenthaltsdauer und die Eingliederung von Wanderern. Zur theoretischen Interpretation soziologischer 'Variablen'', Zeitschrift für Soziologie 10: 76-97.

HOFFMANN-NOWOTNY, H., (1973), Soziologie des Fremdarbeiterproblems. Stuttgart: Enke.

LINDENBERG, S. and R. WIPPLER, (1978), Theorienvergleich: Elemente der Rekonstruktion, pp. 219-231 in K.O. Hondrich and J. Matthes (eds.), Theorienvergleich in den Sozialwissenschaften. Darmstadt: Luchterhand.

LUCKMANN, T., (1979), Soziologie der Sprache, pp. 1-116 in: R. König (ed.), Handbuch der empirischen Sozialforschung, Vol. 13. 2nd ed., Stuttgart: Enke.

MEHRLÄNDER, U., (1981), Situation der ausländischen Arbeitnehmer und ihrer Familienangehörigen in der Bundesrepublik Deutschland, Forschungsbericht der Friedrich Ebert Stiftung, Bonn.

PRZEWORSKI, A., (1974), Contextual Models of Political Behavior, Political Methodology 1: 27-61.

ROSE, A. and L. WARSHAY, (1957), The Adjustment of Migrants to Cities, Social Forces 36: 72-76.

Karl-Dieter Opp

ECONOMICS, SOCIOLOGY, AND POLITICAL PROTEST

Introduction

As long as economics was only concerned with prices, markets, inflation, economic growth etc., it did not challenge the views of any other social science. This peaceful coexistence changed radically at the beginning of the sixties: economists considered economic theory to be a general social theory, as classical writers had already done. Consequently, economics is applied to phenomena like crime, social movements, political processes, rules of conduct (property rights) and marital behavior. These subject matters are also addressed by other social scientists. It is important to note that economic and other hypotheses referring to these phenomena are regarded as theoretical alternatives, that is, as competitors. This view is held by economists as well as by other social scientists. The question arises: which one of the alternative theories is superior?

In this situation one may proceed in two ways. First, one may discuss methodological assumptions and the most general empirical hypotheses underlying economics and the other social sciences. Among the methodological assumptions the postulate of methodological individualism is of primary importance. Thus, if a discussion of this postulate results in the conclusion that it is not tenable, one will not apply economic theory. Different 'models of man' pertain to the basic empirical assumptions in economics and sociology. Thus, if one does not accept a utilitarian perspective, one will not deem economic theory to be fruitful.

If theoretical alternatives exist, one may also proceed in a second way: a specific explanation problem is selected and the competing hypotheses are tested with respect to this problem. For example, an explanation problem may be: why do people engage in some kind of protest or, more specifically, participate in social movements? If this problem is chosen, one may examine the fruitfulness of economic and other hypotheses claiming to answer this question.

In the present paper this second line of reasoning is adopted. In the first
section we shall outline the 'economic model', or, as we prefer to say, the
utilitarian model, as we understand it. In sections 2 and 3 we present data
bearing on the question of the degree to which hypotheses from the utilitarian
model are superior to certain sociological hypotheses dealing with political
protest.

1. The 'economic model of man': some problems and extensions

The hypothesis underlying economic thinking is that preferences and constraints
(or opportunities) determine human behavior (see, for example, Frey, 1980;
Kirchgässner, 1980). Of course, economics does not merely offer the thesis
mentioned above. A great many assumptions are suggested specifying how preferences
and constraints influence behavior. Beyond the specification of such additional
empirical laws or lawlike statements, a further task is to determine the kinds
of preferences and restrictions operating in specific situations, where a certain
kind of behavior is to be explained. It is the opinion of this author that the
fruitfulness of the economic model could be enhanced if certain unnecessary
restrictions which economists impose on this model are relaxed.

(1) The model logically implies that all kinds of preferences and restrictions
may influence behavior. Logically there is no reason to exclude any kind of
preference or constraint, as economists often do. Thus, role expectations,
internalized norms or certain social structures should be considered relevant
factors in utilitarian explanations.

(2) Economists are usually not interested in explaining preferences (or
cognitions). Traditionally this question is addressed by sociologists and
other social scientists. So there is no objection against extending the economic
model with respect to the phenomena to be explained. A fruitful theory which may
be applied is the so-called Ajzen/Fishbein model (see, for example, Ajzen and
Fishbein, 1980).

(3) Economists often assume that preferences are stable and that changes in
behavior can be explained by changing constraints (or opportunities). The
economic model implies that it is a purely empirical question which factors

operate in specific situations. Thus, no restrictions are acceptable concerning the possible explanatory variables.

(4) Social psychological theories like the theory of cognitive dissonance should be applied. These theories specify cognitive structures which are costly or beneficial, or, in other terms, dissonant/consonant or unbalanced/balanced etc. Thus, these theories convey information concerning relevant costs and benefits.

For reasons of space it is not possible to adduce arguments for these suggested extensions of the economic model. But two points seem worth mentioning. First, many more social scientists would probably accept the behavioral model outlined above rather than the narrower models usually applied by economists. Second, our suggested extensions provide the opportunity to integrate a great many findings of various social sciences into a unified model. Among these findings are, for example, sociological investigations of the effects of social structure and social psychological theories or procedures for the measurement of attitudes.

In order to avoid misunderstandings, the extended economic model sketched above will be called 'utilitarian model'. This term is chosen to indicate that the assumptions criticized above are relaxed and that not only economic behavior can be explained. Moreover, the term suggests that a basic assumption of economics is preserved, namely that costs and benefits determine behavior. Obviously, the postulate of methodological individualism is accepted too.

2. The utilitarian model and common sense: some qualitative data and some hypotheses concerning political protest

One way of testing the fruitfulness of the utilitarian model is to examine how far the costs and benefits associated with particular behavior alternatives determine the behavior performed. The usual procedure is that scientists collect data measuring various costs and benefits, and analyse, by applying certain statistical techniques like regression analysis, how far the data are consistent with the hypotheses.

In this section we suggest another procedure. One may ask people performing (or not performing) some kind of behavior why they engage (or do not engage) in this behavior. If they explain their behavior or inactivity by certain kinds of preferences and restrictions, we consider this to be a confirmation of the utilitarian model.

Against this procedure one could make the following objection: actors among themselves may explain their behavior by quite other factors than preferences and restrictions. They may think, for example, that biological predispositions determine behavior like crime. Nevertheless, if scientists collect data on the costs and benefits associated with the respective behavior, the utilitarian model may turn out to be correct. The opposite case may also occur: people may explain their behavior by preferences and restrictions, but scientists may find out that in fact other factors like biological causes are relevant.

We think that this argument is quite implausible. In everyday life people are often asked for reasons for their behavior. This provides incentives to observe the factors associated with their behavior. Although ordinary people do not observe reality as systematically as social scientists do, it is plausible to assume that non-scientists generally will not go totally wrong in identifying the factors influencing their behavior. Thus, if it turns out that a sample of actors generally identify certain kinds of preferences and restrictions as causes for a specific kind of their behavior, this has to be considered to be a confirmation of the utilitarian model, although not a severe test.
Even if one does not accept this argument, informations about common sense hypotheses concerning the causes of behavior may be used as hints at the costs and benefits operating in concrete social situations.

In the explanatory phase of a research project financially supported by the Volkswagenwerk Foundation (Stiftung Volkswagenwerk)[1] we tried to find out how opponents of nuclear energy themselves explain why they acted in some way against atomic energy or why they remained inactive. The aim of this project is to test whether hypotheses based on the utilitarian model are superior to sociological hypotheses explaining inactivity or some kind of protest. In the following we shall present some results of this exploratory phase of the project.

In order to construct a questionnaire, we wanted to obtain some prior information on the costs and benefits connected with inactivity or protest against nuclear energy. We considered the following procedures which may be applied in other investigations too.

A group of opponents of nuclear energy may be asked to discuss the reasons for being active or inactive. The researcher may structure the discussion and ask questions in order to elicit statements about the causal factors as people perceive them. In addition to such group discussions one may conduct a content analysis of documents of protest groups (pamphlets, letters, etc.). In the first place, these documents convey information about the incentives of the protest group. Furthermore, the attempts at mobilizing the constituency reveal what may be incentives for the constituency from the perspective of the mobilizing groups. Also books and articles of activists give hints at relevant factors for protest or inactivity. Another method which could be applied for exploratory purposes is the real contact interview (Kreutz, 1972: 68 ff.). More specifically, the researcher could contact protest groups trying to get their consent to interviewers' becoming active in the protest group. The activities of the interviewers could consist in selling journals, collecting money or getting signatures against atomic plants. In performing these activities the interviewers could ask certain predetermined questions concerning the reasons for buying, not buying, spending, not spending, or signing, not signing. The statements of the interviewers may be recorded afterwards.

In the following we want to present some results of two group discussions and of a qualitative analysis of pamphlets available to us. We did not succeed in conducting real contact interviews because the protest groups in Hamburg refuse to support any kind of empirical research. Furthermore, we propose some hypotheses for which the data were a heuristic base.

2.1. Indirect effects of deprivation

It seems to be a widely accepted common sense hypothesis that protest against nuclear energy is more likely, the more strongly people reject nuclear energy. More generally, the more people are deprived and the higher the deprivation is, the more likely people will act to change the situation.
This is the proposition of the 'grievance theory' in the sociology of social movements. One of the major proponents was Karl Marx, as can be seen in the Manifesto of the Communist Party by Marx and Engels. It is also the major theory of most German political scientists and activists writing on social movements. Social problems like bureaucratization, pollution, crime, alienation of politicians

and people, and unemployment are considered factors leading to widespred discontent and, consequently, to the emergence of protest and particularly social movements. One sometimes has the impression that the writers project their own frustrations onto the people. The deprivation-causes-protest theory was also expressed in the group discussions in various ways.

Frustration with the official energy policy is also a relevant factor according to the utilitarian perspective: the existence of a collective bad (existing or planned atomic plants) or the lack of a collective good (other kinds of energy) are costs people incur and may be incentives for collective action (see particularly Olson, 1971). However, according to hypotheses of modern political economy people may also contribute to the provision of a collective good if they are indifferent to this good. The incentives may be to get a job in a political party or in the government via engaging in the provision of a collective good (see again Olson, 1971; also Tullock, 1974). In the group discussions the overwhelming majority seemed to agree that there is no protest without deprivation. Only one speaker reported the following: he lived in a small village where the protest group was one of the few opportunities to spend free time. A new member, after participating in ten sessions, asked the speaker whether there is a difference between atomic energy and coal energy. One may suppose that for this person the incentive to participate was not the collective good. But it seems that such cases are very rare.

The group discussions suggest that a high degree of deprivation has effects on protest behavior which are not contained in economic writings. The first effect is most succinctly expressed in a pamphlet: where right becomes wrong, resistance becomes a duty. This was expressed in the group discussions in various ways: speakers said they feel responsible as citizens to act if something goes wrong or that they cannot leave it to others to act if bureaucrats or politicians do not act as they should.
We suppose that many individuals have internalized a norm of the following kind: the higher the costs being imposed on an individual by social or political institutions, and the more the individual considers these costs unjust, the more the individual feels obliged to engage in some action against these institutions. In other words, there is a more or less intense preference for realizing a norm in certain kinds of situations. Thus, for a given individual the intensity of the preference depends on the situation: the stronger the deprivation which is regarded

as unjust, the more intense the norm may be. Of course, for a given degree of deprivation people may differ with regard to the intensity with which they feel obliged to protest. At the one extreme, there may be people who do not feel any obligation at all to protest, independently of the intensity of deprivation. At the other extreme, people may feel a very strong obligation to do something, even if their deprivation is very low.

A high degree of deprivation has yet another effect. Let us demonstrate this with some statements from the group discussion. A speaker said that he writes letters to a newspaper even if such letters will not be published. He said that if he feels upset he simply has a desire to write even if it does not have any effect. Other speakers said: 'If one sees that all the ideals of democracy are not realized, I feel so angry that I react to that'. 'It was simply my rage that led to various protest activities'.
These people do not feel any obligation to act if they are frustrated. They simply desire to do something. That is to say, they have learned to react aggressively, if they are frustrated. Put otherwise, the higher the deprivation, the more beneficial it is in itself to express some kind of protest. Again individuals may differ with regard to the intensity of their urge to protest in a given situation.

Thus, a more or less high degree of deprivation has indirect effects: it may actualize norms or it may make protest behavior intrinsically rewarding or it may bring about both reactions. More precisely, people differ to the degree to which, in situations of more or less strong deprivation, they feel obligations or desires to act. If in fact these situations emerge, opportunities are given to realize the norm or desire to act. That is to say, in such situations the benefits of protesting rise.

The preceding considerations imply functions of the following kind: for a given individual a certain intensity of a norm (or desire) is associated with a given degree of unjust deprivation. The functions may differ for different individuals. Let us speculate what these functions may look like (see figure 1). If the deprivation is low, up to a certain point the intensity of felt obligation (or desire) to protest will rise only slowly. If a certain point is reached, the norm (or desire) becomes stronger, that is, the slope of the curve rises. Since the intensity of an obligation (or desire) cannot increase infinitely, the slope will decrease at a certain point.

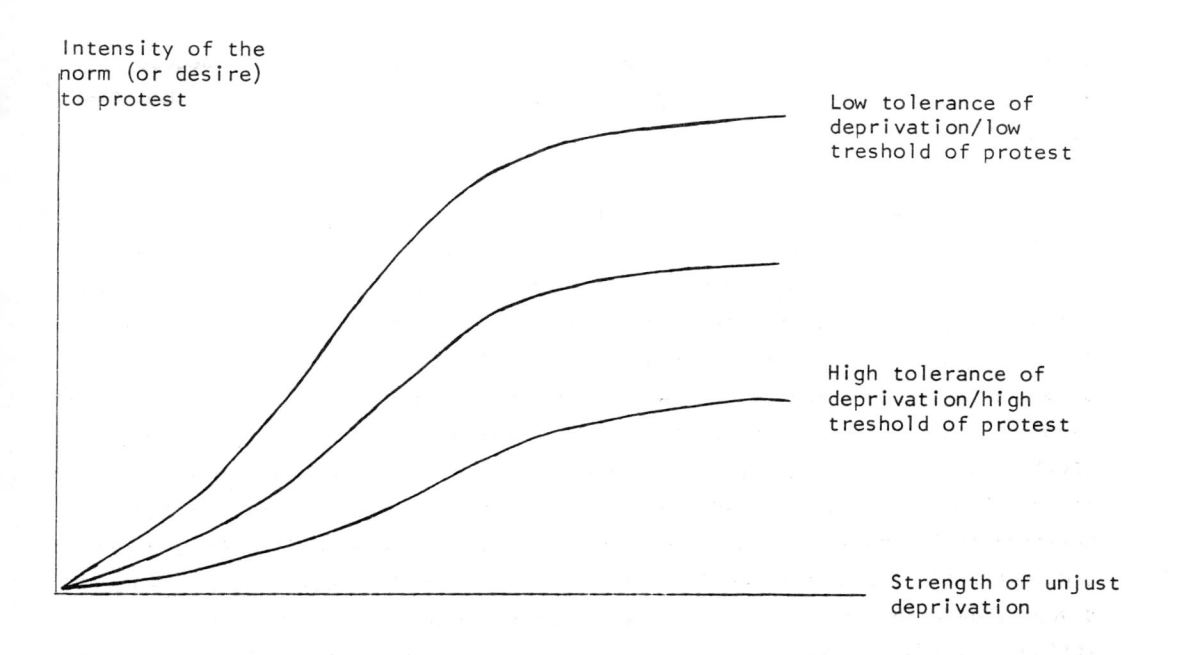

FIGURE-1: Functions specifying the relationship between strength of unjust deprivation and intensity of the norm (or desire) to protest.

(Y-axis: Intensity of the norm (or desire) to protest; X-axis: Strength of unjust deprivation. Curves labeled "Low tolerance of deprivation/low treshold of protest" and "High tolerance of deprivation/high treshold of protest".)

As we said before, the functions may differ for different individuals. The lowest curve in figure 1 represents individuals with a high tolerance of unjust deprivation. In contrast, the highest curve shows a low tolerance of deprivation. In the group discussions participants described how they became involved in protest for the first time. Some of them mentioned events which were rather frustrating to them. Examples are brutal police actions or actions of bureaucrats which are considered to be undemocratic. These reports suggest the following hypothesis: those people with the lowest tolerance of deprivation are the first ones who protest and try to mobilize others. That is to say: their treshold of protest is lowest. They are, so to speak, the political entrepreneurs. These individuals provide incentives of various kinds to others. This again increases the utility of protesting for others with higher tresholds. Thus there is a kind of diffusion process [2].

Our hypotheses imply that a high preference for a collective good indirectly invokes activities directed at the provision of this good, i.e. via actualizing

certain other preferences. Consequently, even if the perceived influence on the
realization of the collective good is negligable and if there are no other
incentives like getting better jobs, protest will emerge.

We said that there are norms specifying that something has to be done in situations
of deprivation. Do these norms coincide with the law or with other commonly
accepted rules of conduct? In several of the pamphlets it is clearly stated that
the existing rules are not considered binding. In one pamphlet it is said that
one does not accept the prescriptions of those furthering the construction of
atomic plants. Sometimes it is claimed that the actions should be nonviolent. This
term is conceived very broadly. It implies: noncooperation (strike, boycott, etc.)
civil disobedience (breaking unjust laws), and nonviolent confrontations
(occupation of places, blockades of streets, sit in, go in). In the pamphlet in
question it is emphasized that nonviolent actions may be unlawful. For example,
a demonstration is considered justified even if it is forbidden. In the group
discussions a speaker said: 'If it is effective, I would also perform illegal
actions'. In fact speakers said that unlawful behavior is most effective. Other
speakers said it would depend on the situation whether they regard violence as
justified. For example, if the police acts violently, counter-violence is
considered legitimate.

2.2. Strategies of coping with efficacy

In modern political economy deprivation, or, in other words, the collective good
aspect is only seen as a possible direct cause for contributing to the provision
of the good. Whether the collective good has an effect depends on the differential
subjective probability of changing the deprivation by protesting. Even a very high
deprivation increases the net utility of protest only if people perceive that the
probability of diminishing the deprivation by protest is higher than the
probability that the deprivation decreases if people remain inactive. How do
people perceive the influence of protest? From the group discussions and the
pamphlets some interesting points emerge.

(1)   People seem to think that their own influence by means of protesting is
        an increasing function of the success of the movement. In short, if the
movement is strong, the individual member is strong too. In the pamphlets much
room is devoted to the achievements of the movement. The authors seem to consider

it an incentive for participation. In the group discussions it was also pointed out that at least a small chance of success of the movement is relevant for participation [3].

Objectively, of course, for a normal member the influence depends not only on the influence of the movement, but also on the size of the movement. For example, assume that the anti-nuclear movement will provide the collective good with certainty. The larger the movement is, the smaller is in fact the influence of the normal member. Thus, presumably, the perceived influence is distorted.

(2)   In the group discussions I provoked the participants by saying that it is quite irrational to participate. The movement is large, so one person more or less has no effect at all. So it would be better to devote one's time to studying or to shopping instead of protesting. One generally accepted reaction to this question was: if everybody thinks this way, no protest will occur. People accepting this statement seem to mean the following: personal influence in the anti-nuclear movement is rather small. If this is realized, the effect may be that no participation will occur. This is an undesirable consequence. Thus, there seems to be a norm that a small influence on the provision of the collective good should not play any role in the decision to participate or to remain inactive. Another speaker seemed to accept this reasonig by saying that a real anti-nuke does not ask the question of influence. Perhaps such statements simply mean that one should participate, even if the influence is small. That is, people say something about the importance of a factor.

Thus people with a strong preference for a collective good seem to be reluctant to recognize that they have a negligable influence on its provision. Perhaps it causes cognitive dissonance to want a collective good and/or to participate in its provision and at the same time to accept having no influence. Individuals seem to reduce the dissonance by attributing to themselves the influence of the movement (see point 1 above) or by refusing to take the degree of influence into account in their decision to participate (see point 2 above).

(3)   There seems to be another possibility for reducing the dissonance: every protest is considered influential. In the group discussions it was said that a protest may not influence the construction of atomic power plants, but one may convince other people that nuclear energy is problematic. The influence on people in the course of interactions seems to be intrinsically rewarding. Thus, the primary aim of the individual is no longer the explicit aim of the movement

or of the protest, but a side effect. If the individual thinks that the movement too has no influence on the energy policy of the government, the explicit goal of the movement is shifted too. One speaker said: the anti-nuclear movement will not have any effect. The government has made its decisions and will not change them. But the movement has instigated a wide discussion about nuclear energy, it has created an awareness of contemporary energy problems, it has led to a greater distrust against the government and political institutions in general. Thus, a third strategy for coping with a small influence on achieving the primary goal of a movement is to emphasize side effects of the movement's activities.

2.3. Other factors

Various other costs and benefits are mentioned in the group discussions. Some speakers deem it important that friends are active too. The company of others in demonstrations is an incentive to participate. If friends are members of a protest group, the probability of participation rises. For many people it seems costly to initiate new contacts. The availability of time was mentioned too. That is, if there is time which can be used without foregoing too much, participation is more probable. One speaker said that a working woman with three small children is in another situation than a student who can dispose of his time more freely without missing too much.

Depending on the occupation they aspired to, some students were afraid of negative sanctions. Getting a job in the public sector may be prevented if one is known as a 'radical'.

Protest not only seems instrumental to contributing to the provision of a public good or for satisfying needs to comply with norms or to 'relieve' aggressions, it also often seems intrinsically rewarding. One speaker said: 'Protest must not only be a duty, it must also be fun'.

Particularly in the pamphlets there is a clear negative evaluation of the state and the economy. The political institutions are regarded as not able and/or not willing to act in the interest of the citizens. The economic institutions act only in their own interest, which consists of maximizing profit. A low loyalty to the political and economic institutions further diminishes the costs of protesting: supposedly protesters consider their activities undesirable for the targets. The lower the loyalty to a target, the less costly it is to cause inconvenience to it.

So far we have distinguished between protest and inactivity. The values of the variables mentioned may be different for different kinds of protest. For example, the time required for participating in a demonstration is lower than the time required for working in a protest group. Moreover, particular kinds of protest may be associated with different costs and benefits. To mention an example, speakers said that in demonstrations they feel the common strength of the movement.

2.4. Conclusion

The striking result of our explanatory analysis of two group discussions and of the pamphlets available to us is that the reasons opponents of nuclear energy give for their engagement or inactivity are kinds of costs and benefits. Sociological variables like social class, integration or relative deprivation were not mentioned. The least we can say is that the utilitarian model is consistent with common sense hypotheses and, accordingly, that costs and benefits seem to influence political protest and inactivity.

3. An empirical confrontation of the 'utilitarian perspective' with some sociological hypotheses concerning social protest

The common procedure of selecting a theory, collecting the relevant data, and determining by statistical techniques like regression analysis the degree to which the theory is consistent with the facts, is faced with the following problem: other theories inconsistent with the theory tested could be supported considerably better.
Thus, to be sure, isolated theory testing gives us some information about the validity of a theory. But the major problem with this kind of theory testing is that we do not get any information about the validity of a theory in comparison with other theories. What is needed, then, is an empirical confrontation of the existing alternative theories. That is, at least two competing theories should be tested in the same situation.

The data presented in the preceding section may be considered to confirm the utilitarian model in comparison with specific competing theories, because certain sociological variables were not mentioned in the group discussions or in the pamphlets analysed. But because of the explorative nature of the data and the qualitative analysis, this test is rather weak. In this section we want to present the results of a secondary analysis which yields a more severe test of alternative theories: we confront some sociological hypotheses with hypotheses derived from utility theory.

It would have been ideal, if we could have tested the hypotheses suggested in the preceding section. This was only partially possible because of missing indicators. The data we use refer to interviews of 2.662 adults in the Federal Republic of Germany in 1974. The interviewees were selected from four rural, two urban and six university communities (with 1.104 students). The data are also analyzed in Muller (1979), where more details can be found (see pp. 8-10 and passim). The data allow a test of a regression equation consisting of variables intended to measure some kinds of costs and benefits influencing conventional and unconventional political participation (CPP and UPP). The equation and the results of the data analysis are represented in table 1. A rough description of the definition of the variables and the results will have to suffice here (for details see Opp et al., 1981).

TABLE-1: A 'utilitarian model' explaining conventional and unconventional political participation and its empirical test.

(1) $UPP = -.70 + .16\ InCt + .30\ Norms + .001\ Exp^{*}$ -

($R^2 = .42$)   ($b_s = .09$)   ($b_s = .12$)   ($b_s = .03$)

(N=1347) $- .76\ Loy - .23\ Eff$
             ($b_s = -.36$) ($b_s = -.28$)

(2) $CPP = -.130 + .11\ InCt + 1.22\ Norms + .004\ Exp$ -

($R^2 = .46$)   ($b_s = .04$)   ($b_s = .34$)   ($b_s = .14$)

(N=1473) $- .36\ Loy - .42\ Eff$
             ($b_s = -.12$) ($b_s = -.34$)

UPP   = Unconventional political participation
CPP   = Conventional political participation
InCt   = Internal control of deprevation by means of UPP (CPP), interaction terms, see text.
Norms   = Acceptance of norms for UPP (CPP).
Exp   = Relevant expectations of others in regard to UPP (CPP).
Loy   = Loyalty to the state.
Eff   = Effort for performing UPP (CPP)
R^2 = Explained variance
N   = Number of cases

The first term in the equation is the constant.
Parameters in front of the variables are the unstandardized regression coefficients.
b_s = standardized regression coefficients
Starred variables: the respective coefficients are not significant.

Under what conditions do people perform (or are ready to perform) CPP (like participating in a petition-signing campaign or in a demonstration) or UPP (like seizure of factories, offices or other buildings, or refusal to pay rent or taxes)? One standard variable in the literature we dealt with in the preceding section is a high deprivation. That means that a certain situation is costly to an individual. The variable 'deprivation' was measured by asking the interviewees whether they feel they get their just desert in regard to housing conditions, medical care, personal income and work satisfaction. The more they denied getting their just deserts with reference to a whole series of kinds of deprivations, the more they were regarded as deprived (and the more points they got).

According to the utility theory, deprivation is not in itself sufficient for being politically active. The perceived effect of CPP (UPP) on reducing the deprivation is of importance. Furthermore, since most of the modes of behavior ascertained in the interviews are directed against the state, the degree to which the state is seen as responsible for the deprivation is relevant. The interaction term, consisting of the three variables mentioned, is called internal control of deprivation by means of UPP (CPP), abbreviated 'InCt'. We hypothesize a positive direct effect of InCt on UPP as well as on CPP.

We saw in the last section that people even protest when they do not perceive any effect on the elimination of the deprivation. There seem to exist internalized norms to the effect that one should protest if institutions deprive people and if this deprivation is considered illegitimate. In terms of the utilitarian model, acting in accordance with internalized norms is intrinsically beneficial and deviating from such norms is intrinsically costly. The variable 'norms' was measured by the question: 'how desirable is it according to your opinion that people like you participate in politics?'. The effect of 'norms' on UPP and CPP is expected to be positive.

Furthermore, there may be expectations on the part of other people the actor knows. These people may exert pressure to participate and it may be costly to the actors not to behave in accordance with these expectations. Furthermore, it may be beneficial to follow the expectations. We term such expectations 'relevant'. This variable was measured by asking the respondents for each of the ten actions how many citizens would approve of it. The variable 'relevant expectations' for UPP (CPP) was formed by adding the percentages for the five unconventional (conventional) behavior items. The higher the relevant expectations, the higher UPP (CPP).

Let us assume, individuals have a positive attitude toward an institution, i.e. they have developed a loyalty (see Hirschman, 1970) to the institution. In the preceding section we hypothesized: the higher the loyalty, the more costly it is for actors if performance of UPP or CPP imposes costs on the institution. We assume that actors perceive that CPP or UPP is costly for the respective institution. Thus, the higher the loyalty, the lower the incentive for UPP and CPP. 'Loyalty' was considerd to be higher, the stronger the interviewees agreed to items like 'in general one can rely upon the government to do the right things' or 'I have great respect and affection for the political institutions in the Federal Republic'.

The last variable in our model we call effort, that is, the time and other resources required to perform UPP and CPP. The higher the effort, the lower the incentive for UPP and CPP. We assumed that, if people have rather much time at their disposal, it is less costly to participate. Accordingly, if people are young and unmarried, and if their work imposes few time restrictions on them (being a student or unemployed), their effort is relatively low.

The model summarized in table 1 is called 'utilitarian', since the independent variables are consistent with utility theory. Calling the model 'utilitarian' does not exclude that some of its variables are also used in other social sciences like sociology. When we say that we confront the utilitarian model with sociological hypotheses, this means the following: we confront the utilitarian model with those hypotheses which are put forward by sociologists and which are not consistent with the utilitarian model.

If we take into account the fact that the measurement of some of the variables was far from ideal, the model can be regarded as confirmed. The explained variance is not too low, compared with other investigations in sociology and political science. Moreover, the effects are in the expected direction.

The more important question, however, is: how far is this model superior to other hypotheses explaining the same behavior. The data showed that our model is superior to hypotheses suggested by Kaase (1976, 1976a) and Muller and Jukam (1977). The results of this empirical confrontation are reported in Opp et al. (1981).

Will the utilitarian model also prove superior if we confront it with other hypotheses? It is typical for sociological investigations to use variables like age, place of living, religious affiliation, sex, family status and in particular socio-economic status as explanatory variables for almost all kinds of phenomena. Political participation is also explained by these variables (see, for example, Verba and Nie, 1972; Barnes and Kaase, 1979). Apparently such explanations seem to be successful. For example, in many empirical studies a positive correlation between SES (Socio-economic status) and political participation is reported.

Nevertheless, one will not accept such a generalization as a lawlike statement. One would rather argue that the (multiple or simple) correlation between demographic variables and political participation (or other kinds of activities) will depend on the values of other variables. Let us assume that there is a positive correlation between SES and UPP. According to the utilitarian model such a correlation would be predicted, if, for example, people with relatively high SES perceive relatively high internal control by means of UPP, have strongly internalized participation norms, are highly illoyal, need little effort to participate, but that the relevant expectations are alike for people with different SES. However, if the variables of the utilitarian model have other values, we would expect a negative correlation or perhaps a zero correlation between SES and UPP[4]. The important proposition is that utility theory or other economic hypotheses are apt to explain certain empirical generalizations of sociology.

We tested this proposition by first constructing a SES scale from items ascertaining occupational prestige, income and education [5]. The data yield a correlation between SES and UPP of .21. If, in fact, this correlation can be explained at least in part by the independent variables of the utilitarian model the correlation must be reduced if the independent variables are 'held constant'. This can be achieved by incorporating SES as an additional variable into the utilitarian model and computing the partial regression coefficients. If the standardized regression coefficient for SES is reduced, that is, smaller than the bivariate correlation between SES and UPP, then this indicates that our model can explain at least in part the correlation between SES and UPP. We carried out a new regression analysis with the additional variable 'SES'. The standardized regression coefficient for SES was .02 (N=1283). The other coefficients were like those of the utilitarian model (see table 1).

The bivariate correlation between CPP and SES was .50 (N=1402). A new regression analysis of the utilitarian model with SES as an additional variable yielded a (partial) standardized regression coefficient of .29. The explained variance increased from .46 (model 1) to .54 (the utilitarian model with SES as an additional variable). The other standardized regression coefficients decreased except for lnCt which remained the same. This result shows that the correlation between CPP and SES is reduced from .50 to .29, which was hypothesized. However, in this model SES has an effect of its own. This is not surprising because the utilitarian model cannot explain the whole variance of CPP. The reason is that some variables of the utilitarian model could not be measured in a desirable way and that other relevant variables are missing. We suppose that an improved utilitarian model would reduce the bivariate correlation between CPP and SES further.

4. Conclusion

It seems to be a fruitful line of inquiry to confront empirically hypotheses based on the utilitarian model with competing hypotheses. So far, isolated theory testing prevails. The major advantage of confronting competing theories is that only this kind of research can yield information about which theory is better. Consequently one may call this kind of research eliminative theory testing. The expression 'comparative theory testing' is too weak: the aim is not simply to look for differences, but to discard theories.

More specifically, the various theories of social movements or, in general, political participation should be analyzed with regard to their relationships to the utilitarian model. Particularly we think of the mass society theory, the grievance (absolute deprivation) theory, the various relative deprivation hypotheses and, above all, the resource mobilization perspective.

Eliminative theory testing may not only yield information about the relative standing of theories. It also opens up the opportunity of utilizing fruitful research results from the various social sciences. For example, sociological theories of social movements seem to specify various kinds of preferences and restrictions which may affect the formation of social movements and which are disregarded in economics. On the other hand, the utilitarian approach will correct sociological hypotheses by pointing out that in sociological theories important variables are missing. Thus, eliminative theory testing may also lead to an integration of research results in the social sciences.

Notes

(1) A copy of a summary of the research proposal in English (12 pages) may be obtained by the author.
(2) On the concept of threshold and its bearing on an utilitarian approach see especially Granovetter (1978).
(3) Let us again speculate about the form of the function. If the x-axis represents the influence of the movement, ranging from 0 to 1, and the y-axis the perceived influence of a person, the curve will be similar to a logistic curve. That is to say, up to a certain influence of the movement, persons perceive their own influence rising, but with a decreasing degree (slope of the curve), until the curve becomes parallel to the x-axis. Assume, for example, that the movement is expected to have an influence of .70. Presumably a member will not perceive a differential subjective probability of .70, but a much lower one.
(4) For a similar argument where economic hypotheses are applied to explain the

positive correlation of income and political participation see Frey (1971) and the exchange in the same journal pp. 113-122. However, Frey does not empirically test whether his proposed explanation is valid.

(5) We used the occupational prestige rankings from Kleining and Moore (1968). Respondents received points according to the kinds of schools they attended ranging from 1 (primary school) to 10 (university) and according to their income ranging from 1 (lowest income category) to 10 (highest income category). The SES scale was constructed by summing up the points for the variables occupational prestige, school attended and income.

References

AJZEN, I. and M. FISHBEIN, (1980), Understanding Attitudes and Predicting Behavior. Englewood Cliffs, N.J.: Prentice Hall.

BARNES, S.H., M. KAASE et al., (1979), Political Action. London: Sage.

FREY, B.S., (1971), 'Why Do High Income People Participate More in Politics?', Public Choice 9: 101-105.

FREY, B.S., (1980), 'Ökonomie als Verhaltenswissenschaft. Ansatz, Kritik und der europäische Beitrag', Jahrbuch für Sozialwissenschaft 31: 21-35.

GRANOVETTER, M., (1978), 'Threshold Models of Collective Behavior', American Journal of Sociology 83: 1420-1443.

HIRSCHMAN, A.O., (1970), Exit, Voice, and Loyalty. Responses to Decline in Firms, Organizations, and States. Cambridge, Mass.: Harvard University Press.

KAASE, M., (1976), 'Bedingungen unkonventionellen politischen Verhaltens in der Bundesrepublik Deutschland', pp. 179-216 in: P. Graf Kielmansegg (ed.), Legitimationsprobleme politischer Systeme. Opladen: Westdeutscher Verlag.

KAASE, M., (1976a), 'Political Ideology, Dissatisfaction and Protest. A Micro Theory of Unconventional Political Behavior', pp. 7-28 in K. von Beyme et al. (eds.), German Political Studies, Vol. 2. London: Sage.

KIRCHGÄSSNER, G., (1980), 'Können Ökonomie und Soziologie voneinander lernen?', Kyklos 33: 420-448.

KLEINING, G. and W.E. MOORE, (1968), 'Soziale Selbsteinstufung (SSE). Ein Instrument zur Messung sozialer Schichten', Kölner Zeitschrift für Soziologie und Sozialpsychologie 20: 505-552.

KREUTZ, H., (1972), Soziologie der empirischen Sozialforschung. Stuttgart: Enke.

MULLER, E.N., (1979), Aggressive Political Participation. Princeton, N.J.: Princeton University Press.

MULLER, E.N. and Th.O. JUKAM, (1977), 'On the Meaning of Political Support', American Political Science Review 71: 1561-1595.

OLSON, M., (1971), The Logic of Collective Action. 2nd ed., Cambridge, Mass.: Harvard University Press.

OPP, K.-D., (1978), 'Probleme und Strategien des Theorienvergleichs', pp. 1128-1147 in: K.M. Bolte (ed.), Materialien aus der soziologischen Forschung. Verhandlungen des 18. Deutschen Soziologentages. Darmstadt: Luchterhand.

OPP, K.-D., K. BUROW-AUFFARTH and U. HEINRICHS, (1981), 'Conditions for Conventional and Unconventional Political Participation: An Empirical Test of Economic and Sociological Hypotheses', European Journal of Political Research 9: 147-168.

TULLOCK, G., (1974), The Social Dilemma. Blacksburg, Virg.: University Publications.

VERBA, S. and N.H. NIE, (1972), Participation in America. Political Democracy and Social Equality. New York: Harper and Row.

Harry B.G. Ganzeboom

EXPLAINING DIFFERENTIAL PARTICIPATION IN HIGH-CULTURAL ACTIVITIES - A CONFRONTATION OF INFORMATION-PROCESSING AND STATUS-SEEKING THEORIES

Introduction

In this paper two theories are developed explaining differential participation in high-cultural activities. In section 1 the propositions are reviewed considering well-known and replicated findings of (mainly) Dutch leisure research [1]. In section 2 results will be given from a recently carried out survey by the author. Throughout this paper, 'culture' has been defined as 'high culture'. In particular, our interest takes into consideration reading books and visiting theatres, concerts, historical places and museums. By tradition, these activities have been known for large overrepresentation of higher status groups in their audiences (cf. Wippler, 1970; CBS, 1981). The most important explanatory problem for the theories therefore is to provide a satisfactory explanation of this overrepresentation.

The first theory to be described has been named the 'theory of information-processing' or 'information theory'. Its main programmatic statement is that differential participation in cultural events between individuals must be explained by the difference in information-processing capacities of individuals. Differences in participation-rates between events may be explained according to the complexity of the information processed. The theory of information-processing has a strong psychological background. The basic ideas on cultural participation as information-processing can be found in Berlyne (1974) and Moles (1958). Similar hypotheses in sociology and economy have been used by Bourdieu (1977) and Becker (1964). These ideas can be summarized in the following statements:

(a) Individuals are rewarded by varied experience. Pleasure increases through variation up to a certain level, when information becomes too complex and pleasure diminishes and tends to become negative.

(b) Information can be arranged according to complexity. More complex stimuli give more varied experience, and tend to displease more likely than less complex stimuli.

(c) Cultural stimuli (works of art) are sources of complex information.
(d) Individuals have different capacities to deal with (cultural) information. Three factors determine these capacities. First, persons have different innate or early trained general skills in processing information. Most prominently, cognitive intelligence is one of these skills. Musical talent is another. According to the information-theory, education is a recruitment of persons with high cognitive skill, and should be highly correlated with cultural consumption. Secondly, persons have different knowledge of and aquaintance with a cultural field, and accordingly a different level of understanding of the information.
Thirdly, a personality characteristic, extraversion, gives a person a general higher preference for complex information, and stimulates his cultural activity.

The second theory to be described, has been named the 'status-seeking theory of cultural consumption', or 'status theory'. Its main programmatic statement is that participation in cultural events is a function of the status a person wants to have, and that differences in participation-rates between events are related to the status-rendering characteristics of these events. This theory has a more sociological background, e.g. in the writings of Veblen and Weber, and the basic ideas can be found in any sociological handbook. Most prominently, they have been formulated by Homans (1974), Bourdieu and Passeron (1977) and Collins (1979). These ideas may be summarized as follows:

(a) Individuals are ranked along status dimensions. Persons tend to conform to social norms associated with their status. Conformation to norms is rewarding in social interaction processes.
(b) Higher status is more attractive than lower status. Persons try to acquire higher status if within reach. If status ranks are inconsistent, persons stress their highest rank, and try to compensate for the lower ones.
(c) Traditionally, high-cultural activities are associated with higher status-groups. Cultural activity is perceived as a social norm belonging to the social standing of these groups. In lower status-groups, social norms discourage cultural activity.
(d) There is a varying degree of status-rendering between cultural activities. Most status is obtained by consuming culture that is attended in a formal manner, like traditional theater. On the other side of the continuum, not much status will be acquired or stressed by reading a book, which is a solo activity.

(e) The most important status dimensions are education, occupation and income. Of these three, occupation is the most important one, being the classical indicator of social standing.

1. Alternative predictions on 9 topics

When considering these two general views on cultural consumption, at least 9 topics can be found, on which they provide different predictions and about which earlier empirical evidence is available.

(1) Overlapping of audience groups

One of the facts well established by Dutch surveys on leisure, as well as in investigations of audience groups is the considerable overlap between these groups. In view of the fact that cultural activities are time-consuming, a certain negative correlation between participation-variables might be expected. However, in general, these correlations are positive and of considerable size. The negative influence of their time-consuming character is obviously compensated by the very strong common factors. Both theories can explain this tendency for positive correlations among attendance variables, since they point towards common factors in cultural activities.

Alternative predictions may be made for certain types of correlation. According to the information theory we might expect a relative higher correlation among activities that demand equal types of skill and knowledge. Typical examples are frequenting movies and theaters, or paying a visit to museums and historical places. According to the status theory we might expect relative higher correlation among activities that demand the same kind of formal attendance. Consequently, a high correlation should occur between visiting a theater and attending a concert. This correlation may act as a crucial experiment between the status- and information-theory, seeing that from the latter we might expect a rather low correlation, since 'the theater' and 'the concert' appeal to quite different types of skill and knowledge.

Empirical evidence shows that concert attendance and theater-going have, in fact, a very strong correlation. But there is also some evidence in favor of the information theory: activities like visiting museums and historical places largely overlap one another.

(2)   The effect of status dimensions

The second well established fact in cultural consumption research is the considerable overrepresentation of higher status-groups among culture consumers. This is true for status-dimensions as different as education, occupation and income. Since these status-dimensions are strongly correlated in modern society, this is quite understandable from both points of view. Possibilities of testing two theories occur in multivariate analysis of the effects of status variables. Quite often, these show a very strong effect of education, and spurious effects of income and occupation, as is predicted in the information theory. However, several other studies may be found, in which the strong effects of occupation and income are decreased by introducing education as a control variable, but where still a certain influence of occupation and income remains, as is predicted in the status theory.

(3)   The status composition of audiences

Although an overrepresentation of higher status-groups among cultural audiences will be found in nearly every cultural consumption investigation, the extent to which this is true may vary. In the information theory we could predict those cultural activities to be most elite, which are complex in information-processing. The more difficult the cultural information is, the stronger the correlation will be between active consumption and education. On the other hand, from status theory we might expect those activities to be elite, that render a higher prestige to the attender.

The scaling of cultural activities along dimensions of complexity and status-rendering may be a difficult problem. Nevertheless, partitioning cultural activities in complex/simple has shown to be useful in empirical research. As far as the distinction between complex and simple activities is valid, this leads to the conclusion that complex activities are far more elite than simple activities. This is especially true when one tries to explain differences within the same cultural branch, for example, serious and popular music, or classical and experimental art. It may be argued that these differences in complexity are at the same time differences in high-browness of these activities, and allow status-theoretical interpretation. Crucial cases in which the theories give alternative predictions are 'off-broadway-theater' and political theater. Formal attendance is not a requirement in these cases, and quite often artists claim to reach lower status groups. On the other hand, the cultural information in off-broadway-theater and political theater may be quite complex to process. Not many comparative studies on this topic have been published, but available evidence seems to point to a desillusion of these artists' claims. Political and off-broadway theater have an elite audience, just as traditional theaters have.

(4) Cultural participation in the life-cycle.

Peaks in cultural consumption may occur at different stages in the life-cycle of an individual. Some of these should be explained from causes external to our theories. Both the drop in activities due to matrimonial status and rearing young children, and the diminishing activities of senior citizens are examples thereof. But several other predictions may be deduced from the two theories. In the information theory, obtaining cultural knowledge and skill are a prerequisite for enjoying culture. People who acquire these in early socialization have a lead over persons with a lack of cultural education. In this theory active participation results in building up human capital (Becker, 1964), thus facilitating enjoyment of more complex cultural events. Another consequence of this human capital formation may be that persons who stop (for some reason) active participation loose contact, and will not likely be able to start again. In summary: 'cultural careers' start in early childhood and are not interrupted for longer periods.

In status theory cultural consumption varies with the status-group one belongs to, or aspires to. Therefore, persons born in higher status-groups will participate in early life-time. But others may begin at stages where they reach or get near these higher status-groups. Status-shifts can be associated with life-cycle events like marriage, migration, attaining a better job, or getting acquainted with members of these higher status-groups.

Empirical evidence reveals that early cultural socialization is a very important factor in stimulating participation as well as preference for more complex forms of culture in a later stage. In these relat.ons, the need to control the effects of education may be essential, because it is highly correlated with status background and cultural consumption. Investigations in which this intermediating variable has been controlled, consistently show a large influence of early culture socialization. Evidence on detail of cultural careers is scarce but gives reason to believe that they very rarely begin once the adolescence phase is over.

(5) Rates of cultural consumption over time

Both theories predict a growth of cultural consumption, at least in the last decades. But the two specify different mechanisms. In the information theory this expectation is based on the fact that the average education has increased very quickly in the last decade, supplying more and more individuals with skill and knowledge in the field of culture. In the status theory, the expectation is based upon the assumption that status-motivation and status-thresholds have declined over the last decades. Assuming that cultural consumption has remained an attractive source of distraction, it is clear that lower status groups have entered into cultural events, and the total consumption has grown.

In fact, cultural consumption rates have declined since the 1950s and this applies to every one of them. This finding may be explained by several other factors, particularly the growing number of alternative attractions (television) is responsible for this decline.

Other predictions on changes over time can be made, especially on those in the status-composition of audience. Will the differences in consumption rates between status groups decline in the long run? In the information theory there is no reason to expect a decline in the difference of consumption between educational groups. In fact, assuming that the rise of the average education goes hand in hand with a more efficient recruitment of intelligent persons, the group with only a lower form of education must be regarded as an intellectual 'residu' with few capacities. This will result in greater differences between educational groups.

On the other hand, owing to the virtual disappearance of status motives in modern society, status theory predicts a declining gap between status groups, in particular between occupational groups.

No thorough investigation has been done in this field. One of the reasons for this omission may be that it is common knowledge that there has been no spreading of cultural consumption in lower status groups, whatever great efforts of government and artists do to reach this goal. Furthermore, available evidence suggests that the position of the information theory is correct in one other respect: differences between educational groups have grown.

(6) The effect of cultural knowledge and skill

The hypothesis that cultural knowledge and skill are a direct cause of cultural consumption is quite important in the information theory. Knowledge and skill act as human capital: they allow the processing of new cultural information and this results in more pleasure from cultural activities.

Many surveys show a very strong correlation between knowledge and/or skill and cultural consumption. Unfortunately, a mere correlation between cultural consumption and cultural knowledge/skill is not a very conclusive argument in favor of the information theory. Although there is no assumption in status theory that knowledge or skill cause cultural consumption, this point of view can be easily reconciled with the rather trivial assumption that consumption increases knowledge and skill. The causal sequence is very critical in choosing between the two theories on this topic.

Available evidence suggests that in some cases, when skill is clearly causally ordered before consumption, there exists a very strong correlation. The fact, that in concert- and museum-audiences professionals and amateurs have a very large overrepresentation, can be cited as the most direct support for this conclusion.

(7) The effect of status background and cultural socialization

Status background and cultural socialization, two correlated variables, reveal to be important factors in several investigations. This can be explained by both theories. But again, the mechanisms are different. According to the information theory, status background influences cultural consumption through cultural socialization, and cultural socialization influences consumption by increasing knowledge and skill. But in the status theory cultural knowledge is an effect of participation, not a cause. The influence of status background and cultural (= status)socialization will be mediated by group norms on cultural consumption.

Although strong effects of status background and cultural socialization on cultural consumption is well documented (even when controlled for the effect of the status ranks of the respondent) no result is known to us that makes either the information-theoretical or the status-theoretical interpretation more plausible.

(8) The effect of extraversion

Extraversion (or preference for complex stimulation) is a personality factor that has been intensively studied by Eysenck and his associates (Eysenck, 1967). Extraverts have a preference for complex stimulation: Their counterparts, introverts, have a preference for a low level of stimulation. If this is true, and cultural consumption is a form of information-processing according to the information theory, extraverts will be more active in cultural events. There is no prediction about the effects of extraversion in the status theory.

There has been no direct test of this hypothesis. But in several surveys, evidence can be found that culture consumers are typical extraverts. Generally, they like new and strange things, and this may be taken as a manifestation of an extravert personality.

(9) The effect of status-inconsistency and social mobility

Status inconsistency and social mobility are examples of the same type of situation: persons have different ranks in status dimensions. In the status theory two combinations of status ranks are expected to increase culture consumption. These are both situations of social climbing ('parvenu', 'nouveau riche'). First, persons may have a higher occupation or income than may be expected from their education. Second, they may have a high education, considering their family background. In both cases, apart from the net effect of the basic status ranks, these combinations should produce a higher degree of culture consumption. There is no proposition in information theory about these effects of status inconsistency or social mobility. Therefore, it will be assumed that cultural consumption is an additive function of status ranks.

Not much work has been done on the interaction effect of status ranks. Some of it gave positive evidence for the status theory, but the analyses are probably flawed by inadequate control of the effect of the basic status dimensions.

2. The research design

We will test the two theories against the data of a recent Dutch survey [2]. Data were collected in June 1981. Except for the effects of non-response (30%), the sample is taken at random from the population of Utrecht. Utrecht is a province capital, 4th largest city in The Netherlands, and in all respects a middle-of-the road place. All respondents (N=347) are over 17 years of age. We cannot think of any special reason why results, as shown by us, would be considerably different in the rest of The Netherlands.

In this paper, variables used in the analysis were measured as follows:

AGE	Coded as a semi-continuous variable, 18-73
EDUCATION	Coded on a 7-point equal-interval scale, from (1) primary school to (7) university degree
OCCUPATION	Coded on a 6-point equal-interval scale, from (1) lower manual, to (6) professionals and managers.
INCOME	Net household income, coded in 6 classes, which are a near log-transformation of the original class-midpoints.
CULTURAL SOCIALIZATION	Four 3-point items on the degree of cultural consumption of the respondent's parents. Reliability: $\alpha= .65$
CULTURAL NORMS	Three 7-point items on the respondent's perception of the cultural consumption of his social interaction partners. Reliability: $\alpha= .68$.
CULTURAL KNOWLEDGE	A 9-item test on knowledge of architecture and history. The reliability of this set of dichotomous items was estimated as $\alpha= .90$.
CULTURAL CONSUMPTION	A set of 45 dichotomous items on cultural consumption was factorized (oblique rotation) in 4 subsets: THEATER & CONCERTS MUSEUMS & EXHIBITIONS BOOKS & MAGAZINES HISTORICAL PLACES The four indices were constructed as the summation of the items. For convenience they are standardized to zero means and unit variance.
EXTRAVERSION	We used five 9-point items, adapted from Eysenck's (1969) Personality Inventory, and local Dutch versions of this test. In spite of several pretests of this short-version instrument, we did not reach a satisfying degree of reliability ($\alpha= .62$).

3. Analysis

Table-1 presents a structural model for the observed correlations, as estimated by the Lisrel-program (Jöreskog and Sörbom, 1978). Most variables were entered as compound indices to accommodate for the assumption of multivariate normality and continuous measurement. Since most variables can be assumed to have approximately the same satisfactory level of reliability (.80/.90), this will not result in a strong bias of the estimated structural coefficients. The original indictors were used in two cases in the estimation procedure, since we had multipoint items here with a more or less unimodal distribution, and a somewhat unsatisfactory level of reliability (CULTURAL SOCIALIZATION; CULTURAL NORMS). Observed variables are in squares, latent variables are in circles.

The structural model, used for evaluating the two theories, does not fit the observed correlation matrix very well (χ^2=217; NDF=117; p<.001). The critical χ^2-criterion is approximately 170. But since any structural effect to be entered in the model would be clearly insignificant, and almost every residual correlation is lower than .10, we feel that we would be overfitting the model by estimating more coefficients.
Following the sequence of topics in section 1, the results may be summarized as follows:

(1) Overlapping of cultural groups

The structural coefficients between the four forms of cultural consumption and the latent variable CULTURAL CONSUMPTION (which are 'factor loadings') are more or less of the same size. With Lisrel a formal test on equality of effects can be run, and the null-hypothesis of equal effects need not be rejected (χ^2=8; NDF=3; p>.05). Therefore it is quite useless to search for patterns as specified by the information theory or the status theory.

But there is one strong confirmation of the status theory in the data: in our preliminary factor-analysis theater-goers and concert-goers were not separated in two groups. We could not find any division between the two, and this finding (which corresponds to earlier results) confirms the status-theoretical interpretation (the same kind of formal attendance), and does not confirm the information-theoretical prediction (very different kinds of required skill and knowledge).

TABLE-1: A structural model for the observed correlations (N=347; χ^2=217; NDF=117; p<.001)

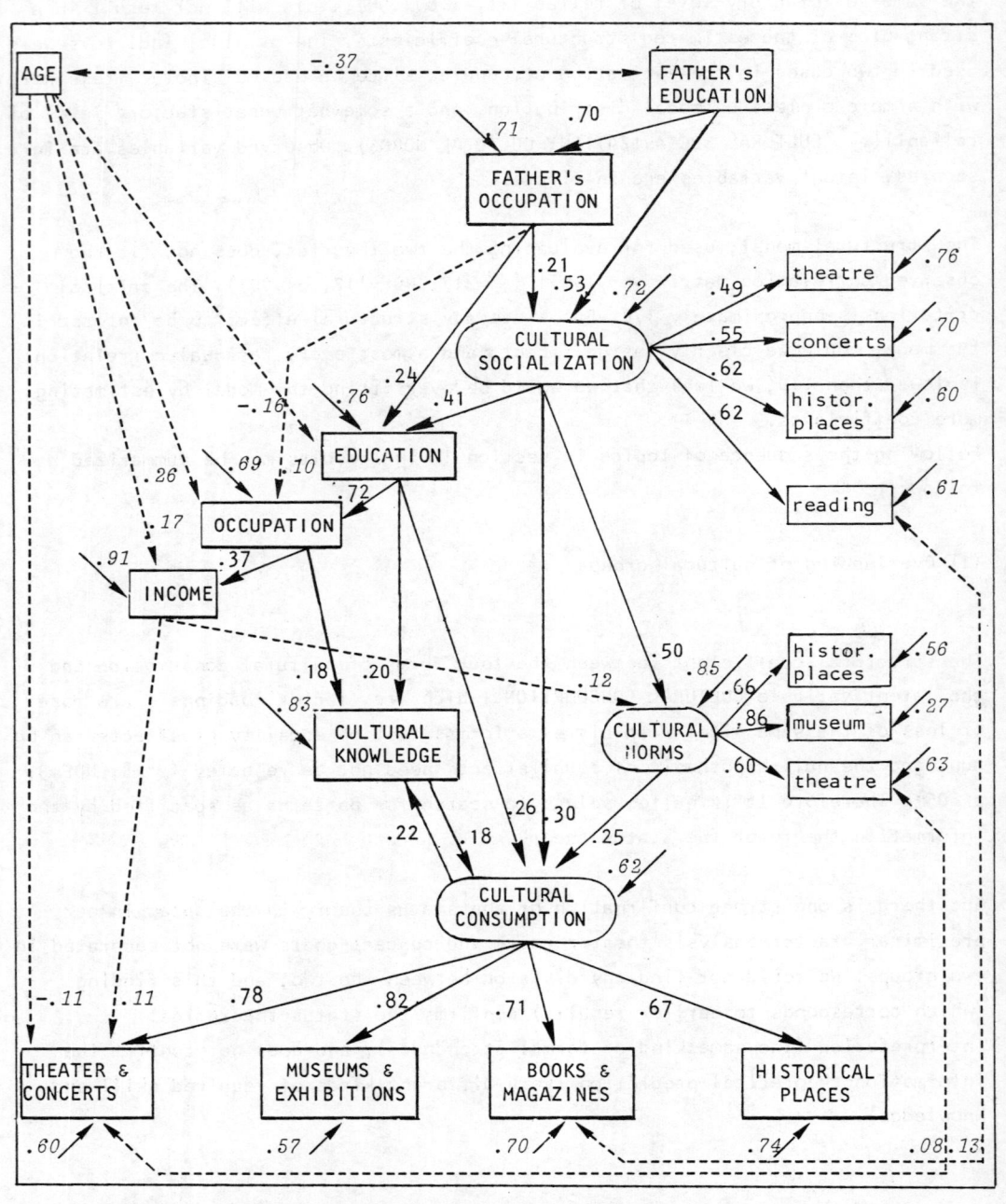

Observed and estimated correlations, means and standard deviations are given in the appendix. Coefficients from a standardized solution. Dashed arrows are not discussed in the text.

(2) The effect of status-dimensions

The effect of status dimensions is very large. Since their relative magnitude may be somewhat unclear from the complex structure in table-1, we single out the estimated effect of status-dimensions on cultural consumption:

	CULTURAL CONSUMPTION	
	estimated correlation	estimated effect
EDUCATION	.61	.33
OCCUPATION	.45	.06 (p<.05)
INCOME	.16	.03 (n.s.)

To a great extent the effects of OCCUPATION and INCOME turn out to be spurious on introducing respondent's EDUCATION and family background variables in the model. This is exactly what the information theory predicts, and it is clearly contradictory to status theory hypotheses. A small effect of OCCUPATION remains after controlling the EDUCATION and the family background. This may be interpreted as a point in favor of the status theory (see however section 2.5).

(3) The status composition of attendance groups

Since all structural coefficients between CULTURAL CONSUMPTION and the four forms of cultural consumption are of the same magnitude, the model gives no information on a different status-composition of audiences. Observed differences are in fact quite small and not relevant for the evaluation of the two theories.

(4) Cultural participation in the life-cycle

The model does not contain any direct information on the degree of cultural consumption in the life-cycle. We did not ask any questions of starting points or interruptions of 'cultural careers'.
However some indirect evidence may be taken from the model. The variable CULTURAL SOCIALIZATION (which does not measure earlier cultural activities of the respondents, but of their parents) does have a large influence on current cultural

activities (direct + indirect effects: .45). This suggests that early experience does play a major part in becoming active in cultural events. This conclusion confirms the information theory predictions. But at the same time it is not a test for the status theory prediction on this topic.

(5) Cultural consumption rates over time

The model gives no information on this topic.

(6) The effect of cultural knowledge and skill

Our measure of cultural knowledge and skill, CULTURAL KNOWLEDGE lies in the field of only one of the surveyed activities, visiting HISTORICAL PLACES. Nevertheless, its correlations with the other activities, particularly visiting MUSEUMS and the reading of BOOKS & MAGAZINES are sufficiently high to warrant it to be a valid measure of general cultural skill and knowledge.
The hypothesis that cultural knowledge and skill are a major cause of cultural consumption, and intermediate the effect of status dimensions and family background, is partly substantiated by the model. The direct effect of CULTURAL KNOWLEDGE on CULTURAL CONSUMPTION is .31, and it intermediates the total effect of OCCUPATION and part of the effect of EDUCATION on CULTURAL CONSUMPTION. This result is an important confirmation of the information theory. The fact that CULTURAL KNOWLEDGE intermediates the effect of OCCUPATION is somehow surprising, since we assumed that the differences in occupation, apart from confounding effects of educations, are differences on a prestige dimension, and not on an information-processing capacity scale. This finding is a windfall for the information theory, since it clearly shows that persons with higher occupations are more culturally active, in as far as they have acquired more cultural knowledge and skill.

However, there may be alternative interpretations of this part of the model, in which cultural activity is the cause and not the effect of cultural knowledge and skill. We can test this interpretation by introducing a feedback effect in the causal structure. A Lisrel maximum likelihood estimation procedure allows for modelling of this type, although at the cost of introducing some multicollinearity and correlated estimates. In as far as this procedure is correct (and it is the best thing to do in the present situation), a Lisrel-test shows this feedback-effect (and the original direct effect) to be significant ($\chi^2=5$; NDF=1; p<.05). The mutual causation gives a nice picture of the process of human capital formation, as assumed by the information theory.

But there is another part of the model that is clearly a refutation of the information theory. CULTURAL KNOWLEDGE is a result of the respondents' EDUCATION and OCCUPATION, but not of their family background (FATHER's EDUCATION/OCCUPATION), or the CULTURAL SOCIALIZATION their parents gave them. Whatever the respondents have learned from their parents, when they were young, it is not measured in our CULTURAL KNOWLEDGE-variable, as was predicted by the information theory.

(7) The effect of status-background and cultural socialization

As we can deduce from the model in table-1 status background, as indicated by FATHER's EDUCATION and FATHER's OCCUPATION plays a great part in becoming culturally active. The total effect of family status, net of the status characteristics of the respondents themselves, is estimated on .28. All of this is intermediated by CULTURAL SOCIALIZATION. As we have seen in section 2.6. the information theory fails to explain this part of the observed relations. Family background and cultural socialization do not increase cultural knowledge, as was assumed in the information theory.

To test a status-theoretical interpretation of the effects of family background and cultural socialization, we introduce a CULTURAL NORMS-variable in the model. This variable is equal to the respondent's perception of his interaction partners' cultural consumption. As its information-theoretical counterpart, CULTURAL NORMS has a strong effect on CULTURAL CONSUMPTION (.25). In the same way as in section 3.6., we suspected that CULTURAL NORMS also may be an effect, instead of a cause of CULTURAL CONSUMPTION. Again we introduced a feed-back effect, but this time it turned out to be nearly zero, and clearly insignificant. In more than one way CULTURAL NORMS acts as a counterpart of CULTURAL KNOWLEDGE. It fails to account for the effect of the status characteristics of the respondents themselves, but does give a fairly good interpretation of family background and CULTURAL SOCIALIZATION effects.

(8) The effect of extraversion

The short-version test on EXTRAVERSION has only a weak correlation with CULTURAL CONSUMPTION (.15), and this effect is confounded by effects of AGE and EDUCATION. Conclusion: no positive evidence for the information theory can be submitted to this topic. Since we are dealing with a variable with a low reliability, we have doubts to interpret this as a strong refutation of the information theory.

(9) The effects of status-inconsistency and social mobility

The possible effects of status inconsistency and social mobility are a unique prediction of the status theory. Table-2 gives the impact of the two relevant combinations of ranks. To get around the identification problem, well known from the discussion on comparable analysis problems (Lenski, 1964; Blalock, 1967), we used dummy regression, as recommended by Jackson and Burke (1965). EDUCATION was regressed on FATHER's EDUCATION, and OCCUPATION on EDUCATION. The highest quintile of the residuals was split off to form the group of inconsistents/social climbers in dummy regression.

TABLE-2: The effect of status inconsistency and social mobility (N=347)

	CULTURAL CONSUMPTION	
	B	β
FATHER's EDUCATION	.12	.24
EDUCATION	.20	.41
SOCIAL CLIMBERS (22%)	.14	.06 (p>.10)
R=		.61
EDUCATION	.33	.69
OCCUPATION	-.06	-.09 (p>.30)
INCONSISTENTS (23%)	.48	.21
R=		.60

In the first analysis, just a small and insignificant interaction effect occurs. CULTURAL CONSUMPTION seems to be an additive function of the education of the respondents and their fathers. In the second analysis, the INCONSISTENTS have a higher rate of CULTURAL CONSUMPTION than might have been expected from their EDUCATION and OCCUPATION. The effect of OCCUPATION becomes insignificant on the introduction of the dummy variable for inconsistency. This means that the effect of OCCUPATION as modelled in table-1, is restricted to persons whose OCCUPATION is on a high level in relation to their EDUCATION.

4. Discussion

We have started with two competitive explanatory theories of cultural consumption. In assessing the relative empirical value of the two alternatives, we reviewed results from Dutch leisure research and a recent survey on cultural consumption. The theory of cultural consumption as information-processing gives the best prediction on a majority of topics. In particular, its explanation of the differential effect of the status ranks of the respondents (education, occupation, income) is far more confirmed by the research findings than the status-theoretical explanation. On the other hand, there is one part of our own result, in which it turned out to be the other way around. Both the effect of status background and cultural socialization, apart from the effect of the own status ranks of the respondents, are best explained by the status theory.

Since the direct effects of family background and cultural socialization are rather smaller than that of the respondents' own status we have the general impression that the information theory somehow gives a better explanation. Nevertheless, the status theory cannot be discarded. In future research, we will try to reconcile both viewpoints, and find new testable predictions, and try to give information on topics which now have remained in the background.

Notes

(1) Since almost all of the literature reviewed here is written in Dutch, we will refrain from citing any sources. Persons able to read Dutch are invited to request the original papers:

H. Ganzeboom, Culturele activiteiten als verwerving van status en verwerking van informatie (paper voor de Werkgemeenschap Verklarende Sociologie, Utrecht, Sociologisch Instituut, 1982).

H. Ganzeboom, Cultuurdeelname als verwerking van informatie of verwerving van status - een confrontatie van twee alternatieve verklarende theorieën aan de hand van reeds verricht onderzoek (Mens en Maatschappij, 57-4, 1982).

(2) A full account of all methodological aspects of this study will be given in:
H. Ganzeboom, Beleving van Monumenten-II (Utrecht, Sociologisch Instituut, 1983).

References

BECKER, G.S., (1964), Human Capital, New York: Columbia University Press.

BERLYNE, D.E. (ed.), (1974), Studies in the New Experimental Aesthetics, New York: Wiley.

BLALOCK, H.M., (1967), 'Status Inconsistency, Social Mobility, Status Integration and Structural Effects', American Sociological Review 32: 790-801.

BOURDIEU, P., (1976), 'Elemente einer soziologische Theorie der künstlerischen Wahrnehmung', pp. 58-86 in: A. Silbermann, Theoretische Ansätze der Kunstsoziologie. Stuttgart: Enke.

BOURDIEU, P. & J.C. PASSERON, (1977), Reproduction in Education, Society and Culture. London: Sage.

CBS (NETHERLANDS CENTRAL BUREAU OF STATISTICS), (1981), Recreation Participation and Personal Characteristics, An Explorative Analysis. The Hague: Staatsuitgeverij.

COLLINS, R., (1979), The Credential Society. New York: Academic Press.

EYSENCK, H.J., (1967), The Biological Basis of Personality. Springfield, Ill.: Thomas.

EYSENCK, H.J., (1969), Personality Structure and Measurement. London: Routledge.

HOMANS, G.C., (1974), Human Behavior: Its Elementary Forms. New York: Harcourt.

JACKSON, E.F. & P.J. BURKE, (1965), 'Status Inconsistency and Symptoms of Stress: Additive and Interactive Effects', American Journal of Sociology 20: 556-564.

JÖRESKOG, K.G. & D. SÖRBOM, (1978). LISREL IV, Users Guide. Chicago, Ill.: National Educational Resources.

LENSKI, G., (1964), 'Comment', Public Opinion Quarterly 28: 326-330.

MOLES, A.A., (1971), 'Informationstheorie und ästhetische Wahrnehmung'. Köln: Dumont Schauburg.

WIPPLER, R., (1970), 'Leisure Behavior, A Multivariate Approach', Sociologica Neerlandica 4: 1-ff.

Appendix A: Observed correlations, means, standard deviations and *residuals*

	(1)	(2)	(3)	(4)	(5)	(6)	(7)	(8)	(9)	(10)	(11)	(12)	(13)	(14)	(15)	(16)	(17)	(18)
(1) FATHER's EDUCATION	1.0	-.00	.03	.03	.01	-.04	.02	-.05	-.10	.06	-.05	-.06	-.00	.07	-.02	.04	-.05	.00
(2) FATHER's OCCUPATION	.70	1.0	-.00	.06	-.01	-.05	-.00	.00	-.06	-.04	-.04	-.02	-.05	-.07	.01	.07	-.02	-.02
(3) CULTURAL SOC. THEATRE	.37	.29	1.0	-.05	.08	-.02	-.10	-.06	-.00	-.03	.01	-.01	.05	.05	-.05	.02	.02	-.03
(4) CULTURAL SOC. CONCERTS	.41	.40	.22	1.0	-.05	.09	-.01	.01	-.07	-.04	-.06	-.02	-.01	-.05	-.05	.00	-.10	.03
(5) CULTURAL SOC. MUSEUMS	.44	.36	.39	.30	1.0	-.03	.03	.01	-.04	-.02	-.01	-.04	.05	.07	.01	.01	.04	.18
(6) CULTURAL SOC. READING	.38	.31	.29	.44	.36	1.0	.04	.09	.02	.06	.02	.03	.06	.02	-.01	.02	-.04	-.10
(7) EDUCATION	.53	.52	.19	.31	.42	.41	1.0	-.00	-.04	.00	.01	.01	.06	.04	-.05	-.07	-.00	.00
(8) OCCUPATION	.29	.41	.14	.23	.27	.35	.68	1.0	.00	.01	-.07	-.02	-.00	.06	-.00	.07	.01	-.00
(9) INCOME	-.04	.05	.04	-.01	-.07	.09	.15	.37	1.0	.05	-.04	-.05	-.03	-.01	.00	-.03	-.05	-.00
(10) CULTURAL KNOWLEDGE	.33	.32	.20	.15	.23	.27	.46	.42	.19	1.0	.02	-.03	-.01	-.05	.00	.05	.04	-.08
(11) CULTURAL NORMS HIST. PLACES	.18	.16	.18	.13	.20	.24	.22	.10	.09	.18	1.0	.01	-.05	.03	-.02	-.03	-.04	-.04
(12) CULTURAL NORMS MUSEUM	.24	.24	.21	.23	.23	.24	.30	.29	.20	.10	.16	1.0	.00	-.02	-.03	-.06	-.04	-.09
(13) CULTURAL NORMS THEATRE	.21	.24	.20	.16	.25	.25	.26	.15	.14	.13	.36	.52	1.0	.06	.03	.07	.06	.00
(14) THEATRE & CONCERTS	.47	.43	.31	.23	.40	.34	.52	.37	-.01	.37	.30	.37	.39	1.0	.02	.01	-.03	.02
(15) MUSEUMS & EXHIBITIONS	.37	.37	.21	.25	.34	.32	.45	.36	.13	.45	.27	.35	.30	.66	1.0	-.02	.05	.04
(16) BOOKS & MAGAZINES	.38	.38	.25	.26	.30	.44	.51	.42	.14	.44	.23	.27	.30	.56	.57	1.0	-.02	.03
(17) HISTORICAL PLACES	.28	.32	.24	.14	.32	.24	.41	.31	.06	.41	.28	.27	.28	.50	.60	.46	1.0	.01
(18) AGE	-.37	-.24	-.10	-.17	-.34	-.06	-.34	-.00	-.17	-.04	-.03	-.01	-.07	-.31	-.21	-.18	-.15	1.0
Means	2.6	3.4	1.5	1.5	1.7	2.1	3.3	3.2	3.0	0	5.0	5.0	5.5	0	0	1	1	40
Standard deviations	2.0	1.6	.7	.5	.8	.8	2.0	1.5	1.8	1	2.6	2.6	2.4	1	1	1	1	18

Appendix B: Estimated correlations for the model in table-1

	(1)	(2)	(3)	(4)	(5)	(6)	(7)	(8)	(9)	(10)	(11)	(12)	(13)	(14)
(1) FATHER's EDUCATION	1.0													
(2) FATHER's OCCUPATION	.70	1.0												
(3) CULTURAL SOCIALIZATION	.68	.58	1.0											
(4) EDUCATION	.51	.52	.59	1.0										
(5) OCCUPATION	.34	.40	.42	.68	1.0									
(6) INCOME	.06	.10	.11	.20	.37	1.0								
(7) CULTURAL KNOWLEDGE	.27	.28	.34	.46	.42	.14	1.0							
(8) CULTURAL NORMS	.35	.31	.52	.32	.26	.19	.23	1.0						
(9) CULTURAL CONSUMPTION	.48	.44	.65	.61	.45	.16	.55	.54	1.0					
(10) THEATRE & CONCERTS	.41	.36	.52	.49	.31	.00	.43	.41	.78	1.0				
(11) MUSEUM & EXHIBITIONS	.39	.36	.53	.50	.37	.13	.45	.44	.82	.64	1.0			
(12) BOOKS & MAGAZINES	.34	.32	.47	.44	.32	.11	.39	.38	.71	.56	.58	1.0		
(13) HISTORICAL PLACES	.32	.30	.44	.41	.30	.11	.37	.36	.67	.53	.55	.48	1.0	
(14) AGE	-.37	-.26	-.25	-.33	-.01	-.17	-.12	-.11	-.21	-.29	-.17	-.15	-.14	1.0

Ute Kort-Krieger

STRUCTURAL DETERMINANTS OF OBJECTIVE AND SUBJECTIVE STATUS

Introduction

In this paper we stress two points, a theoretical and a methodological one. The theoretical discussion analyses the relationship between an individual's objective and subjective social status. We review relevant literature and develop a causal model with the structural determinants of social status. For the analysis we use the program LISREL which combines characteristics of factor-, path- and regression-analysis. Data are from a representative sample of the West-German election population in 1980. Results so far show that -by modifications in applying LISREL- the fit between the theoretical model and the data can considerably be improved.

1. Theory

1.1. From 'false consciousness' to 'subjective reality'

Up to the present day, social structure analysis has been profoundly stimulated by Marx' "discovery" and analysis of false consciousness. False consciousness occurs when the subjective positioning in the class structure is not in accordance with the objective class situation of a social group in terms of the social relations of production. Marx (1965: 125) began his class analysis with the description of the social and political situation of the lower peasantry in 19th century France. He argues that only the existence of class consciousness constitutes a social class (class-for-itself). If such a consciousness does not exist in a group with the same social and economic background, a latent class (class-in-itself) is constituted. The non-owning classes can fulfil their historical role in the development of class-conflict only if they recognize (and act in accordance with) their objectively true class interests. In the Marxist view objectivity is given when consciousness and action are in accordance with the historical stages of the development of class conflict. In the final stage there will be no false consciousness, that is, the objective conditions will determine the subjective minds and actions. But until today people always have different perceptions of their social position in contrast to their 'objective' class situation. However, this raises the question of the subjective reconstruction of reality, and of the causes for motivation and action of people in a particular society. Lukacs (1970: 127) was aware of this problem and pointed out the practical significance of the contradiction between the objective economic totality and the subjective interpretation of reality for both political attitudes and action.

Today the analyses of social reality, irrespective of the approach used, show that 'false consciousness' is inherent in every society. The problem is to explain this phenomenon and demonstrate consequences for both the social and political structure and the action of the members of the society concerned.

One rather 'radical' solution for this problem is offered by the subjectivistic approach in arguing that there is no such a thing as an 'objective' social structure, that the 'real' or 'significant' social reality (in terms of relevance for social action) is to be found in the subjective perception of the people. Lloyd Warner's (1949) 'Jonesville' is an example of a totally subjectivistic analysis of social structure. The criteria are taken from different persons' subjective judgements about the social position of an individual and no 'objective' data are reviewed. Coxon and Jones (1978: 12) argue in their study of occupational structure that it is possible that the 'objective' characteristics may only be 'seemingly' so and that cognitions may vary according to the people's own experience with the social system. Of course, the variations of experience are -in turn- dependent on the social position in the social structure, but may not be totally explicable by this because different experiences can be observed within the same class. So the stress is not so much on the 'objective' positioning of persons as in classical Marxist analysis but on trying to identify different 'subjective' interpretations of the individual's situation in society.

Apart from the solely subjectivistic approaches, the center of the debate is still constituted by the Marxist categories of the individual's subjective and objective classification in society, basically assuming that there is or should be a correlation of social position, interests and motivation for action. However, this does not deny the existence of social processes leading to the gap between 'objective' and 'subjective' worlds and the constitution of different subjective realities.

In West-Germany there are two recent rather 'pure' Marxist approaches to class analysis designed with the aim of developing appropriate strategies for Communist agitation and action (Projekt Klassenanalyse, 1975 and Institut für Marxistische Studien und Forschungen, 1974). Capital ownership as the main criterion for the definition of social classes is used in both studies. Data are taken from the official statistics; methods of analysis and results differ in some ways we cannot discuss here. The common general conclusion was, however, that 'objectively' a growing proletarisation but 'subjectively' a growing embourgeoisement of the West-German population between 1950 and 1970 can be observed. That is: false consciousness is growing. The 'solution' is seen in the Marxist or rather Leninist elitist strategy of political agitation of the Communist party to overcome the gap between the subjective (false) ideas of the people and 'restore' the law of history.

The pluralistic approach -on the other hand- denies the relevance of the Marxist criteria of capital ownership because in differentiated modern society it is overruled by overlapping group membership. So class-identification does not emerge as there is no single group dominating an individual's consciousness. Consequently, dimensions of top and bottom are widely neglected as Hodge and Treiman (1968) illustrated by noting that 80 percent of the US-population claim to belong to the middle class. The interest-group approach modifies both the Marxist and the pluralistic view, stating that the economic factor (not necessarily restricted to capital ownership) principally determines the basic interest conflicts not only between the classes but also the variations of social and economic chances within the non-ownership classes (Jackman and Jackman, 1973).

This idea corresponds with Mill's (1962) theoretical analysis that not pure ownership but control of production means is the core of modern capitalism. For our analysis we follow Mill's critical remarks on Marx' theory and philosophy, arguing that his categories for class analysis are still relevant even though his theories and speculations about the development of capitalist society have not yet been verified.

From the foregoing discussion of the different theoretical and empirical approaches we conclude for our present analysis that neither approach answers all questions about the gap between the 'objective' and 'subjective' social structure or -to put it in Marx' terms- the development of false consciousness. Therefore we try to integrate different approaches to find some explanation for the existence and development of this gap. After the analysis of structural determinants of objective and subjective status in this paper the consequences of a certain state of subjective consciousness for the individual's perception of social economic and political conditions and the development of (class-) interests in a society are investigated in the following paper (Schmidt, 1982).

With this kind of analysis we try to integrate three traditions of sociological research: the empirical social research tradition which often lacks a theoretical foundation; the Marxist tradition which generally lacks precision; and the utilitarian tradition which frequently ignores both the basic structural conditions for the formation of individual interests and the cognitions determining the individual's preferences (Ultee, 1980).

The hypotheses developed so far for the construction of our theoretical model of features of social structure have the character of 'low level laws'. But we hope that after clarifying these structures -and this is what the paper is about- we can procede to integrate the results (Opp, 1982) into a more general theory of behavior to explain what has not been explained so far. This general theory would have to state the conditions under which our low level laws are true. In the paper of Schmidt (1982) the cognitive-hedonistic approach is proposed as such a general theory to be applied to our problem for explanation: the gap between the objective status of individuals and their subjective judgements about this.

1.2. A causal model for people's social ranking

Using basic ideas of the theoretical approaches discussed above we can now construct a causal model to specify the relation between the 'objective' and 'subjective' positioning of individuals in the social structure of West-German society.

We measure an individual's 'objective' status by the indicators education, occupation and income, and 'subjective status' by two different judgements of the individual about his own place in society. 'Objectivity' is thus defined in a very relativistic sense: the status may be called 'objective' only because the criteria for measurement are relatively less dependent on individual perceptions than the ones for measuring 'subjective status'. To some extent we follow the analyses of Hodge and Treiman (1968) and Jackman and Jackman (1973). Although objective status has regularly been measured by multiple indicators, subjective status only occurs in one indicator. Kluegel et al. (1977) criticized this, arguing that it is closer to social reality to assume that people also judge their subjective status according to different dimensions. Moreover, they hoped that a multidimensional measurement of subjective status would strengthen the relation between subjective and objective status. They used the Weberian categories 'class' (occupation, income), 'status' (life style) and 'power' (influence). Although they got stronger correlations between the subjective and objective indicators, the relation between the theoretical or latent constructs for status did not improve. Sörbom and Jöreskog (1980) reanalyzed Kluegel's et al. data with LISREL, a program for the analysis of LInear Structural RElationship among quantitative variables. The advantage of LISREL is that it tests simulaneously the so-called 'measurement model' (the relations between the indicators and their latent variables) and the 'structural model' (the relations between the latent or theoretical variables). By controlling for measurement errors and analyzing subjective and objective status multidimensionally, they did not get significantly stronger correlations between objective and subjective status.

From a theoretical point of view we find this basic model consisting of two variables rather unsatisfying. We think we can explain more of the social structure when considering a wider social context. An individual's social position is not only defined by more or less objective or subjective judgements but additionally by interaction and communication with members of different social background. Moreover, the individual's own social background is an essential predisposition for determining his final position in society and his ideas about this position. So the formation of an individual's subjective consciousness about his social position is influenced by the 'milieu' of his socialization and of his actual communication outside the family as well as by some 'objective' criteria. We therefore add two variables to the original model:

social origin (indicated by father's education and father's occupation) and contact status (indicated by the 'average' of the values for the occupational positions of the three closest friends). Now our basic model contains the following variables (with indicators) and paths:

FIGURE-1: The basic model

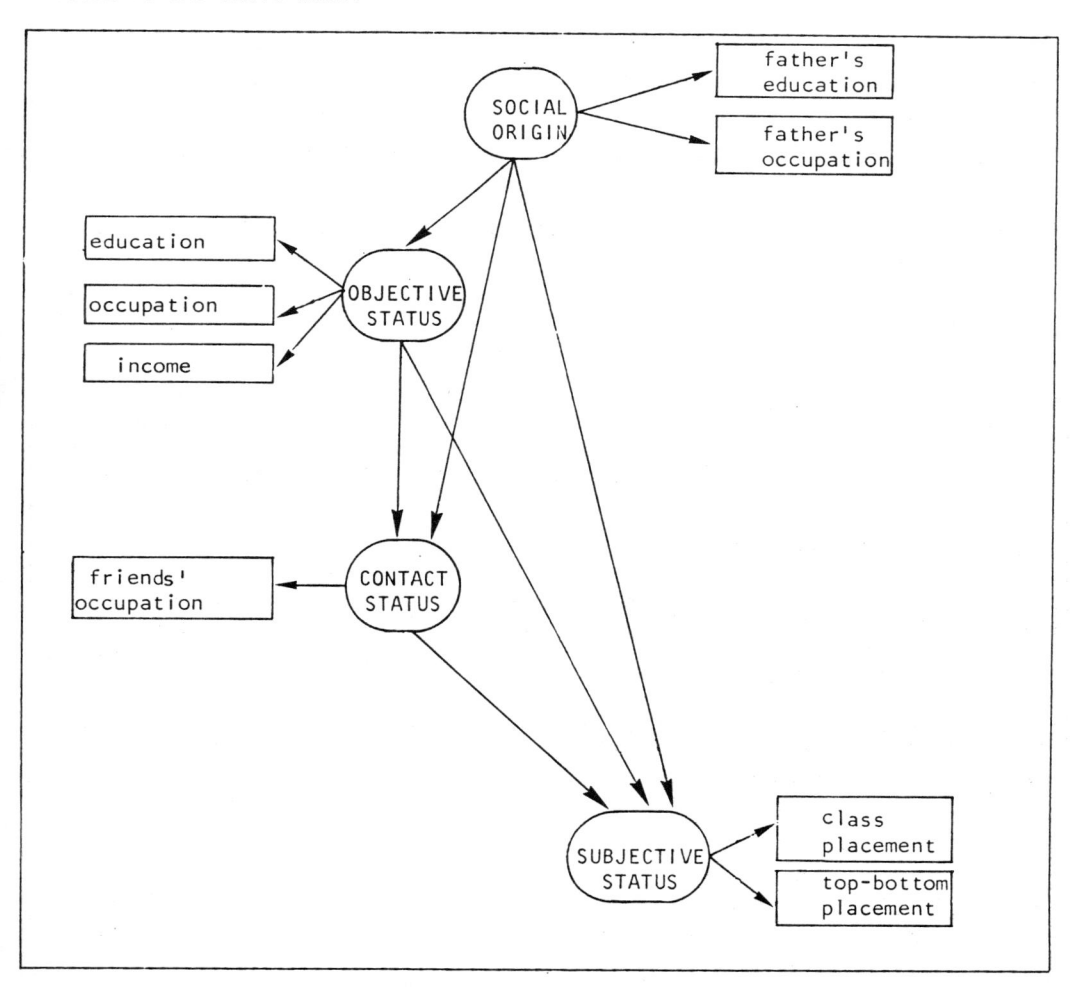

2. Sample and measurement procedures

Data are taken from the National Social Survey 1980, done by the Zentrum für Umfragen, Methoden und Analysen (ZUMA) in Mannheim (West Germany). The sample consists of 2955 persons and is representative for the election population of West Germany. For the test of the model we used only the subgroup of employees in the sample: 1409 individuals. We did this because we think that the status indicators used, such as occupation and income, which refer directly to an employment situation, have different meanings for those employed and those who are not employed. Later, we intend to compare these two groups. All eight variables shown above in the model (cf. Figure 1) are measured by interval scales. The appendix contains the questions and frequency distributions for all variables.

Table 1 shows measurement procedures, means and standard deviations for the eight variables.

TABLE-1: Scales, means and standard deviations

	variable	measurement procedure	mean	standard deviation	N	missing cases
social origin	FATHER's EDUCATION	5-point scale	2.32	.83	1172	237
	FATHER's OCCUPATION	5-point scale	2.55	1.03	1174	235
objective status	EDUCATION	6-point scale	2.50	1.32	1394	15
	OCCUPATION	5-point scale	2.68	1.02	1365	44
	INCOME	5-point scale	2.19	.84	1206	203
	FRIENDS' OCCUPATION	5-point scale	2.10	.93	1194	215
subjective status	CLASS PLACEMENT	5-point scale	2.83	.61	1355	54
	TOP/BOTTOM PLACEMENT	5-point scale	3.20	.74	1386	23

Table 1 can best be interpreted by the people's perception of their self in the hierarchy of the social structure. First people tend to place themselves subjectively higher (2.83 and 3.20 respectively on the two subjective indicators), than their status is measured objectively (2.68). The friends' status -on the other hand- ranks lowest (2.10) whereas the social origin (as indicated by father's occupation) is seen in a medium position (2.55). It must be borne in mind that the subjective indicators are measured by other scales than the objective indicators for occupation of self, father and friends (see Appendix) and, therefore, are not strictly comparable. Still, the comparison may be taken as showing -if only tentatively- the trend discussed first.

Looking at the frequency distributions (in the Appendix) reveals that the subjective ranking of the own position centers around the medium categories: more than 50 percent consider themselves to be middle class. Accordingly the extremes of the scale at the top and bottom ends are rather ignored. The objective indicators suggest only 36 percent to belong to the middle categories, whereas the objective ranking of top and bottom gives a more distinct impression of social hierarchy. Therefore we cannot readily agree with the conclusion that we live in a middle-class society because most people say they are middle-class. There might be other social criteria contradicting this judgement. At least it seems that social reality is a little more complex!

3. Data analysis

3.1. The basic model

Essentially a LISREL-model consists of two parts: the structural model with the exogenous and endogenous variables (in circles), and the measurement model with the indicators (in squares). The structural model contains the causal structure we propose and want to test, namely -all relations between the variables being positive-:

(a) The OBJECTIVE and SUBJECTIVE STATUS of an individual are dependent on his SOCIAL ORIGIN.
(b) The OBJECTIVE STATUS influences the SUBJECTIVE and the STATUS of the social CONTACTS.
(c) The STATUS of the social CONTACTS influences the SUBJECTIVE STATUS.

In addition to this causal structure, LISREL tests the measurement model. As our variables in the structural model are latent variables, i.e. are not measured directly but by indicators, we have to test whether our specifications of the measurements (and errors) are adequate.

For data input we use the intercorrelation matrix of the eight indicators.

We begin the interpretation of the results by looking at the structural model
containing our basic hypotheses. The Beta-coefficients can be interpreted as
standardized regression coefficients.

The 'main' relation between the OBJECTIVE and SUBJECTIVE STATUS amounts to a
Beta-coefficient of .60. Thus, the OBJECTIVE STATUS rather strongly influences
the SUBJECTIVE STATUS of an individual, although -as in other analyses- the
relationship is not 'perfect'. There are also -as we proposed- influences from
SOCIAL ORIGIN on the SUBJECTIVE and OBJECTIVE STATUS. The SOCIAL ORIGIN (in
terms of father's occupation and education) strongly determines the individual's
OBJECTIVE STATUS (.56) but much less so the SUBJECTIVE STATUS (.15).

What about the role of social contacts in defining a person's status? We
proposed that the OBJECTIVE STATUS determines choices people make in selecting
friends and that the status of friends -on the other hand- adds to the subjective
definition of one's own status. The first part of our hypothesis was found to be
evident as the relation between the OBJECTIVE STATUS and CONTACT STATUS is rather
strong: .45, but there is no sizable coefficient between the CONTACT STATUS and
the SUBJECTIVE STATUS: At least with this model structure we could not prove that
the status of one's friends in any way influences the subjective consciousness
about one's own position. On the other hand we found a relation between the
SOCIAL ORIGIN 'determining' in some (rather weak) way (.09) the social status
of one's friends.

Before considering the results in detail we have to realize that the overall
fit of our basic model is rather poor: with 16 degrees of freedom there is a
Chi-square of 86. A good fit would approach a 1:1 ratio between the degrees of
freedom and the Chi-square value. The LISREL program provides information to be
utilized for a reformulation of the model to achieve a better fit. Moreover we
think that another reason for the bad fit of the basic model might be that there
are also relations between the indicators, not only between the theoretical
constructs they measure, and that the construct variables such as SOCIAL ORIGIN
are dependent on their indicators and not vice versa as in the basic model. For
instance, in the basic model we assume that SOCIAL ORIGIN influences FATHER's
EDUCATION and OCCUPATION. Now we want to specify that SOCIAL ORIGIN is dependent
on FATHER's EDUCATION and OCCUPATION and FATHER's EDUCATION influences his
OCCUPATION. In the generalized form LISREL allows this kind of specification.

TABLE-2   Intercorrelation Matrix (Pearson standardized correlation coefficients).

	(1)	(2)	(3)	(4)	(5)	(6)	(7)	(8)
(1) FATHER's EDUCATION	1.000							
(2) FATHER's OCCUPATION	.542	1.000						
(3) EDUCATION	.362	.318	1.000					
(4) OCCUPATION	.305	.377	.537	1.000				
(5) INCOME	.192	.166	.436	.515	1.000			
(6) CONTACT STATUS	.254	.262	.360	.410	.300	1.000		
(7) CLASS PLACEMENT	.287	.343	.409	.504	.314	.322	1.000	
(8) TOP/BOTTOM PLACEMENT	.111	.136	.165	.246	.230	.120	.352	1.000

LISREL tests the specified structure of the model by maximum-likelihood estimation of the coefficients. The adequacy of the fit between the specified model and the data is indicated by a Chi-square test and some other informations in the program. The results for our basic model and the fit according to the Chi-square test are shown in Figure 2.

FIGURE-2:   Results for the basic model ($\chi^2 = 86$; NDF = 16; p = 0.0)

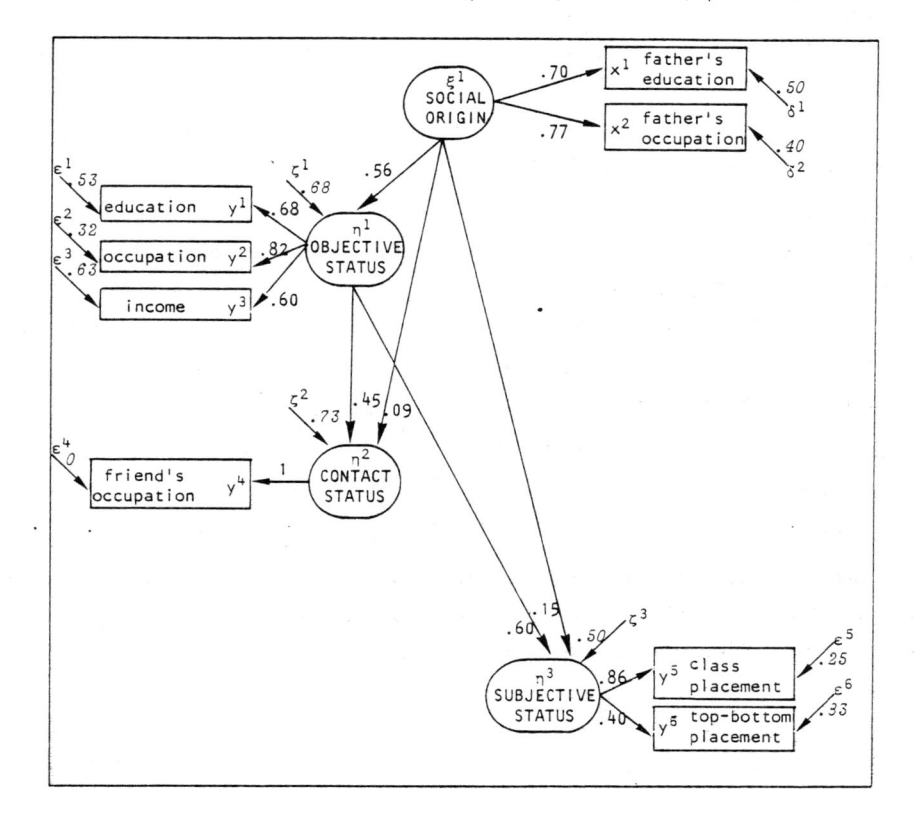

3.2. The generalized model

The main difference between the basic and the generalized models is that six of the previous eight indicators are specified as latent variables measured by only one indicator each. Only the SUBJECTIVE STATUS remains unchanged with two indicators. Now we can alter the causal direction in the indicated way for SOCIAL ORIGIN and OBJECTIVE STATUS. The hypotheses (a), (b), (c) (see section 3.1) about the causal structure of the basic model remain the same in the generalized model. Hypotheses about the 'inner' causal structure of the SOCIAL ORIGIN and OBJECTIVE STATUS are added.

(d) SOCIAL ORIGIN is dependent on FATHER's EDUCATION and OCCUPATION.
 FATHER's EDUCATION influences his OCCUPATION.
(e) OBJECTIVE STATUS is dependent on EDUCATION, OCCUPATION and INCOME.
 Additionally OCCUPATION is dependent on EDUCATION, INCOME on EDUCATION and OCCUPATION
(f) SOCIAL ORIGIN influences OBJECTIVE STATUS (see (b)) and also its indicators EDUCATION, OCCUPATION and INCOME.

The fit for the generalized model is much better than in the basic model: 13 degrees of freedom and a Chi-square of 46 (instead of 16 df and Chi-square of 86). In addition, we found direct relations between the variables FATHER's EDUCATION and EDUCATION and OCCUPATION of the respondent. By adding these two paths (indicated by the two broken lines in Figure 3) we could improve the fit with 11 degrees of freedom and a value for Chi-square of 25.

Basic model	16 df	$chi^2 = 86$	$p = 0.0$
Generalized model 1	13 df	$chi^2 = 46$	$p = 0.0$
Generalized model 2	11 df	$chi^2 = 25$	$p = 0.0086$

Table 3 shows the residuals for both models. The differences between S and Sigma are all less than .10, which is a quite satisfactory result for the fit of the theoretically specified models and the data.

Figure 3 represents our basic model in generalized form.

FIGURE-3: Results for the generalized model ($\chi^2 = 25$, NDF = 11, p = .0086).

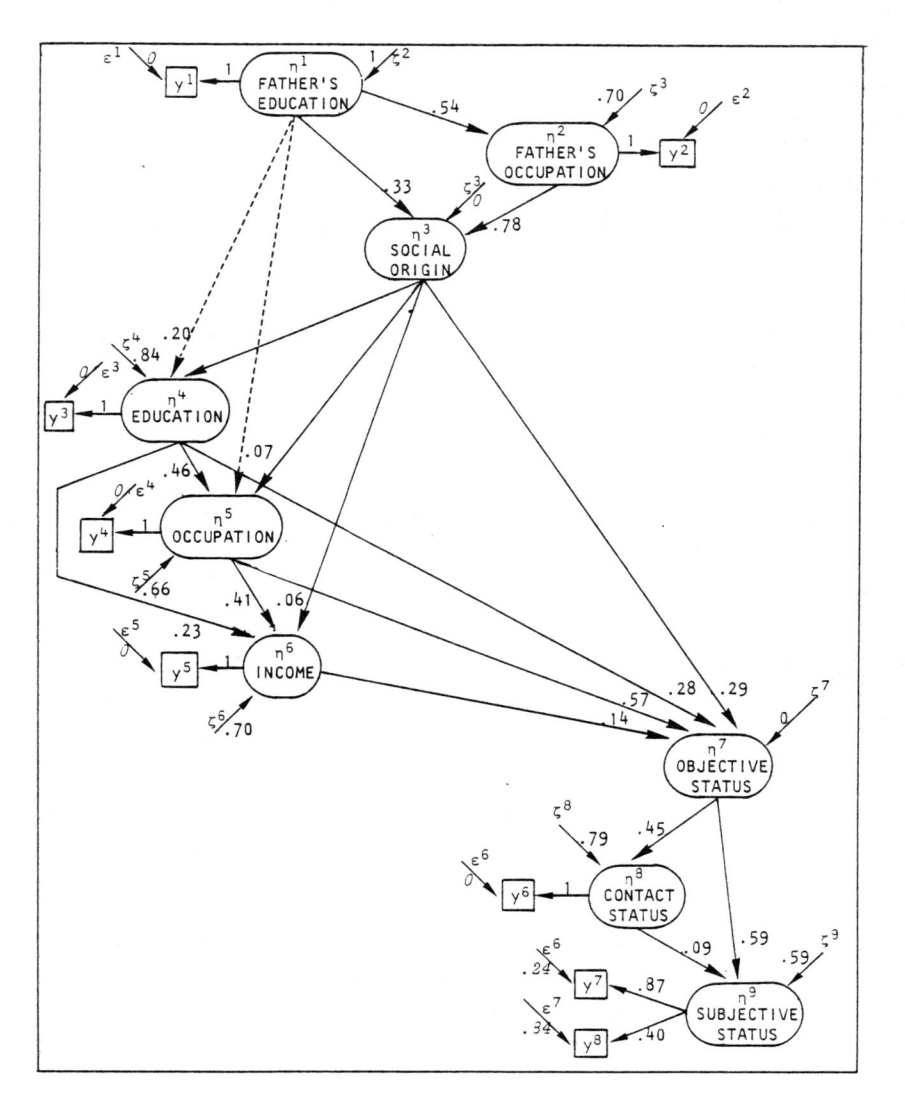

TABLE-3: Residuals (S - Sigma) for the Basic Model (below the diagonal) and for the Generalized Model (above the diagonal)

	(1)	(2)	(3)	(4)	(5)	(6)	(7)	(8)
(1) EDUCATION		-.000	-.000	.014	-.006	-.028	.000	-.000
(2) OCCUPATION	-.023		-.000	-.007	.004	.014	-.000	-.000
(3) INCOME	.024	.019		.019	-.023	.074	.024	-.010
(4) CONTACT	.014	-.006	-.007		.004	-.028	.017	-.016
(5) CLASS PLACEMENT	.001	.013	-.048	.010		-.000	.003	.009
(6) TOP/BOTTOM PLACEMENT	-.028	.014	.059	-.027	-.000		-.021	-.019
(7) FATHER's EDUCATION	.092	-.020	-.047	.009	-.012	-.030		-.000
(8) FATHER's OCCUPATION	.021	.020	-.097	-.007	.014	-.019	.000	

Now we look at the results in detail to compare them with the basic model. The relations between OBJECTIVE and SUBJECTIVE STATUS remain nearly the same (.59) as in the basic model (.60), also the influence of the OBJECTIVE on the CONTACT STATUS: .45 in both models. In contrast to the basic model there is a -although low- relationship between CONTACT and own SUBJECTIVE STATUS (.10). The rather 'strong' influence of SOCIAL ORIGIN on OBJECTIVE STATUS in the basic model (.56) was, however, halved to .29 in the generalized model. This might be an effect of the additional estimate of the direct relations between SOCIAL ORIGIN and the indicators of OBJECTIVE STATUS: EDUCATION (.22), OCCUPATION (.28) and INCOME (.06). There is no direct influence any more from SOCIAL ORIGIN to SUBJECTIVE STATUS. (.15 in the basic model).

Another important point about the adequacy of the model is the explained variance of the dependent variable SUBJECTIVE STATUS, indicated by the residuals. In the basic model it is 75% (1 - $.50^2$), in the generalized model 65% (1 - $.59^2$). So less variance of subjective status is explained in the generalized model. However, the generalized model gives us information about the 'inner structure' of the theoretical constructs or latent variables SOCIAL ORIGIN and OBJECTIVE STATUS. As Figure 3 shows, the indicators have rather strong relations between each other as well as rather strong effects on their latent variable. In the case of SOCIAL ORIGIN: FATHER's EDUCATION influences his OCCUPATION .54, the SOCIAL ORIGIN as well with .33. FATHER's EDUCATION influences SOCIAL ORIGIN .78. In the case for OBJECTIVE STATUS: EDUCATION influences OCCUPATION .46, INCOME .23. OCCUPATION influences INCOME .41. All three indicators influence their latent variable OBJECTIVE STATUS: EDUCATION .28, OCCUPATION .57 and INCOME .14.

The results discussed so far should suffice to demonstrate the rather complex relations between the structural determinants of people's objective and subjective status in the social hierarchy, indicated especially by the different weights of the coefficients. Although the basic causal direction has been confirmed:

SOCIAL ORIGIN → OBJECTIVE STATUS → CONTACT STATUS → SUBJECTIVE STATUS

the various indicators contribute with different weights to this result. One clear example is to be seen in the case of INCOME. The higher the INCOME, the higher the OBJECTIVE STATUS, although the coefficient is only .14, while the OCCUPATIONAL status contributes strongest (.57) to the OBJECTIVE STATUS, followed by the EDUCATIONal status (.28).

4. Theoretical conclusions

Now we want to draw some conclusions concerning the theoretical problems we started with: false consciousness, subjective reality and the structural determinants for the gap between the objective and subjective status. As we proposed, social background and the social status of the friends do in fact directly determine and explain to a certain extent the relation or the gap between the objective and subjective status of an individual. However, the objective status is more strongly affected by these determinants than is the subjective: either as dependent variable (from social origin) or as independent variable, influencing the choice of friends according to social status. That is to say: the status of the social contacts is strongly dependent on the individual's own objective status, but does not seem to influence the subjective judgements people make about their place in the social hierarchy significantly. Also the social background -while strongly affecting people's objective status- does not (at least not directly) seem to play a comparable role in these subjective judgements.

In other words and to stress this important point a little further: having achieved a position in society, the individual's ideas about this differ from what society would 'concede' he has achieved and the individual's ideas seem to be rather 'independent' of his social background.

The same holds for the communication pattern: people choose friends similar to their own objective status but this -too- has little effect on their own subjective ideas about their social position in society.

Maybe these are reasons for the occurence of the 'gap' between the two kinds of status we analysed. Although they are not independent -on the contrary they are strongly related (.60)- structural determinants affect the objective and subjective status differently. Whereas the objective status seems to be -as ever and contrary to all ideology about equal chances- strongly dependent on social background, people subjectively have other ideas about their place in society. Obviously people believe in this ideology that -irrespective of their social background- they get ahead. Therefore we did not find a sizeable relation between social origin and subjective status in our analysis. Moreover, people choose friends similar in status who do not influence them otherwise and -very important- they think of themselves as being in a higher social position than 'objective' criteria would concede.

This is, of course 'good' for a society in terms of its stability! In terms of 'false consciousness' and 'subjective reality' we cannot help but ask for the reasons for this kind of 'objective reality'. Obviously, even without applying Marxist criteria for objectivity we find evidence for a social process that 'produces' a gap between these kinds of realities.

Whether it is called 'false consciousness' in terms of Marxist theory, which is designed to guide actions aiming at changing society, or whether it is expressed as 'subjective reality', with the relation between objective and subjective status being 'far from perfect', is a matter of theoretical and/or political taste. The Marxist inquires into the political and social interests that are in favor of producing and keeping up the 'false consciousness' of the people. Others are satisfied with knowing what kind of subjective reality is responsible for motivation and actions.

We think it would be most reasonable to combine these kinds of thinking. It might then be possible to learn not only what reality looks like for the people but also why reality looks like that. As mentioned before, the application of a more general theory of behavior could probably serve as the combining link between these two kinds of reasoning. For instance, the cognitive-hedonistic approach (cf. Schmidt, 1982) would state that the formation of individual cognitions concerning social structure is guided not only by those objective and subjective but also by other criteria involved in the social situation.

One example may be that -because of egalitarian values of the society concerned- people tend to place themselves neither at the top nor at the bottom of social hierarchy. There might be other similar determinants of a more general character which help to explain the gap.

References

COXON, A.P.M. and Ch.L. JONES, (1978), The Images of Occupational Prestige. London: MacMillan.

GRAFF, J. and P. SCHMIDT, (1982), A Generalized Model for Decomposition of Effects, in: K.G. Jöreskog and H. Wold, (eds.), Systems under Direct Observation. Amsterdam: North Holland.

HODGE, R.W. and J. TREIMAN, (1968), Class Identification in the United States, American Journal of Sociology 73: 535-547.

INSTITUT FUER MARXISTISCHE STUDIEN UND FORSCHUNGEN (IMSF), (1974), Klassen- und Sozialstruktur der BRD 1950-1970. Frankfurt: Verlag Marxistische Blaetter.

JACKMAN, M.R. and R.W. JACKMAN (1973), An Interpretation of the Relation between Objective and Subjective Social Status, American Sociological Review 38: 569-582.

JAEGGI, U., (1976), Sozialstruktur und Politische Systeme. Köln: Kiepenheuer und Witsch.

KLUEGEL, J.R., R. SINGLETON, and Ch.E. STARNES (1977), Subjective Class Identification: A Multiple Indicator Approach, American Sociological Review 42: 599-611.

LUKACS, G., (1970), Geschichte und Klassenbewusstsein. Neuwied: Luchterhand.

MARX, K., (1965), Der 18. Brumaire des Louis Bonaparte. Frankfurt: Insel (first published 1852).

MILLS, C.W., (1962), The Marxists. New York: Dell Publishing Company.

MUELLER, W., (1975), Familie-Schule-Beruf. Opladen: Westdeutscher Verlag.

OPP, K.-D., (1982), Economics, Sociology and Political Protest, in this volume.

PROJEKT KLASSENANALYSE, (1974), Materialien zur Klassenstruktur der BRD. West Berlin: Verlag für das Studium der Arbeiterbewegung.

SCHMIDT, P., (1982), Subjective Status Identification, Class Consciousness and Political Attitudes, in this volume.

SÖRBOM, D. and K.G. JÖRESKOG, (1980), The Use of LISREL in Sociological Model Building, pp. 179-199 in: E.F. Borgatta and D. Jackson (eds.), Factor Analysis and Measurement in Sociological Research. Beverly Hills: Sage.

ULTEE, W.C., (1980), Fortschritt und Stagnation in der Soziologie. Neuwied: Luchterhand.

WARNER, E.L., M. MECKER and K. ELLS (1949), Social Class in America. New York: Science Research Association.

Appendix

Questionnaire

FATHER's EDUCATION

'What kind of school did your father finish?'

	FREQUENCY		
	abs.	relat. (%)	adjusted (%)
1. none	23	1.6	2.0
2. elementary	930	66.0	79.4
3. middle	115	8.2	9.8
4. polytechnic	29	2.1	2.5
5. secondary	75	5.3	6.4
0	237	16.8	missing
	1409	100.0	100.0

FATHER's OCCUPATION

'When you were 15 years old: Which occupational status did your father have?'
(Originally 30 occupation categories were used, then recoded into a 5-point scale).

	FREQUENCY		
	abs.	relat. (%)	adjusted (%)
1. un-, semi-skilled	176	12.5	15.0
2. skilled	423	30.0	36.0
3. middle qualif.	385	27.0	32.0
4. high qualif.	132	9.4	11.2
5. professional	58	4.1	4.9
0	235	16.7	missing
	1409	100.0	100.0

EDUCATION

'What kind of occupational training did you finish?'
(Originally 8 occupational training categories were used, then recoded into a 6-point scale).

	FREQUENCY		
	abs.	relat. (%)	adjusted (%)
1. none	191	13.6	13.7
2. elementary	799	56.7	57.3
3. secondary: low	141	10.0	10.1
4. secondary: high	108	7.7	7.7
5. polytechnic	58	4.1	4.2
6. university	97	6.9	7.0
0	15	1.1	missing
	1409	100.0	100.0

OCCUPATION

'Which occupational status do you have?'
(For recoding see: FATHER's OCCUPATION).

	FREQUENCY		
	abs.	relat. (%)	adjusted (%)
1. un-, semi-skilled	171	12.1	12.5
2. skilled	421	29.9	30.8
3. middle qualif.	501	35.6	36.7
4. high qualif.	212	15.0	15.5
5. professional	60	4.3	4.4
0	44	3.1	missing
	1409	100.0	100.0

INCOME

'What is your monthly net income after withholding taxes and social security?'
(income was measured in German marks and recoded into the following groups).

	FREQUENCY		
	abs.	relat. (%)	adjusted (%)
1. - 1.000 DM	202	14.3	16.8
2. 1.001 - 2.000 DM	672	47.7	55.7
3. 2.001 - 3.000 DM	258	18.3	21.4
4. 3.001 - 4.000 DM	45	3.2	3.7
5. 4.001 and more	29	2.1	2.4
0	203	14.5	missing
	1409	100.0	100.0

FRIENDS' OCCUPATION

Sum of the occupational status of the 3 closest friends, divided by 3.
(For recoding see: FATHER's OCCUPATION).

	FREQUENCY		
	abs.	relat. (%)	adjusted (%)
1. un-, semi-skilled	344	24.4	28.8
2. skilled	492	34.9	41.2
3. middle qualification	261	18.5	21.9
4. high qualification	87	6.2	7.3
5. professional	10	.7	.8
0	215	15.3	missing
	1409	100.0	100.0

(SUBJECTIVE) CLASS PLACEMENT

'Nowadays there is much talk about social strata of the population. To which social strata do you think you belong more: the lower, the working, the middle, the upper middle or the upper strata?'

	FREQUENCY		
	abs.	relat. (%)	adjusted (%)
1. lower	5	.4	.4
2. working	369	26.2	27.2
3. middle	835	59.3	61.6
4. upper middle	139	9.9	10.3
5. upper	7	.5	.5
0	54	3.8	missing
	1409	100.0	100.0

(SUBJECTIVE) TOP/BOTTOM PLACEMENT

'Now our last question: in our society there are groups in the population more at the top and more at the bottom of the society. Here is such a scale. If you think about yourself: where on this scale would you place yourself?'
(Originally a ten-point scale was used, then recoded into five points).

	FREQUENCY		
	abs.	relat. (%)	adjusted (%)
1. bottom	16	1.1	1.2
2. ..	185	13.1	13.3
3. ..	728	51.7	52.5
4. ..	420	29.8	30.3
5. top	37	2.6	2.7
0	23	1.6	missing
	1409	100.0	100.0

Peter Schmidt

SUBJECTIVE STATUS IDENTIFICATION, CLASS CONSCIOUSNESS AND POLITICAL ATTITUDES

Introduction

"When a traditional positivist applied his criteria of testability to such 'nebulous' visions of social and psychological reality as are involved in Marxism or psychoanalysis, he could formulate only one conclusion; being untestable in their large areas and additionally loaded with value assumptions they have little in common with scientific thinking. They constitute spurious knowledge, belonging rather to the areas of Weltanschauung or ideology than to science. The best thing a real science can do is therefore to get rid of them and to start formulating real -i.e. testable, falsifiable- theories, free of evaluations and therefore unrelated to anything but empirical facts. But are things so simple?" (Nowak, 1982: 6-7).

We believe not and therefore want to explicate the fruitful but vague ideas concerning class consciousness by discussing firstly the relation between subjective status identification, class consciousness and political attitudes. Our model can be regarded as an attached model to Kort-Krieger's (1982) model on the structural determinants of objective and subjective status. In a next step we specify a structural equation model based on this theoretical discussion. The application of a general behavioral theory to the explanation of our lower level propositions relating subjective status identification, class consciousness and political attitudes is dealt with in the next section.

Section 2 contains information concerning the study design, the sampling and the measurement instruments. The core of our empirical analysis is the test and the modification of Structural Equation Models. In our theoretical conclusions we discuss whether by using the more general individualistic theory an increase in the explanatory power of our tested models can be achieved.

1. Theoretical background

1.1. Subjective status identification, class consciousness and political attitudes

The pioneering studies of class consciousness were done by Centers (1949; Swanford et al., 1952) and Converse (Campbell et al., 1960, 1964; Maccoby et al., 1958). All these studies were inspired by the Marxist conception of class structure and class conscience. The central research question was whether a high intensity of class identification or consciousness lead to extreme political views. The just mentioned relationships can be formulated more precisely in the following way:

H_1 Strong working class identifiers tend to associate themselves with positions of the left and strong middle class identifiers tend to associate with positions of the right.

Studying subjective class attitudes Centers found (Swanford et al., 1952) that subjective class differences in attitudes could be summarized by 'two opposite philosophies of government - an individualistic one and a collectivistic one".

H_2 The working class tend to identify with the collectivist philosophy while the middle class tend to identify with the individualistic philosophy.

Centers measured collectivist philosophy by support for federal aid, hostility toward big business, warmth toward unions and support for the Democratic as opposed to the Republican party. Converse essentially agreed with Centers' views and stated that 'differences between liberal and conservative tend to focus on the degree to which the government should assume interest, responsibility and control over these sectors of endeavor'. The sectors where government should intervene referred to natural resources, trade and income distribution . He further stated that

H_3 'people of lower status predominate both among those who rank as liberal in their social welfare attitudes and among the adherents of the liberal party. Citizens in higher strata tend to preserve 'conservative' alternatives to such questions, and give primary support to the conservative party' (Campbell et al., 1964: 116).

Both Centers and Converse postulate a three stage model in which class identification affects ideology and ideology affects voting so that much of the relationship between class and voting may be explained by ideology. They both stated as a background assumption that ideological positions were often poorly developed among the american population and that the model worked best among persons who were knowledgeable and involved in politics.

The major differences between Centers and Converse arose over an issue of methodology and not of theory. Converse argued (Maccoby et al., 1958: 389) that Centers failed to distinguish between what he called 'class consciousness' and 'class awareness', for persons may be willing to place themselves in classes without class membership being salient in their lives. Converse and his co-authors (Campbell et al., 1964: 186) suggested that class-aware persons should differ from unaware but class-identifying persons in a manner consistent with a general hypothesis: The higher the identification of the individual with the group, the higher the probability that he will think and behave in ways which distinguish members of his group from nonmembers. Therefore class-aware persons should represent the most extreme examples of the general view that the working class persons represent a liberal ideology and vote for their class party, the Democrats, while middle class persons represent a conservative ideology and vote for their class party, the Republicans.

Guest (1974) tested these propositions by using longitudinal survey data from 1956 to 1968. He divided the respondents into four groups based on identification with the working class versus the middle class and on admission of awareness of social class membership as opposed to unawareness. Consistent with previous research, working-class identification is associated with collectivist views on the role of government and voting for the Democratic party. Awareness however, contrary to previous research, increases the collectivist tendencies of both the working and middle classes. Furthermore he found that the effects of class identification and awareness on political attitudes show little change over time, although they do seem to have different effects on presidential voting in a Democratic as opposed to Republican majority.

Finally let us discuss a proposal for clarification and explication of the terms class consciousness, class awareness and subjective class identification by Giddens (1979) which supplements the contributions of Centers, Converse and Guest. Giddens (1979: 137) differentiates between three stages of class consciousness. The least developed form implies only the conception of a class identity and differentiation. The perception of class identity is defined in the same way as the concept of awareness by Converse and Gould.

The next stage is characterized by the inclusion of the perception of class conflicts.

The third stage is the revolutionary class consciousness which is characterized by the perceived possibility of a fundamental reorganization in power structure of society and the belief that actions of a class can reach such a reorganization. As Giddens states, Marx did not differentiate between these three forms of class consciousness (Giddens, 1979: 137).

Contrary to Marx, who assumes that subjective class identification leads automatically to perception of class conflicts and that the perception of class conflicts will directly lead to the creation of a revolutionary class consciousness, Giddens argues that there is no deterministic relation between these two concepts. The following proposition can be therefore explicitly formulated:

H_4 The higher the subjective class identification the less people tend to perceive class conflicts.

Furthermore it is important to note that this differentiation is not identical with the differentiation between a class-in-itself (Klasse an sich) and a class-for-itself (Klasse für sich) (See Kort-Krieger, 1982).

1.2. Specification of our model

Using basic ideas of the theoretical approaches discussed we can now construct a causal model to specify the relations between subjective class identification, perception of class conflicts, collectivist/left attitudes and relative deprivation.

Subjective class identification is measured by two different indicators based on judgements of the individual about its own place in society. It is the exogenous latent variable in model. This variable should influence directly the left-right placement of the individuals and the perceived class conflicts measured by three indicators (class conflicts between poor and rich, capitalists and workers, and employer and employees). We can formulate more precisely, that the lower the subjective status identification the more people tend to be left oriented, the more they perceive class conflicts the more they are against the expansion of the private sector and the more they feel relatively deprived. These two variables should influence directly deprivation and collectivistic attitudes measured by degree of approval toward an enlarged private economic sector. Now our basic model is given in figure 1. Latent variables are encircled, whereas indicators are within a rectangle.

FIGURE-1: Specification of our model

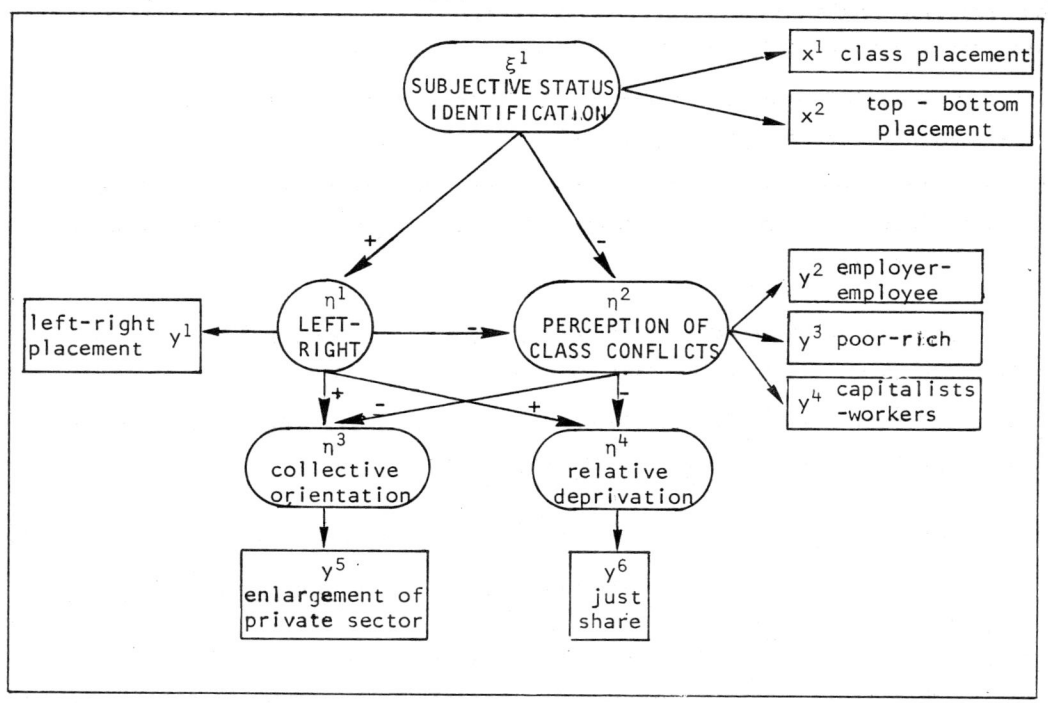

The propositions developed so far for the construction of our theoretical model about class consciousness and political attitudes have the character of 'low level laws'.

In the next section we shall proceed to integrate the results into a more general theory of behavior by trying to explain the lower level propositions. A cognitive-hedonistic theory (Kaufmann-Mall, 1978) is used as such a general theory to be applied to our problem of explanation: the relations between subjective class identification, left-right-attitude, perception of class conflicts, collectivist philosophy of government and relative deprivation.

1.3. Relation between the Marxist (lower-level) propositions and the individualistic research program

The individualistic research program can be characterized by three main theses (see Raub and Voss, 1981: 16-19).

a) Singular social science explananda can be explained by using propositions dealing with individual behavior.

This does not imply the selection of one general behavior theory but only the statement that individual level propositions have to be used for the explanation of singular events.

b) Generalizations (low-level laws) in the social sciences can be explained or modified by using propositions dealing with individual behavior.

This second thesis was first worked out and applied by Malewski (1967) and is seen as a central part of the individualistic program.

The third thesis refers not to explanation but to reconstruction.

c) Collective terms can be reconstructed (explicated) by individual terms.

Collective terms are terms characterizing collectivities like the class consciousness of West German workers, whereas individual terms refer to individual persons. An example is the class consciousness of one person (worker A).

The most important consequence of this research program is the idea of an integration of social scientific knowledge (Malewski, 1967; Opp, 1970; Kaufmann-Mall, 1978). Such an integration seems to have two main advantages (Raub and Voss, 1981: 20) which go beyond a mere cumulation of knowledge. In the first place, one can apply propositions concerning individual behavior to new fields and applications which offer new and more severe possibilities of testing the propositions. In addition, by confronting the empirical generalizations with general propositions one can work out the conditions under which the generalizations are valid.

Referring to the Marxist research program Israel (1971: 145) vigorously defended the thesis, 'which at first may appear to be strange, that in order to base sociology (and knowledge) on Marxian epistomology one has to accept on an ontological level the position of methodological individualism and on a metatheoretical level a position of non-reductionism'. Israel (1971: 150) argues that the position of methodological individualism accounts for the notion of the active, creative human being and stresses the role of the subject. The non-reductionist approach tries to explain human action in terms of the total social situation. According to Israel, combining methodological individualism and non-reductionism allows for theories in which human actions as well as social events may be treated as independent variables and in which their interaction in an ongoing process can be emphasized. This is the way we want to proceed later.

A very informative and interesting analysis comparing propositions of the Marxist research program with propositions from the tradition of empirical social research can be found in Ultee (1978, 1980). Ultee compares sequences of propositions from both programs but does not confront them with a more general theory. Now the question comes up, which general theory we can use for the confrontation with our reconstruction of the empirical generalizations of the Marxist research program. For our purposes we have selected the cognitive-hedonistic theory of Kaufmann-Mall (1978), which is an integrative theory dealing with behavior, valences of consequences, expectations and cognitions. It is a general behavioral theory containing propositions concerning the relations between the just mentioned concepts. The theory is more general than value-expectancy theory and a mere decision theory as it also contains determinants of cognitions, valences of consequences and expectations.

Figure 2 offers at least a short overview of the structure of the theory. On the right side in the causal sequence we have behavior. As intervening variables called determinants of behavior Kaufmann-Mall uses cognitions, valences of consequences and expectations. On the left side one finds the determinants of valences, of consequences, expectations and cognitions.

FIGURE-2: Structure of the cognitive-hedonistic theory

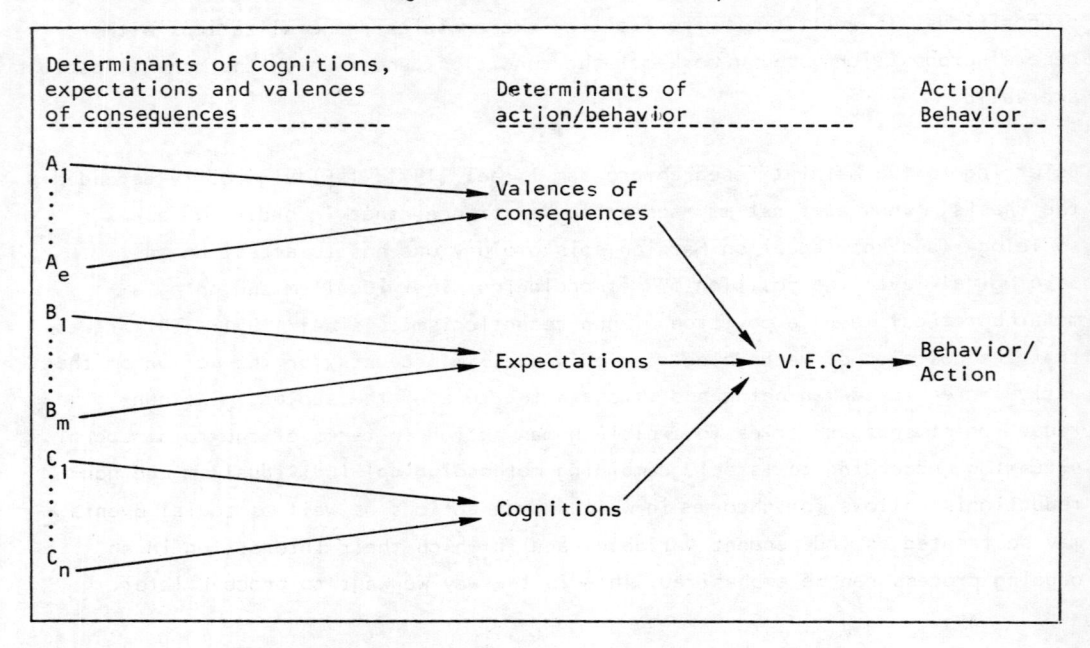

```
Determinants of cognitions,
expectations and valences        Determinants of                    Action/
of consequences                  action/behavior                    Behavior

A_1 ─────────────────────►  Valences of
 .                           consequences ─────────┐
 .                                                  │
A_e ─────────────────────►                          │
                                                    ▼
B_1 ─────────────────────►  Expectations ────────► V.E.C. ──► Behavior/
 .                                                  ▲          Action
 .                                                  │
B_m ─────────────────────►                          │
C_1 ─────────────────────►  Cognitions ─────────────┘
 .
 .
C_n ─────────────────────►
```

All the latent and measured variables of our model in figure 1 can be interpreted as cognitions in the language of cognitive-hedonistic theory. Cognitions are defined as perceptions, attributions or general attitudes. They are not linked with consequences of specific actions in the same way as expectations or valences of consequences (Kaufmann-Mall, 1978). A compact overview of the relations between the terms is given in table 1.

TABLE-1: Coordination of terms

terms of lower level propositions		terms of cognitive hedonistic theory
latent variable	observed variable	latent variable
subjective status identification	class placement, top-bottom	cognition
left-right	left-right placement	cognition
perception of class conflict	poor-rich, capitalist-worker, employer-employee	cognition
private vs public sector	enlargement of private sector	cognition
relative deprivation	fair share statement	cognition

Now we must pose the question how the relations between the latent variables of our lower level propositions such as subjective status identification and perception of class conflicts, which we interpret as cognitions, can be explained. For explaining the formation of cognitions like the perception of class conflicts the following theoretical postulate (TP) from cognitive-hedonistic theory seems to be useful:

TP_1 The higher the relevance of a cognition, the higher is the probability of the formation of a cognition.

'Relevance' is defined as the product of the expectations of the consequences of a cognition and the valences of the consequences of the same cognition.

As we have no direct measurements for the relevance of the cognitions we cannot directly apply TP_1 for the explanation of our lower level propositions. However, we propose a potential explanation, which can be tested in later empirical studies.

As an example we use the relationship between subjective status identification
and perception of class conflicts. Those people who identify themselves as
working class will have a higher relevance (expected utility) for acquiring the
cognition of class conflicts than those who identify themselves as middle-class.
In other words: Working-class people perceive more class conflicts than middle-
class people, since this fits better to their interests. What is important to
note however is that the subjective status identification is not the only
determinant of the relevance (expected utility) of that cognition. Other
determinants will include attributes of the social network of the interviewed
persons such as the professions of the three best friends, their education,
income, and their perception of class conflicts.

It is very plausible from this explanatory sketch that the strength of the
relations between the latent variables in figure 1 will not be very high, since
many relevant explanatory variables are missing. These missing variables are
additional determinants of the expected utility of acquiring the cognitions.

2. Study design, sampling and measurement instruments

For the test of our propositions we used data from a representative field study
(ALLBUS, 1980; see Mayer and Schmidt, 1983). ALLBUS (previously National Social
Survey) is a research program to collect and distribute data on topics in the
social sciences for research and teaching. The basic design provides for repeated
surveys of the West German population with partly constant, partly variable content
to cover central areas of social research. There are three primary purposes of
ALLBUS:

(1)   The scientific goal of studying social change.
(2)   Providing key data for researchers and students who have no direct access
        to national samples.
(3)   Providing a social report for informed policy decisions.

Data for the first ALLBUS were collected during January and February of 1980. The
population sampled consisted of all individuals of German nationality who had
completed their 18th year of life by January 1, 1980, and were resident in the
Federal Republic or West Berlin. A random sample was drawn on the basis of the

multi-stage ADM-Sample using voting districts or artificially created districts from 1978. A total of 2955 interviews were completed.

The first ALLBUS contained, in addition to basic background items, questions regarding the importance of the various domains of life, educational goals, orientations toward work, contacts with and attitudes toward authorities and foreigners working in the FRG ('guest workers'), attitudes toward marriage and family, the perception of social conflict, political interests, voting intentions, evaluations of parties, ideological orientations, political goals and problems, attitudes toward the welfare-state, a subjective self-classification of social status, the perception of social justice and social networks.

We shall now describe the measurement instruments which we shall use in our empirical analysis. There are two operationalizations of subjective status identifications. The first of these is the 'classic' operationalization:

'There is a lot of talk today about different classes of people. What class would you put yourself in - the lower class, the working class, the middle class, the upper middle class, or the upper class?'

1. Lower class
2. Working class
3. Middle class
4. Upper middle class
5. Upper class
6. None of these classes
8. Don't know
7. Refused to classify himself/herself.

The second one was developed for Germany by Klingemann (1980):

'To come to the last question: In our society there are groups of people who rank higher and groups who rank lower. Here we have a scale that runs from high to low. When you think about yourself, where do you rank yourself on this scale? (10 point scale)(Interviewer: Note any comments the respondent makes in answering this question below.)'.

Perception of class conflicts is operationalized in the following way:

'It is often said that there are conflicts of interest between different groups in the Federal Republic - for example, between political groups, between men and women, etc. However, these conflicts are not equally strong. I'll list a few such groups and please tell me whether, in your opinion, these conflicts are very strong, rather strong, rather weak, or whether you think there is no conflict at all between these two groups.

- between employer and employees
- between poor people and rich people
- between capitalists and the working class'.

Relative deprivation is measured as follows:

'In comparison to how other people in the Federal Republic live: Do you believe that you receive a just share of the pleasant things of life, more than your just share, somewhat less or much less than your just share?

1. Just share
2. More than a just share
3. Somewhat less than a just share
4. Much less than a just share
8. Don't know'.

A general left-right orientation also developed by Klingemann (1980, 1982) is operationalized in the following way:

'Many people think of political attitudes as being on the 'left' or on the 'right'. Here is a scale stretching from the 'left' to the 'right'. When you think of your own political attitudes, where would you put yourself. Please mark the scale in the box (01 = left to 10 = right)'.

Finally the attitude toward private vs. state ownership was measured by the following item:

'We would like to hear your views on some important political problems. With the help of this scale tell me to what extent you agree with the following statements. Number 1 means that you don't agree at all with the statement and number 7, that you agree completely with it. You can use any number between 1 and 7 for your answers.
More public services, such as, for example, garbage collection, postal services, or mass transportation, should be taken over by private firms'.

3. Empirical results

3.1. Descriptive results

In the Appendix we present the code values, the absolute frequencies, the relative frequencies, the adjusted frequencies and the cumulative frequencies for our 8 measured variables. In Figure 3 one can find a graphic illustration of the frequency distributions we have just discussed.

FIGURE-3: Frequency distributions of the observed variables

SUBJECTIVE STATUS IDENTIFICATION	class placement | 1 | 2 | 3 | 4 | 5 | *lower* *upper* top - bottom placement | 1 | 2 | 3 | 4 | 5 | *bottom* *top*
LEFT - RIGHT	left - right placement | 1 | 2 | 3 | 4 | 5 | 6 | 7 | 8 | 9 | 10 | *left* *right*
PERCEPTION OF CLASS CONFLICTS	employer - employees | 1 | 2 | 3 | 4 | *none* *very strong* poor - rich | 1 | 2 | 3 | 4 | *none* *very strong* capitalists - workers | 1 | 2 | 3 | 4 | *none* *very strong*
COLLECTIVE ORIENTATION	enlargement of private sector | 1 | 2 | 3 | 4 | 5 | 6 | 7 | *don't agree* *agree complete*
RELATIVE DEPRIVATION	just share | 1 | 2 | 3 | 4 | *much less* *more than a just share*

We shall now discuss some of the results in figure 3. In our sample of full and part-time working people, 26.2% identify themselves as explicitly working class, whereas 59.3 consider themselves as middle class. When one compares the distribution of the two indicators of subjective status identification, one can see that the percentage in the higher middle class in the first and 'classical' indicator is much lower than in the comparable category of the top-down placement. This seems to be an effect of the different question format and scaling technique used in the two items. The distribution of the left-right placement shows that there is a slight tendency in the direction of the right end of the scale, as the mean is 5.839. The comparison between two of those items measuring perceived class conflict reveals the potential effect of variations in question wording. The approval rate to the question whether there are conflicts is much higher when the words capitalist versus worker are used instead of employer versus employee.

Table 2 contains Measurement Procedures, Means, Standard Deviations, Number of Persons and Missing Cases for our subsample of full and part-time working people.

TABLE-2: Means, Standard Deviations, N and Missing Cases

latent variable	observed variable	Measurement Procedure	Mean	Standard Deviation	N	Missing Cases
subjective status	class placement (X_2)	5-point scale	2.833	.61	1355	54
	top bottom placement (X_1)	5-point scale	3.200	.74	1386	23
left-right	left-right placement (Y_1)	10-point scale	5.839	1.88	1378	31
perception of class conflicts	conflicts between employer/employee (Y_2)	4-point scale	2.931	.77	1376	33
	conflicts between poor and rich (Y_3)	4-point scale	3.061	.87	1365	44
	conflicts between capitalists and workers (Y_4)	4-point scale	3.197	.83	1333	76
collective orientation	privatization of state-owned companies and services (Y_5)	7-point scale	2.187	1.10	1405	4
relative deprivation	just share (Y_6)	4-point scale	2.718	.60	1328	81

It is interesting to note that the missing values vary considerably between the items. The question with the highest number of missing cases is also the most 'difficult' question (conflicts between capitalists and workers). As we suspect that the missing cases are not randomly distributed, these differences may have some effect on the parameter estimates. However, as we have no additional information, we cannot empirically test such effects and must therefore be very cautious in the interpretation of our results. To get an impression of the amount of the bivariate associations we present in the Appendix the Correlation matrix.

One can see from the Appendix that the correlations are without exceptions under .50. The determinant of the correlation matrix is .47, which additionally indicates that no problem of multicollinearity exists.

3.2. Specification and test of the LISREL models

The specification of our models has to follow certain rules, which we now describe. A LISREL model is defined by

1. the model specifying the structural relationships among the latent variables (the structural equation model);
2. the measurement model specifying the structural relationships between latent variables and observed variables (the measurement model);
3. assumptions referring to 1 and 2 (see Jöreskog and Sörbom, 1982).

Our structural model contains the causal relations we hypothesized in section 1.2 (see also figure 1). As our variables in the structural model are latent variables, we have to specify a measurement model between our eight observed variables and the five latent variables. In the case of three of our latent variables only one indicator is available. This implies -due to identification problems- that we assume a measurement error of zero and a one to one relationship between latent variable and observed variable. However, subjective social status and perception of class conflicts are measured by two resp. three items. It is therefore possible to test the amount of random and systematic measurement error for these latent variables. LISREL (version V) tests the specified model by maximum likelihood or unweighted least squares estimation of the coefficients (Jöreskog and Sörbom, 1982). Here we have used maximum-likelihood estimation as we have a large sample and furthermore there were no indications of severe violations of the assumption of multinormality of the observed variables.

Given these assumptions the maximum-likelihood estimators are optimal in the sense of being most precise in big samples.

The assessment of the fit of the model is one important part in the application of LISREL. The first way of assessing the model is to examine the results of the following quantities (Jöreskog and Sörbom, 1982: 1.36):

1. Parameter estimates
2. Standard errors
3. Squared multiple correlations
4. Coefficients of determination
5. Correlations of estimates

As in the model none of the above quantities has an unreasonable value in the sense that there is no estimated correlation bigger than one, no negative variance, no extremely large standard errors, and the estimates do not correlate too highly, we can accept it. The second part of the model evaluation concerns the assessment of the overall fit of the model to the data. It may be judged by means of three measures of overall fit. The first and usual one is the overall χ^2-measure and its associated degrees of freedom and probability level. Instead of regarding χ^2 as a test statistic in the strict sense, one should regard it as a goodness of fit measure in the sense that large χ^2-values correspond to bad fit and small χ^2-values to good fit. The degrees of freedom serve as a standard by which to judge whether χ^2 is large or small. The other two measures of overall fit are the goodness-of-fit index GFI and the root mean square residual RMR. GFI is a measure of the relative amount of variances and covariances jointly accounted for by the model and should be between zero and one. RMR is a measure of the average of the residual variances and covariances. The root mean square (RMR) residual can be used to compare the fit of two different models for the same data. The goodness of fit index can be used for this purpose too but can also be used to compare the fit of models for different data.

In figure 4 one finds the estimated standardized coefficients with the corresponding paths. Furthermore one finds in figure 4 all three measures of the goodness of fit of the model.

FIGURE-4: Maximum likelihood estimates for model 1 ($\chi^2=14.70$, NDF=14, p=.399, GFI=.997, RMR=.014)

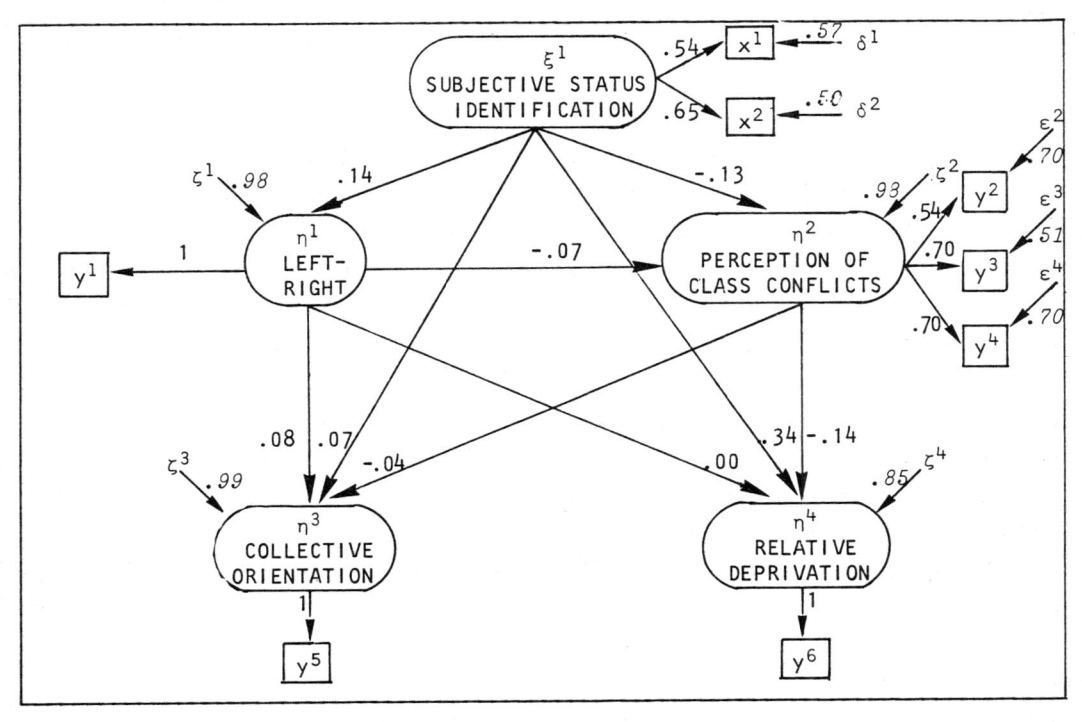

We shall now discuss the interpretation of the results, beginning with the coefficients related to the structural model. The signs of all coefficients are as predicted. The positive coefficient of .14 between subjective status and left-right orientation indicates that people with rising subjective status tend to become more right-wing whereas the negative coefficient between subjective status and perception of class conflicts of -.13 tells us that with rising subjective status people tend to perceive less intensive class conflicts. As expected, people who have a more left-wing orientation tend to perceive more intensive class conflicts. However, the strength of the relationship is very small (-.07). Subjective status has the strongest effect (.34) on relative deprivation whereas the left-right orientation has no and the perception of class conflicts a less strong influence (-.14) in the sense that the higher the perception of class conflicts the less people think that they get their fair share.

The coefficients of the relations of collective orientation with subjective status, left-right orientation and perception of class conflicts have all the predicted signs. However they are without exception very small, that is lower than .10.

When one looks to the residuals of the latent endogenous variables one can see that they are all very high. They vary from .85 for relative deprivation to .99 for collective orientation. Correspondingly the explained variances of left-right, class conflicts, collective orientation and relative deprivation are .020, .026, 0.016, 0.148. This indicates that in our model the most relevant variables are still left out.

Potential explanations for the high amount of unexplained variance have been discussed in section 1.3. Furthermore, some of the objective status variables of Kort-Krieger's model may have an additional effect on our 'cognitive' variables. In addition some of the attributes of the personal networks of persons and memberships in certain organizations like trade unions and parties should have some effect.

However, for a deeper explanation of the relations between the latent endogenous variables in our model it would be more fruitful to apply a general theory like cognitive hedonistic theory than an ad-hoc strategy characterized by searching for 'relevant' additional variables. This point is taken up in section 4.

The measurement model seems to be much better than the structural model when one looks at the coefficients and the residuals. The formal validity of the observed variables expressed by the size of the coefficients is satisfactory and ranges between .54 and .70. Furthermore it is interesting to note that the coefficients themselves do not differ too much. This demonstrates that the formal validity of the items is rather similar.

The three goodness of fit indices indicate different things. Whereas the probability level of .39 demonstrates that an improvement of the model should be attempted, the two other indices are very satisfactory. The Goodness of Fit Index (GFI) is near the ideal value of one (.997). This means practically that the relative amount of variances and covariances jointly accounted for by the model is nearly one and that -in other words- a change in the model cannot improve the amount of explained variance in the model. The message of the Root Mean Square

Residual goes in the same direction. The value of 0.014 says that the average of the residual variances and covariances is very low in relation to the size of the observed variances and covariances.

Now the question comes up whether and how the model should be modified. Our proposed modifications refer to two different strategies. First, we delete those paths which are nearly zero and have not been significant. Secondly, we look at the modification index in LISREL V, which indicates at which place in the model a change from a fixed to a free parameter would result in the strongest improvement of the model in terms of goodness of fit of the whole model. According to this index, the zero path from left-right attitude to the first item of perceived class conflicts (conflicts between employers and employees) is wrong. There seems to be a unique covariance between these variables which cannot be explained by the latent variable class conflict. From a theoretical point of view it makes also sense that people who are more left oriented tend also to perceive more conflicts between employers and employees.

Now we have run two more models. Model 2, in contrast to model 1, has two zero paths specified between left-right orientation (η^1) and relative deprivation (η^4), and between perception of class conflicts (η^2) and collective orientation (η^3).

Model 3 is with one exception identical with model 2. It allows for a direct path from left-right orientation (η^1) to perception of conflict between employers and employees (y^2).

Table 3 contains a comparison of the goodness of fit indices of the three models.

TABLE-3: Comparison of Goodness of Fit of the three models

	Model 1	Model 2	Model 3
χ^2	14.70	15.91	11.39
df	14	16	15
p-level	.3999	.459	.724
GFI	.997	.997	.998
RMR	.014	.016	.013

According to all three criteria: p-level, GFI and RMR, the third model is best. For comparative model fitting one can use the χ^2 in the following way. When one compares two models (for example model 2 and model 3) one compares the differences in degrees of freedom and χ^2. A large drop in χ^2 compared to the differences in number of degrees of freedom indicates that the improvement in fit is obtained by 'capitalizing on chance', and the added parameters may not have real significance and meaning (Jöreskog and Sörbom, 1982: I.40). By using this rule for the comparison of our three models, one can see that model 1, which has two degrees of freedom less than model 2, is no improvement, since χ^2 does not diminish more than the degrees of freedom. Model 3 is however an improvement compared with model 2, since the reduction in χ^2 (4.52) is greater than the loss in degrees of freedom (1). In figure 5 one finds the standardized coefficients for model 3.

FIGURE-5: Standardized maximum likelihood estimates for model 3 (χ^2=11.39, NDF=15, p=.724, GFI=.998, RMR=.013)

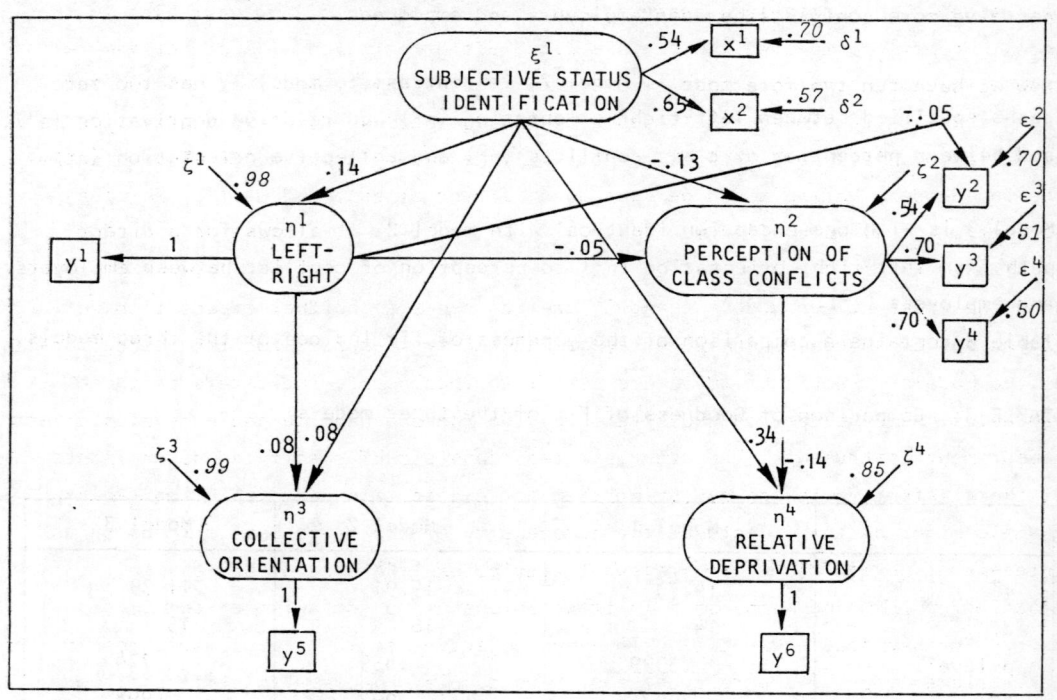

By comparing figure 4 with figure 5 it is easy to verify that the coefficients have not changed drastically by this respecification. Anyway, we think that a cross validation of our model 3 is necessary to test the stability of the model structure and the coefficients.

4. Theoretical conclusions

It is obvious from the results of our empirically tested models that the relations between the different components of class consciousness are rather low. The high unexplained variances (residuals) demonstrate that the most relevant variables in the model are still missing. At this point we have to ask whether the general framework of cognitive-hedonistic theory gives us some hints for explaining this result.

According to the postulate discussed in section 2, persons are more likely to perceive one cognition C_1 as causal for at least one other cognition C_2 the higher the relevance (expectation x valence of consequences) of this cognition.

Let us apply this postulate again to the relation of two of our variables in the model. We have postulated that people with left orientation will perceive more intensive class conflicts than people with middle, upper middle or upper class identification. Obviously the valence of consequences and the expectation of the cognition of class conflicts is not directly measured in our model. The effect of the independent variable can be seen as an effect of expected utility for the perception of class conflicts.

When one looks at our models 1 and 3, one can see that neither expectation nor valence of consequences are directly or indirectly measured. For the respecification of the models it would be therefore useful to incorporate indicators of these variables. Here we can use two strategies. On the one hand we could develop direct measurement instruments. The other strategy consists of specifying determinants of these latent variables and using them for explanation and prediction. An example might be the effects of the homogeneity of the three best friends of an interviewed person concerning relevant attributes like type of profession, election behavior and membership in trade unions, in a socialist or communist party. Furthermore, the social origin and objective social status variables in Kort-Krieger's paper are relevant too. Such complex models with different types of latent variables could be tested by the generalized LISREL model, assuming that the identification problem is solved.

Another point of interest is the chosen measurement theory. According to Converse instead of assuming an invariant measurement theory for the whole sample, one has

to assume different consistencies of attitudes in groups differing in education
and political interest (Converse, 1964, 1970). Therefore one would have to test
the stability of the coefficients of our measurement theory in subsamples. An
alternative measurement theory would be Marx' own ideas of influencing the
attitudes of people (Bewusstsein) by asking them questions about their social
situation (see Weiss, 1936). By formalizing this idea via structural equation
models one would specify causal arrows from observed variables to lagged
endogenous latent variables.

So instead of ending with no more than the old motto 'further research is needed',
we end up by saying something which is hopefully more informative. By using the
approach outlined in our explanatory sketch in section 1.2 one should attempt to
develop a more satisfactory model from the point of view of explained variance
and explanatory power.

References

AJZEN, I. and M. FISHBEIN, (1980), Understanding Attitudes and Predicting Behavior,
    Englewood Cliffs, N.J.: Prentice Hall.

CAMPBELL, A., E. CONVERSE, W.E. MILLER and D. STOKES (1960, 1964 abr.), The American
    Voter. New York: Wiley.

CENTERS, R., (1949), The Psychology of Social Classes. New York: Russell and
    Russell.

CONVERSE, Ph.E., (1964), 'The Nature of Belief Systems in Mass Publics', pp. 75-169
    in D.E. Apter (ed.), Ideology and Discontent. Glencoe, Ill.: Free Press.

CONVERSE, Ph.E., (1970), 'Attitudes and Nonattitudes: Continuation of a Dialogue';
    pp. 168-189 in E.R. Tufte (ed.), The Quantitative Analysis of Social Problems.
    Reading, Mass.: Addison-Wesley.

GIDDENS, A., (1979), Die Klassenstruktur fortgeschrittener Gesellschaften.
    Frankfurt a.M.: Suhrkamp.

GUEST, A.M., (1974), 'Class Consciousness and American Political Attitudes',
    Social Forces 52: 496-510.

ISRAEL, J., (1971), 'The Principles of Methodological Individualism and Marxian
    Epistemology', Acta Sociologica 14: 145-150.

JÖRESKOG, K.G. and D. SÖRBOM, (1982), LISREL Version V, User's Guide. Chicago:
    International Educational Services.

KAUFMANN-MALL, K., (1978), Kognitiv-hedonistische Theorie menschlichen Verhaltens.
    Bern: Huber (Beiheft 3 der Zeitschrift für Sozialpsychologie).

KLINGEMANN, H.D., (1980), Links-Rechts und Oben-Unten, Mimeo.

KLINGEMANN, H.D., (1982), 'What 'Left' and 'Right' Means to Mass Publics: Variations in the Understanding of Political Symbols'. Mimeo (paper read at the XII th World Congress of the International Political Science Association, Rio de Janeiro, Brazil).

KORT-KRIEGER, U., (1982), 'Structural Determinants of Objective and Subjective Status', in this volume.

MALEWSKI, A., (1967), Verhalten und Interaktion. Tübingen: Mohr.

MAYER, K.U. and P. SCHMIDT, (1983), Allgemeine Bevölkerungsumfrage der Sozialwissenschaften. Beiträge zu methodischen Problemen des Allbus 1980. Kronberg: Athenäum.

NOWAK, S., (1982), 'Introduction', pp. 1-26 in T. Bottomore, S. Nowak and M. Sokolowska (eds.), Sociology: The State of the Art. London: Sage.

OPP, K.D., (1970), Soziales Handeln, Rollen und soziale Systeme. Stuttgart: Enke.

RAUB, W. and Th. VOSS, (1981), Individuelles Handeln und gesellschaftliche Folgen. Darmstadt: Luchterhand.

SÖRBOM, D. and K.G. JÖRESKOG (1980), 'The Use of LISREL in Sociological Model Building', pp. 179-199 in E.F. Borgatta and D.J. Jackson (eds.), Factor Analysis and Measurement in Sociological Research. London: Sage.

SWANSON, G.E., T. NEWCOMB and E.G. HARLEY (eds.), (1958), Readings in Social Psychology. New York: Holt, Rinehart and Winston.

ULTEE, W.C., (1978), 'Erkenntnisfortschritt durch Vergleich von Hypothesensequenzen. Das Problem des Wählerverhaltens in der Tradition der empirischen Sozialforschung und im revisionistischen Zweig des historischen Materialismus', pp. 107-118 in K.O. Hondrich and J. Matthes (eds.), Theorienvergleich in den Sozialwissenschaften. Darmstadt: Luchterhand.

ULTEE, W.C., (1980), Fortschritt und Stagnation in der Soziologie. Darmstadt: Luchterhand.

WEISS, H., (1937), 'Die "Enquete Ouvriere" von Karl Marx', Zeitschrift für Sozialforschung 5: 76-98.

Appendix

1. Frequencies for the eight variables

class-placement	Code	absolute freq.	relative freq. (PCT)	adjusted freq. (PCT)	cum. freq. (PCT)
lower	1.	5	0.4	0.4	0,4
working	2.	369	26.2	27.2	27.6
middle	3.	835	59.3	61.6	89.2
higher middle	4.	139	9.9	10.3	99.5
upper	5.	7	0.5	0.5	100.0
missing	6.	54	3.8	missing	100.0
total		1409	100.0	100.0	

Top-Bottom Placement	Code	absolute freq.	relative freq. (PCT)	adjusted freq. (PCT)	cum. freq. (PCT)
down	1.	16	1.1	1.2	1.2
"	2.	185	13.1	13.3	14.5
"	3.	728	51.7	52.5	67.0
"	4.	420	29.8	30.3	97.3
top	5.	37	2.6	2.7	100.0
missing	6.	23	1.6	missing	100.0
total		1409	100.0	100.0	

Left-Right Placement	Code	absolute freq.	relative freq. (PCT)	adjusted freq. (PCT)	cum. freq. (PCT)
left	1.	20	1.4	1.5	1.5
"	2.	36	2.6	2.6	4.1
"	3.	98	7.0	7.1	11.2
"	4.	154	10.9	11.2	22.4
"	5.	251	17.8	18.2	40.6
"	6.	353	25.1	25.6	66.2
"	7.	203	14.4	14.7	80.9
"	8.	156	11.1	11.3	92.2
"	9.	68	4.8	4.9	97.2
right	10.	39	2.8	2.8	100.0
missing	97.	17	1.2	missing	100.0
"	98.	3	0.2	missing	100.0
"	99.	11	0.8	missing	100.0
total		1409	100.0	100.0	

	Code	absolute freq.	relative freq. (PCT)	adjusted freq. (PCT)	cum. freq. (PCT)
Perceived conflicts between employer and employees					
none at all	1.	33	2.3	2.4	2.4
moderate	2.	358	25.4	26.0	28.4
rather strong	3.	656	46.6	47.7	76.1
very strong	4.	329	23.3	23.9	100.0
missing	8.	31	2.2	missing	100.0
"	9.	2	0.1	missing	100.0
	total	1409	100.0	100.0	
Perceived conflicts between poor and rich					
none at all	1.	69	4.9	5.1	5.1
moderate	2.	269	19.1	19.7	24.8
rather strong	3.	537	38.1	39.3	64.1
very strong	4.	490	34.8	35.9	100.0
missing	8.	43	3.1	missing	100.0
"	9.	1	0.1	missing	100.0
	total	1409	100.0	100.0	
Perceived conflicts between capitalists and workers					
none at all	1.	44	3.1	3.3	3.3
moderate	2.	217	15.4	16.3	19.6
rather strong	3.	504	35.8	37.8	57.4
very strong	4.	568	40.3	42.6	100.0
missing	8.	72	5.1	missing	100.0
"	9.	4	0.3	missing	100.0
	total	1409	100.0	100.0	
Privatization of firms					
don't agree at all	1.	368	26.1	26.2	26.2
"	2.	143	10.1	10.2	36.4
"	3.	138	9.8	9.8	46.2
"	4.	209	14.8	14.9	61.1
"	5.	178	12.6	12.7	73.7
"	6.	142	10.1	10.1	83.8
agree completely	7.	227	16.1	16.2	100.0
missing	97.	2	0.1	missing	100.0
"	99.	2	0.1	missing	100.0
	total	1409	100.0	100.0	

	Code	absolute freq.	relative freq. (PCT)	adjusted freq. (PCT)	cum. freq. (PCT)
Just share					
much less than just share	1.	50	3.5	3.8	3.8
some what less than a just share	2.	327	23.2	24.6	28.4
just share	3.	899	63.8	67.7	96.1
more than a just share	4.	52	3.7	3.9	100.0
missing	8.	80	5.7	missing	100.0
"	9.	1	0.1	missing	100.0
total		1409	100.0	100.0	

2. Correlation matrix

	Y_1	Y_2	Y_3	Y_4	Y_5	Y_6	X_1	X_2
Y_1	1.000							
Y_2	-0.091	1.000						
Y_3	-0.050	0.377	1.000					
Y_4	-0.050	0.375	0.494	1.000				
Y_5	0.091	-0.031	-0.029	-0.046	1.000			
Y_6	0.064	-0.125	-0.115	-0.141	0.011	1.000		
X_1	0.093	-0.043	-0.042	-0.040	0.055	0.193	1.000	
X_2	0.083	-0.100	-0.068	-0.047	0.060	0.240	0.352	1.000

NOTES ON CONTRIBUTORS

Hartmut Esser

Universität Essen
FB 1 - Empirische Sozialforschung
4300 Essen
Federal Republic of Germany

(b. 1943) studied sociology and economics in Cologne. 1970-1974 Wissenschaftlicher Assistent at the University of Cologne. Dr. rer. pol. 1974 with a dissertation Soziale Regelmässigkeiten des Befragenverhaltens. 1974-1978 first Wissenschaftlicher Assistent, then Akademischer Rat at the University of Bochum. 1978-1982 Professor for Empirical Social Research at the University of Duisburg. 1981 habilitation with a thesis Assimilation und Integration. Since 1982 Professor for Empirical Social Research at the University of Essen

Harry B.G. Ganzeboom

Rijksuniversiteit Utrecht
Sociologisch Instituut
Heidelberglaan 2
3584 CS Utrecht
The Netherlands

(b. 1953) studied sociology in Utrecht, where he has been a research associate at the university since 1978.

Ute Kort-Krieger

Technische Universität München
Institut für Sozialwissenschaften
Lothstrasse 17
8000 München
Federal Republic of Germany

(b. 1943) studied sociology and political science in Hamburg and Mannheim. 1969-1974 research associate at the University of Mannheim. Dr. phil. 1973 with a dissertation Akademische Bürokratie. 1975-1978 research associate at the Gesamthochschulrat Baden-Württemberg in Heidelberg and Karlsruhe. Since 1978 Akademischer Rat at the Munich Technical Institute.

Siegwart Lindenberg   Rijksuniversiteit Groningen
                             Sociologisch Instituut
                             Grote Markt 23
                             9712 HR Groningen
                             The Netherlands

(b. 1941) studied sociology, philosophy and social psychology in Freiburg i. Br. and Mannheim. Subsequently studied at Harvard University, where he acquired a PhD. with a thesis Aspects of the Cognitive Representation of Social Structures. From 1969-1973 he taught sociology and philosophy at Princeton University. Professor of Sociology at the University of Groningen since 1973.

Karl-Dieter Opp   Universität Hamburg
                             Seminar für Sozialwissenschaften
                             Sedanstrasse 19
                             2000 Hamburg 13
                             Federal Republic of Germany

(b. 1937) studied sociology and economics in Cologne. 1963-1967 Wissenschaftlicher Assistent at the University of Cologne. Dr. rer. pol. 1967 with a dissertation Zur Erklärung delinquenten Verhaltens von Kindern und Jugendlichen. 1967-1971 Wissenschaftlicher Assistent at the University of Erlangen-Nürnberg. 1970 habilitation with a thesis Soziales Handeln, Rollen und soziale Systeme. Since 1971 Professor of Sociology at the University of Hamburg.

Werner Raub   Universität Erlangen-Nürnberg
                               Sozialwissenschaftliches Institut
                               Findelgasse 7-9
                               8500 Nürnberg
                               Federal Republic of Germany

(b. 1953) studied social sciences and philosophy in Bochum. 1980-1982 Wissenschaftlicher Assistent at the University of Hagen, since 1982 at the University of Erlangen-Nürnberg.

Peter Schmidt   Universität Giessen
                               FB Gesellschaftswissenschaften
                               Karl-Glöckner-Strasse 21
                               6300 Giessen
                               Federal Republic of Germany

(b. 1942) studied sociology, economics and philosophy in Cologne and Mannheim. 1970-1971 research associate at the University of Mannheim. 1972-1979 Wissenschaftlicher Assistent at the University of Hamburg. Dr. phil. 1977 with a dissertation Zur praktischen Anwendung von Theorien. 1979-1981 research associate at the Zentrum für Umfragen, Methoden und Analysen (ZUMA) in Mannheim. Since 1981 Professor for Empirical Social Research at the University of Giessen.

Frits Tazelaar   Rijksuniversiteit Utrecht
                               Sociologisch Instituut
                               Heidelberglaan 2
                               3584 CS Utrecht
                               The Netherlands

(b. 1946) studied sociology in Groningen. Since 1974 research associate and wetenschappelijk medewerker at the University of Utrecht. In 1980 doctoral dissertation Mentale incongruenties - Sociale restricties - Gedrag.

Thomas Voss   Universität München
                                    Institut für Soziologie
                                    Konradstrasse 6
                                    8000 München
                                    Federal Republic of Germany

(b. 1955) studied social sciences and philosophy in Bochum. Wissenschaftlicher Assistent at the University of Munich since 1980.

Reinhard Wippler   Rijksuniversiteit Utrecht
                                    Sociologisch Instituut
                                    Heidelberglaan 2
                                    3584 CS Utrecht
                                    The Netherlands

(b. 1931) studied sociology in Groningen. 1963-1971 wetenschappelijk medewerker at the University of Groningen. Doctoral dissertation in 1968 on Sociale determinanten van het vrijetijdsgedrag. 1968-1969 post-doctoral studies at Harvard University and at the University of California at Berkeley. Professor of Sociology at the University of Utrecht since 1971.

NAME INDEX

Abelson, R.P., 102, 126, 127
Acock, A.C., 121, 122
Ajzen, I., 102, 121, 122, 124, 167, 184, 248
Albert, H., 4, 10, 19, 36
Albrecht, G., 122
Albrecht, S.L., 121, 122, 124
Andrews, K.H., 121, 122
Apter, D.E., 248
Arrow, K.J., 10, 36, 85, 98
Arts, W., 39, 60, 61
Aya, R., 73, 74

Ballachey, E.L., 125
Bames, S.H., 181, 184
Bansford, H.E., 121, 125
Barry, B., 61
Barth, F., 10, 36
Black, J.S., 121, 124
Blalock, H.M., 13, 34, 36, 162, 163, 164, 200, 202
Blau, P.M., 10, 33, 36, 79, 80, 81, 82, 98
Becker, G.S., 10, 17, 32, 36, 38, 96, 186, 190, 202
Belassa, B., 99
Bemberg, R.E., 122
Bennett, P.D., 122, 124
Benninghaus, H., 121, 122
Bentham, J., 39
Berlyne, D.E., 186, 202
Berman, J.J., 122, 125
Boissevain, J., 84, 98
Bolte, K.M., 185

Bonfield, E.H., 122, 123
Boorman, S.A., 84, 98
Borgatta, E.F., 164, 222, 249
Borger, R., 36, 37
Boudon, R., 6, 9, 11, 20, 21, 22, 23, 24, 26, 27, 29, 30, 31, 34, 35, 36, 44, 49, 50, 57, 60, 61, 158, 164
Bourdieu, P., 186, 187, 202
Boyd, H., 131, 150, 153, 164
Brannon, R., 121, 122, 123
Brehm, J.W., 102, 127
Brenner, M., 37
Brigham, J.C., 121, 123
Brinton, G., 72
Buchanan, J.M., 10, 36
Buffalo, M.D., 121, 123
Burgess, R.L., 10, 36
Burke, P.J., 200, 202
Burow-Auffarth, K., 185
Bushell, D., 10, 36
Butts, R.E., 37

Campbell, A., 121, 123, 228, 229, 248
Carpenter, K.E., 121, 122
Cartwright, D., 12
Casinelli, C.W., 43, 61
CBS (Netherlands Central Bureau of Statistics), 186, 202
Centers, R., 228, 229, 230, 248
Chein, I., 121, 123
Chowdry, K., 121, 123
Cioffi, F., 36, 37

Clark, A.L., 121, 123
Coase, R.H., 83, 98
Coleman, J.S., 5, 7, 9, 10, 13, 31, 32, 34, 36, 39, 60, 61, 62, 96, 98
Cohen, A.R., 121, 123
Collins, B.E., 125
Collins, R., 96, 98, 187, 202
Converse, Ph.E., 123, 228, 229, 230, 247, 248
Cook, S.W., 102, 121, 123, 128
Coser, L.A., 74, 75
Corey, S.M., 121, 122, 123
Coxon, A.P.M., 207, 221
Crutchfield, R.A., 125
Cyphers, G., 123

Daheim, H., 122
Darroch, R.K., 122
Davies, J.C., 64, 65, 66, 67, 72, 73, 74, 75
Davis, J.A., 12, 36
Defleur, M.L., 121, 122, 123
Defriese, G.H., 121, 122, 123
Demsetz, H., 83, 97, 98
Deutsch, M., 121, 123
Deutscher, I., 121, 122, 123, 125
Devinney, L.C., 127
De Vos, H., 33, 37
Downs, A., 10, 20, 37
Durkheim, R., 22, 23, 24, 31, 33, 39, 76, 77, 78, 79, 81, 87, 92, 96, 98
Duvall, R., 68, 74

Ehrlich, H.J., 121, 124
Eichner, K., 38
Eisenstadt, S.M., 135, 164

Ells, K., 222
Elster, J., 12, 27, 34, 37
Engels, F., 170
Erbring, L., 160, 161, 163, 164
Esser, H., VII, IX, 32, 134, 135, 137, 164, 254
Ewens, W.L., 121, 124
Eysenck, H.J., 193, 194, 202

Faris, R.E.L., 37
Feather, M.T., 14, 37
Feldman, S., 124, 126
Fendrich, J.M., 121, 122, 124
Ferguson, A., 10
Festinger, L., 124
Fishbein, M., 102, 121, 122, 124, 167, 184, 248
Ford, W.S., 121, 122, 123
Franc, D.E., 121, 127
Fey, B.S., 13, 37, 167, 184
Frideres, J.S., 122, 124
Frost, R.T., 122, 124
Furubotn, E., 13, 37, 83, 98

Ganzeboom, H.B.G., IX, X, 202, 254
Garcia, L., 121, 124
Gasson, R.M., 121, 124
Geschwender, J.A., 73, 74
Gerats, G.E., 122, 127
Gibbs, J.P., 121, 123
Giddens, A., 230, 248
Gilbert, E., 122, 127
Gould, C., 230
Gouldner, A.W., 80
Graff, J., 221
Graham, H., 74
Granovetter, M.S., 84, 98, 183, 184
Griffith, W., 121, 124
Groser, M., 60, 61

Gross, S.J., 121, 124
Grunwald, M., 43, 55, 61
Guest, A.M., 229, 230, 248
Gurr, T., 66, 67, 68, 73, 74

Habermehl, W., 38
Hagan, J., 122, 124
Hall, N.E., 121, 128
Haller, A.O., 121, 124, 128
Hamm, B., 164
Hands, G., 43, 61
Hannan, M.T., 33, 37
Harary, F., 12
Hardin, R., 79, 98
Harley, E.G., 249
Harrell, G.D., 122, 124
Harrison, R., 36
Harsanyi, J.C., 16, 18, 19, 34, 37, 93, 96, 98
Hayek, F.A., 77, 98
Hyman, H., 121, 125
Heath, A., 81, 98
Haberlein, T.A., 121, 124
Heider, F., 12
Heinrichs, U., 185
Hempel, C.G., 8, 22, 33, 37
Herder-Dorneich, Ph., 46, 57, 60, 61
Hesse, S., 123
Hesselbart, S., 123
Himelstein, Ph., 122, 125
Hintikka, J., 37
Hirsch, F., 29, 37
Hirschman, A.O., 45, 54, 60, 61, 180, 184
Hobbes, Th., 77
Hodge, R.W., 208, 210, 221
Hoffmann-Nowotny, H., 132, 164
Holland, P.W., 36

Homans, G.C., 5, 6, 8, 9, 10, 33, 34, 36, 37, 187, 202
Hondrich, K.O., 165, 249
Hornik, I.A., 122
Hovland, C.I., 102, 121, 127
Hume, D., 10, 81
Hummell, H.J., 6, 38

Insko, C.H.A., 102, 121, 125
Institut für Marxistische Studien und Forschungen, 208, 221
Israel, J., 233, 248
Iversen, R., 131, 150, 153, 164
Jackman, R., 208, 210, 221
Jackman, W., 208, 210, 221
Jackson, D.J., 164, 222, 249
Jackson, E.F., 200, 202
Jaeggi, U., 221
Jeffries, V., 121, 125
Jones, Ch.L., 207, 221
Joyce, W.F., 100
Jöreskog, K.G., 194, 202, 210, 221, 222, 241, 242, 246, 248, 249
Jukam, Th.O., 181, 184

Kaase, M., 181, 184
Kahle, L.R., 122, 125
Kandel, D.B., 121, 122
Katz, D., 121, 125
Kaufmann-Mall, K., 232, 233, 234, 248
Keane, R., 123
Kelley, H.H., 10, 39, 82, 83, 99
Kelman, H.C., 122, 125
Kendler, H.H., 121, 125
Kendler, T.S., 121, 125
Keuth, H., 34, 38
Kielmannsegg, P. Graf, 184
Kiesler, C.A., 121, 125
Kirchgässner, G., 167, 184

Kleining, G., 184
Klingemann, H.D., 237, 238, 248, 249
Kluegel, J.R., 210, 221
Kort-Krieger, U., IX, X, 227, 230, 244, 247, 249, 254
Kothandapani, V., 121, 125
König, R., 165
Krech, D., 121, 125
Kreutz, H., 170, 184
Kunkel, J., 12, 38
Kurz, M., 96, 99
Kutner, B., 122, 125

Laing, R.D., 121, 125
Lapiere, R.T., 122, 125
Larson, O.N., 74, 75
Lauer, R.H., 121, 125
Lee, A.R., 125
Lee, W., 34, 38
Leinhardt, S., 36
Lenk, H., 36
Lenski, G., 200, 203
Lesourne, J., 12, 38
Lévy-Garboua, L., 38
Lewis, D., 7, 38, 93, 99
Lilge, H.G., 61
Lindenberg, S., VIII, X, 5, 7, 8, 9, 11, 12, 19, 20, 32, 34, 38, 39, 48, 59, 61, 62, 69, 74, 75, 94, 97, 99, 131, 165, 255
Linn, L.S., 122, 125
Lipset, S.M., 44, 55, 60, 62
Liska, A.E., 121, 126
Luce, R.D., 88, 99
Luckmann, G., 132, 165
Lukacs, G., 207, 221

Maccoby, E.E., 228, 229

Magura, S., 121, 126
Makowsky, M., 96, 98
Malewsky, A., 10, 33, 38, 232, 233, 249
Mann, J.H., 121, 126
Marx, K., 33, 74, 170, 206, 208, 209, 221, 230, 248, 249
Matthes, J., 40, 62, 165, 249
May, J.D., 43, 62
Mayer, K.U., 236, 249
McGuire, W.J., 102, 126, 127
Mecker, M., 222
Meckling, W.H., 12, 38
Meinefeld, W., 121, 126
Mehrländer, U., 132, 165
Merton, R.K., 61, 126
Michael, R.T., 17, 38
Michels, R., VIII, 43, 44, 45, 47, 48, 49, 50, 53, 54, 55, 57, 62
Midlarsky, M., 73, 75
Miller, N., 125
Miller, W.E., 123, 248
Mills, C.W., 208, 221
Moles, A.A., 186, 203
Monk, M., 121, 126
Moore, B., 75
Moore, J.C., 70, 73, 122, 125
Moore, W.E., 184
Mueller, D.C., 10, 38
Mueller, W., 221
Mulder, M., 55, 62
Muller, E.N., 178, 181, 184
Münch, R., 87, 90, 99, 102, 126

Nelson, R., 99
Newcomb, Th.M., 102, 121, 123, 126, 249
Nie, N.H., 181, 185
Niman, C.M., 121, 124

North, D.C., 83, 99
Nowak, S., 227, 249
Nozick, R., 87, 99

Olson, M., 7, 10, 20, 38, 48, 62, 69, 75, 171, 184
Opp, K.-D., VII, IX, 10, 33, 34, 38, 95, 96, 99, 178, 181, 185, 209, 221, 233, 249, 255
Ordeshook, P.G., 10, 39
Ostrom, T.M., 121, 126
Ouchi, W.G., 84, 100

Parsons, T., 76, 77, 81, 87, 99
Passeron, J.C., 187, 202
Pejovich, S., 13, 37, 83, 98
Pilkington, G.W., 122, 126
Polsby, N.W., 75
Popper, K.R., VIII, IX
Poppleton, P., 122, 126
Portes, A., 73, 75
Posner, R.A., 85, 99
Precker, J.A., 121, 126
Project Klassenanalyse, 208, 222
Przeworski, A., 165

Raiffa, H., 88, 99
Raub, W., 9, 26, 34, 35, 38, 39, 60, 62, 96, 99, 232, 233, 249, 256
Reiss, I.L., 127
Riker, W.H., 10, 39
Rogers, J.W., 121, 123
Rose, A., 135, 165
Rosenbaum, M.E., 121, 127
Rosenberg, M.J., 102, 121, 127
Rossi, P.H., 61
Rudé, G., 70, 75

Runciman, W.G., 24, 39

Sack, F., 122
Saenger, G., 122, 127
Salert, B., 73, 75
Sample, J., 121, 127
Savage, L.J., 14, 31, 39
Scheff, T.J., 7, 39, 121, 127
Schmidt, P., IX, X, 209, 221, 222, 236, 249, 256
Schneider, L., 10, 39
Schopler, J., 102, 121, 125
Schotter, A., 7, 39, 86, 88, 89, 90, 92, 93, 94, 97, 99
Schulte, W., 38, 61, 75
Schuman, H., 121, 123, 127
Schumpeter, J.A., 20, 39
Schütte, H.G., 6, 9, 19, 34, 39
Schwarz, D., 73, 75
Selltiz, C., 102, 121, 123
Sewell, W.H., 124
Sherif, C.W., 128
Sherif, M.S., 128
Shubik, M., 97, 99
Silbermann, A., 202
Simon, H.A., 13, 39, 97, 99
Singleton, Jr., 221
Skocpol, T., 70, 71, 73, 75
Smith, A., 10, 69
Sörbom, D., 194, 202, 210, 222, 241, 242, 246, 248, 249
Sokolowska, M., 249
Speare, A., 122, 127
Spencer, H., 76
Spohn, W., 14, 16, 17, 39
Star, S.A., 127
Starnes, Ch.E., 221
Steffensmeier, D.J., 122

Steffensmeier, R.H., 122, 127
Stegmüller, W., 4, 39
Steiner, I.D., 124
Stokes, D.E., 123, 248
Stotland, E., 121, 125
Stouffer, S.A., 22, 23, 24, 31, 122, 127
Suchman, E.A., 127
Svehla, G., 121, 126
Swanson, G.E., 249

Tanter, R., 73, 75
Taylor, M., 89, 90, 92, 99
Tazelaar, F., IX, 12, 39, 102, 106, 120, 121, 122, 127, 128, 256
't Hart, M., 74
Thibaut, J.W., 10, 39, 82, 83, 99
Thomas, R.P., 83, 99
Tilly, Ch., 70, 73, 74, 75
Tilly, L., 75
Tilly, R., 75
Tocqueville, A. de, 22, 24, 31, 72
Tognacci, L.N., 128
Topitsch, E., 36
Treiman, J., 208, 210, 221
Triandis, H.G., 121, 128
Trow, M., 62
Tufte, E.R., 248
Tullock, G., 10, 36, 70, 75, 171, 185
Tversky, A., 19, 39

Ullmann-Margalit, E., 97, 99
Ultee, W.C., 209, 222, 233, 249

Vanberg, V., 7, 10, 39
Van der Ven, A., 100
Verba, S., 181, 185

Verbeek, A., 106, 120, 121, 122, 127
Veblen, T., 187
Vernon, D.I.A., 128
Vicarro, T., 123
Voss, Th., VII, IX, 35, 60, 62, 96, 99, 232, 233, 249, 257
Vroom, V.H., 122, 128

Waldo, G.P., 121, 128
Walras, L., 77
Warland, R., 121, 127
Warner, E.L., 207, 222
Warner, L.G., 124
Warshay, L., 135, 165
Weber, M., 33, 99, 197
Weigel, R.H., 121, 128
Weiss, H., 248, 249
Westie, F.R., 123
Wicker, A.W., 121, 128
Wilken, P.H., 13, 34, 36, 162, 163, 164
Wilkins, C., 125
Williams jr., R.M., 127
Williamson, O.E., 84, 99, 100
Wippler, R., VIII, 9, 12, 33, 34, 39, 40, 43, 56, 57, 60, 61, 62, 106, 121, 122, 128, 131, 165, 186, 203, 257
Wittman, D., 84, 100
Woelfel, J., 121, 128
Wold, H., 221
Woodmansee, J.J., 121, 128
Wright, D., 123

Yaari, M.E., 17, 40
Yarrow, P.R., 125
Young, 160, 161, 163, 164

Zimmermann, E., 73, 75

SUBJECT INDEX

ALLBUS	X, 212, 236, 237
assimilation of migrant workers	
- by language acquisition	132, 133, 134, 135, 136
- causal model	135, 136, 137, 138, 139, 140
- theory of action	134, 135
behavioral assumptions, general utility-theoretical	22
behavioral sociology	10
behavioral theory of learning	6, 9, 10
branching point	21
class consciousness	X, 206, 227, 228, 229, 230, 232, 247
classical attitude-behavior hypothesis, theoretical suggestions	101
cognitive consistency, theory of	6, 103
cognitive dissonance, theory of	168
collective decisions	7, 31
collective effects	5, 7, 8, 9, 11, 20, 21, 22, 24, 27, 30, 32, 35
competition model	23, 24, 25, 26, 27, 28, 29, 31
- further development	29
- idealizing assumptions	25
conditions	
- environmental	163
- initial	158, 161
- initial and boundary	3, 4, 5, 6, 7, 8, 9, 27, 30
- institutional	VII, VIII, 20, 21, 59
- of individual behavior	3, 8, 20, 21, 27, 30, 103
- social-structural	131
- structural	VII, VIII, 44, 59, 103, 132
coordination, problem of	131, 158, 163, 164

coordination rules	8, 9, 20, 21, 32
corporate actors	7, 31, 88
cultural consumption	189, 190, 191, 192, 193, 195
cultural events	197, 198, 201
- explanation of participation in	IX, 186 ff.
- information	189, 192
- knowledge	192, 198
- participation	190
- socialization	190, 192, 201
decision rule	12
decision theory	6, 233
disposition theory	103, 105
- boundary conditions	104
- general theory of behavior	105, 110
distribution rule	25, 27
dominant strategy	26, 27, 79, 87, 88, 89
dominant pure strategy	26, 27, 89
dynamization of subjective probabilities	17
economic model of man	
- problems and extensions	167, 168
- utilitarian model	IX, 168, 169, 178, 180, 181, 182, 183
- the case of opponents of nuclear energy	196 ff.
eliminative theory testing	183
- confronting sociological with utilitarian hypotheses	178 ff.
emergence of norms	
- exchange solution	77
- Hobbesian anarchy	77, 87, 95
- Prisoners' dilemma game	78, 79, 87
- quasi-functionalistic arguments	82
- rational-choice approach	87 ff.
- supergames (iterated PD-games)	88, 94
- supergame strategies	88, 89, 90, 91, 92, 93
- conditions of cooperation	91, 92, 93, 94

emergence of norms, economic approach	
- general principles	85
- property-rights paradigm	83, 84, 96, 97
- social exchange theory	81, 82
- transaction cost approach	84
empiricist model of man	11
expectancy-value theory	IX, 233
explanandum	4, 5, 8
explanans	4, 5, 8, 25
explanation	
- of collective social phenomena	VII, VIII, 3, 4
- covering-law	4
- deductive-nomological	4, 5, 8, 9, 33
- exchange-theoretical	81
- inductive-statistical	33
- potential	22
- structural-individualistic	8, 30, 32, 34, 158
- utility-theoretical	20
explanatory sociology	VII, VIII
functionalistic model of man	11
game theory	10, 16, 24, 76, 78
general behavioral assumptions	3, 8, 9, 11, 27, 35
- empirical test of	VIII, IX, 9
grievance theory	170, 183
individual behavior, general assumptions concerning	5, 6
individual effects	4, 7, 8, 9, 11, 21, 22, 27, 32
individualism, methodological	166, 168
inequality of educational opportunity	11, 21, 31
information processing (information theory)	IX, 186, 187, 201
- confronting with status-seeking theory	188 ff.
- empirical test	193 ff
- structural model	194, 195, 196

interdependencies	
- between individuals	6, 7, 11, 22, 25, 77, 82, 83, 84, 86, 97
- examples of language acquisition	7
- absorption of migrants	IX, 134
- effect of context variables	150 ff.
- environmental/context effects	131, 132, 140, 141, 146, 147, 148, 149, 150, 153, 158, 159, 162, 163, 164
- environmental/context variables	131, 133, 138, 141, 144, 150, 151, 152, 153, 154, 155, 156, 157, 158, 159, 161, 162, 163
- individual variables	131, 133, 138, 140, 141, 144, 146, 147, 148, 149, 150, 141, 152, 153, 154, 155, 156, 157, 158
- influence of individual variables	144 ff.
- social conditions	132
limited rationality	13
LISREL	194, 195, 198, 199, 206, 210, 213, 214, 215, 241, 242, 247
macrosociological explananda	5, 30
maximizing behavior	13
mental incongruity model	111, 112, 113, 114, 115, 116, 117
- empirical test of the	117, 118, 119
- general model of behavior	119, 120
- incongruity reduction	115, 116
mental incongruity, theory of	102, 103, 104, 105, 106, 117
- application of the	104, 105
- empirical test	117, 118, 119
- mental elements	104, 105
- postulates and hypotheses	106, 107, 108, 109, 110
metrization theorem	15, 16
microsociological explananda	5, 30
naturalistic program	3, 4

oligarchic phenomena, model of	44, 45
- behavioral alternatives	45, 46, 47, 58
- boundary conditions	50, 57, 58
- change of structural and environmental assumptions	54, 55, 56, 57, 59
- dynamization	49, 50, 51, 52
- homogeneity of organizations	48, 49, 51, 55
- organizational network density	48, 49, 51, 52, 55, 61
- simplifying assumptions	47
- size of organization	48, 51, 52, 55
- types of organization	45
oligarchic structures	
- in democratic organizations	VIII, 43, 44
- or tendencies as unintended consequences	56, 57
oligarchic tendencies	VIII, 43, 44, 45, 47, 54, 55, 56, 57, 59, 60
- enhancing conditions	45, 46
- inhibiting conditions	54, 55, 56
oligarchy, iron law of	43
Prisoners' dilemma	78, 79, 80, 82, 85, 87, 94, 96
probability function	16
problem of dominant loyalties (Harsanyi)	18, 20, 21
psychological theory of action	15
rational action, theory of	34, 69
rational-choice theory	IX, 87 ff.
reference group (Runciman)	24
relative deprivation	22, 23, 24, 35, 66, 231, 243, 246
revolution, theory of	64, 67, 68
- adequate theory of action	67, 68, 69
- frustration-aggression hypothesis	67
- major-group hypothesis	63, 64, 67, 68
- negative transfer system	71, 72, 73
- revolution as unintended consequence	70, 71
- theory of rational action	69

SEU-theory	14, 31
social exchange theory	10, 80, 81, 82, 84
- model of man	81
social phenomena, deductive models of social status, subjective and objective	4
- basic causal model	209 ff.
- false consciousness	206, 207, 208, 209, 219, 220
- generalized model	216 ff.
- general theory of behavior	209
status-seeking theory of cultural consumption (status-theory)	IX, 187, 201
- confronted with the theory of information-processing	188 ff.
- empirical test of the	193 ff.
- structural model	194, 195, 196
structural-individualistic approach	VII, 3, 4, 5, 6, 9, 10, 11, 12, 20, 22, 29, 32, 33, 34, 60, 232
- central task of the	3, 9
- consequences of the	32
- open problems of the	31, 32, 33
- summary of basic elements and exemplary applications of the	29, 30, 31
structural-individualistic program	76, 227, 232, 233
structural-individualistic sociology	3, 21
subjective probabilities	15, 17
- dynamization of	16, 17
subjective status identification and political attitudes, explanation of	
- causal model of	230, 231, 232
- test of the model	241 ff.
- interpretation of results	243 ff.
- cognitive-hedonistic theory of behavior and	232, 233, 234, 235, 244, 247
- individualistic research program and	227, 232, 233
- measurement instruments	237, 238, 239, 240, 241
- theoretical backgrounds	228, 229, 230
subjective utilities	15, 18
synthetic theory formation	3, 9

total deprivation rate	24, 27, 28, 29, 30, 35
transformation, problem of	131, 164
transformation rules	9, 27, 32, 33
unintended consequences	9, 56, 57, 70, 71
utility argument	13, 18, 19, 20, 57
utility function, subjective	16, 17, 21
utility theory	VIII, IX, 3, 6, 10, 11, 12, 13, 14, 16, 19, 30, 31, 32, 34, 44, 76, 179, 181, 182
- application in sociology	18, 19, 20, 166, 167, 180, 181, 182
- basic assumptions	13, 34
- dynamization of the	16, 17
- empirical assertion of the	15
- survey of related theories	13, 14
utility-theoretical explanations, symplifying and idealizing assumptions	21, 22